D1175414

DATE DUE

The Illusion of Attitude Change
Towards a response contagion theory of persuasion

European Monographs in Social Psychology

Series Editor HENRI TAJFEL

E. A. CARSWELL and R. ROMMETVEIT
Social Contexts of Messages, 1971

J. ISRAEL and H. TAJFEL
The Context of Social Psychology: A Critical Assesment, 1972

J. R. EISER and W. STROEBE
Categorization and Social Judgement, 1972

C. HERZLICH
Health and Illness: A Social Psychological Analysis, 1973

M. VON CRANACH and I. VINE
Social Communication and Movement

In preparation

H. GILES and P. F. POWESLAND
Social Evaluation through Speech Characteristics

J. INNES
Bias in Psychological Research

J. K. CHADWICK-JONES
Social Exchange Theory

SERGE MOSCOVICI
Social Influence

Louvain Psychology Series Studia Psychologica

Series Editor JOSEPH (R.) NUTTIN

Co-editor for Social Psychology: JOZEF M. NUTTIN, JR.

The Illusion of Attitude Change

Towards a response contagion theory of persuasion

JOZEF M. NUTTIN, JR.
with the collaboration of Annie Beckers
University of Leuven (Louvain, Belgium)

 1975

Published jointly in cooperation with the
EUROPEAN ASSOCIATION
OF EXPERIMENTAL SOCIAL PSYCHOLOGY
by
ACADEMIC PRESS   *and*   LEUVEN UNIVERSITY PRESS
London, New York and San Francisco

Publishers

UK edition published and distributed by
ACADEMIC PRESS INC. (LONDON) LTD.
24–28 Oval Road
London NW1

US edition published and distributed by
ACADEMIC PRESS INC.
111 Fifth Avenue,
New York, New York 10003

Benelux edition published by
LEUVEN UNIVERSITY PRESS
Krakenstraat 3,
B-3000 Leuven/Louvain (Belgium)
Wettelijk Depot Nummer 1974/1869/6

Sole Distributors for the Benelux countries:
Martinus Nijhoff, PO Box 269,
The Hague, The Netherlands.

Library of Congress Catalog Card Number 74 29186
ISBN: (Academic Press) 0 12 522940 2
ISBN: (Leuven University Press) 90 6186 017 2

PRINTED IN GREAT BRITAIN BY
PAGE BROS (NORWICH) LTD, NORWICH

Foreword

It was at Frascati, Italy in 1964 that I first learned of Jozef Nuttin Jr.'s research on attitude change. He presented a paper before a small scientific meeting reporting the results of his earliest studies on the effects of rewards for counter-attitudinal advocacy on subsequent attitude change. The paper stimulated vigorous discussion since it had implications for the then lively controversy between dissonance and reinforcement theorists. Though the findings supported neither theory very well they were more easily assimilated by dissonance theory, and reinforcement theorists were motivated to discredit the results to protect their position. However, research characterized by such theoretical sophistication and methodological rigour is not readily discredited and Nuttin was easily able to defend the research against his critics.

But a defensive posture for a competent scientist is after all not very difficult. He has only to point to the flaws in his opponent's analysis, reaffirm the validity of his findings, and simultaneously attack the critic's own research. Science is not much advanced but collleagues are entertained and one's reputation remains intact. To his credit Nuttin did not limit himself to such a defensive stance; nor did he permit himself, as a reaction against the reinforcement critics, to be seduced into the dissonance camp. He instead continued to pursue independently, and without doctrinaire theoretical constrictions, the leads uncovered in his early studies, gradually building up evidence for a fresh and exciting new theoretical position which ironically more resembles "reinforcement" theory than dissonance theory. The present monograph presents the results of this painstaking, persistent, and systematic experimental and theoretical attack on the classic social psychological problems of attitude and attitude change.

The monograph will certainly make an important theoretical and empirical contribution but in addition, it should serve as a model of how to conduct systematic, integrated and theoretically meaningful research programmes. The methodological sophistication is impressive, the careful analysis of theoretical issues is brilliant, and the experiments are creative and exciting. The new theoretical ideas will provide inspiration and guidance for future research on attitude change and should serve, more generally, as a corrective for overly "cognitive" biases in theorizing about social behaviour. Professor Nuttin has done the field a service by demonstrating again how careful, systematic research and incisive theoretical analysis can clarify problems made murky by the conceptual and methodological shortcomings of earlier research.

The monograph may anger some colleagues, but it will be widely read and very influential, especially as it is admirably suited for teaching purposes. Both graduate and advanced undergraduate seminars, stressing either substantive or methodological issues, will find much here that is exciting and instructive.

John T. Lanzetta

Preface and Acknowledgements

In the present monograph some thirteen unpublished experiments are reported which represent the core of a long term research project on attitude change undertaken by the author in close collaboration with Dr. Annie Beckers at the Laboratorium voor Experimentele Sociale Psychologie of the University of Leuven (Louvain, Belgium). The starting point of this programme has to be situated in Leon Festinger's 1957 book "A Theory of Cognitive Dissonance" in which a challenging theory on cognitive integration and change is offered as a common conceptual framework for the understanding of an impressive amount and wide variety of psychological phenomena. The four main classes of research problems which were covered in the original publication are: the consequences of decisions, the effects of forced compliance, the voluntary and involuntary exposure to information and the role of social support. This publication undoubtedly has stimulated more research and theoretical controversy than any other single contribution to the field of social psychology. Our own research developed from a scepticism with regard to the experimental foundation of the cognitive dissonance interpretation of the effects of forced compliance upon post-advocacy attitude change. The relevance of the first part of our research project for the cognitive dissonance controversy was so obvious that we originally wanted to make this salient in the title of the monograph, which at one moment read "Attitude Response Contagion: an a-cognitive dissonant view of persuasion". We finally decided not to refer in the title to Festinger's theory and chose "The Illusion of Attitude Change: towards a response contagion of persuasion". Although the title might appear an ambitious overstatement—the most important single term probably being "towards"—we thus wanted to emphasize the more recent developments of our theorizing effort which hopefully will have an impact, well beyond the traditional forced compliance paradigm, upon the vast area of behaviour modification and persuasion research, both fundamental and applied.

We would like to express our gratitude to those who helped us in achieving this project and its publication.

Annie Beckers, whose collaboration is acknowledged on the title page, was the main experimenter for the reported research. Moreover, Chapter Two is essentially based on her doctoral dissertation. Most important however, was her continuous scientific and personal commitment and enthusiasm which made her inspiring collaboration essential for the successful development of the project.

vii

It would be difficult to overestimate our debt to John T. Lanzetta: we simply would not have published this monograph without his constant encouragement and his critical reading of the various drafts of the manuscript. Those who know the very demanding editor of the Journal of Personality and Social Psychology, will realize that only the author is to be blamed for the gaps and inadequacies left in the text.

The University of Leuven, the Ford Foundation and the Nationaal Fonds voor Wetenschappelijk Onderzoek (Belgian National Science Foundation) have financially sponsored the research project and/or contributed to the indispensable technical and personnel infrastructure.

On a more personal level, we would like to take this opportunity to acknowledge the influence of Professors Joseph (R.) Nuttin and Leopold Knops. The outstanding theoretical and methodological training received at their hands, together with their constant concern for the development of Social Psychology and the proper research facilities at the University of Leuven, have contributed more to this monograph than anyone can measure.

The first experiments were reported at the formal foundation conference of the European Association of Experimental Social Psychology, Frascati 1964. All along the Association played an important role in providing a scientific milieu to a rather isolated social psychologist.

A large part of the writing was done while the author was a Filene Visiting Professor in Human Relations at Dartmouth. A sabbatical leave awarded by the University of Leuven left no choice but to finish the manuscript. At the same time it enabled us to present and discuss the crucial data with stimulating friends and colleagues at the social psychology laboratories of the Universities of Oslo, Wisconsin, Michigan, Delaware, Princeton, Massachusetts, Yale, Harvard, Stanford, and the University of California at Los Angeles and Santa Barbara.

Finally, we thank Jos Feys for his precious technical and statistical assistance and Eddy De Greef who never seemed discouraged when typing, retyping and typing again an ever changing manuscript.

Leuven, May 1974   JOZEF M. NUTTIN, Jr.

Contents

Aan Monika

1

The Cohen-Rosenberg Controversy and our 1964 Research

Psychology students exposed to American general or social psychology text-books cannot afford to ignore the famous Festinger and Carlsmith (1959) experiment in which subjects were paid either one or twenty dollars for telling a waiting stooge that a boring task they had just performed, was enjoyable and exciting. This study was the first experimental test of Festinger's hypothesis concerning the negative relationship between amount of reward offered for forced compliance and magnitude of subsequent attitude change. Since the subjects merely had to formulate a few counterattitudinal assertions (prepared by the experimenter) concerning a simple laboratory task, one can hardly consider the role playing involved in this experiment as an instance of elaborate advocacy. In view of the fact that all experiments presented in this monograph deal with the written or oral presentation of a more elaborate essay in which the respondent is invited to generate himself arguments concerning a debatable issue, we decided to initiate the reader in the problem area via the campus-riot experiment of A. Cohen (1962) which was the first cognitive dissonance study using a more elaborate form of advocacy, while closely following the Festinger and Carlsmith paradigm.

Besides a general presentation of the cognitive dissonance view upon the relation between reward for counterattitudinal advocacy and attitude change, a major part of this first chapter will be devoted to a report of our hitherto unpublished 1964 dissonance research. Although some readers might wish to skip the present chapter entirely, we feel that the incorporation of this research is justified since we intend to give a report

of the progressive development of a long range research project whose
starting point is to be found in our 1964 experiments. Also, these early
experiments remain relevant, it seems to us, for a critical evaluation of
the widely quoted research of Rosenberg (1965) who was among the first
to challenge the cognitive dissonance interpretation of Cohen's experiment. The fact that our 1964 research on the effect of reward for elaborate advocacy upon subsequent attitude change has only been made
public in mimeographed or oral presentation (Nuttin, 1964 and 1965)
might explain that its conclusions often have been quoted erroneously in
the more recent literature.

1. Festinger's cognitive dissonance theory (1957) and the campus-riot experiment of Cohen (1962)

A rather detailed presentation of the Cohen experiment (Brehm and
Cohen, 1962, p. 73–78) provides us with a simple and appealing
example to familiarize the reader with the core notions of Festinger's
theory and the derived hypothesis concerning the negative relationship
between the amount of reward offered for a counterattitudinal plea and
the magnitude of the subsequent attitude change in the advocated
direction. Moreover, the experimental paradigm of Cohen's study will
serve as a basic point of reference for all research presented in the
remaining chapters. We will first present the data of Cohen's experiment. After that it will be shown how the main propositions of Festinger's theory are used to explain these facts.

Cohen's campus-riot experiment: data

The subjects of this experiment were Yale students known to be upset by
what they called the unwarranted brutality of the local police during a
campus riot. They were individually approached by a member of a
research team of "The Institute of Human Relations" inviting them to
write a short unilateral essay in favour of the police action. The experimenter who hinted at the student's negative attitude towards the issue,
argued that a scientific approach of this "human relations" problem
would profit from a full inventory of arguments for and against and that
the best way to reach this goal consisted of asking people to write essays
favouring only one side of the issue. Under the pretext that the experimenter had already a full complement of anti-police essays, each subject
was induced to write the "strongest, most forceful, most creative and

thoughtful essay you can, unequivocally against your own position and in favour of the police side of the riots" (Brehm and Cohen, 1962, p. 75). The experimenter went on to say that he had some research funds available and was prepared to pay the subject a specified amount for writing the essay against his own position. Each subject was furthermore told that the decision to write the essay was entirely his own choice. In order to prevent any considerable differential loss of subjects, the experimenter insisted upon the fact that he needed the subject's cooperation in the study since he was a student and the research was part of his research paper.

Cohen who did not report on the possible differential loss or self-selection of his subjects, succeeded in obtaining the cooperation of 30 students who were submitted to one of four monetary reward conditions: 6 were offered $10.00; 10 were offered $5.00; 6 were offered $1.00 and 8 were offered $.50 for writing the essay. It should be noted that the monetary reward was not delivered until after the experiment.

As soon as the subject had written an essay on a sheet entitled "Why the New Haven Police Actions Were Justified" he was told "Now that you have looked at some of the reasons for the actions of the New Haven Police, we'd like to get some of your reactions to the issue; you may possibly want to look at the situation in the light of this. So, would you please fill out this questionnaire". The first and critical self-rating question invited the subject to indicate on a 31-point scale how justified he thought—considering the circumstances—the New Haven police actions were in the recent riot. At every fifth point, the scale was labelled by the following terms: completely justified; very justified; quite justified; somewhat justified; little justified; very little justified; not justified at all.

Each attitude response was converted into a numerical value from 7 (completely justified) to 1 (not justified at all). The mean attitude responses toward the police actions obtained for the four experimental conditions were as follows: $10.00 offered reward: 2.32; $5.00: 3.08; $1.00: 3.47 and $.50: 4.54.

For the 14 subjects of the baseline condition, who were simply given the attitude self-rating (they neither had been invited to write an essay nor had they been offered a reward), the mean attitude response was 2.70. Using the latter data as a baseline or estimation of the pre-experimental attitude response of the differentially rewarded subjects, Cohen concluded that the subjects of the reward conditions had changed their attitude in the direction advocated in the essay, the change being inversely related to the magnitude of the reward. This linear trend proved to be significant at less than the 0.01 level by F test. After further testing of the differences between specific experimental conditions—using the Duncan Multiple Range Test—Cohen summarizes his results as follows: "The $10.00 and $5.00 conditions are not significantly different from each other or from the control condition, but the $1.00 condition is different from the control ($p < 0.10$) as is the $.50 condition ($p < 0.01$). Furthermore, the $1.00 and the $.50 conditions are both different from the $10.00 condition ($p < 0.05$ and < 0.01 respectively). Finally, the $.50 condition is itself different from the $1.00 condition ($p < 0.05$) as well as from the $5.00 condition ($p < 0.01$)" (*ibid.*, p. 77).

The only other data reported by Cohen aim at providing a check of the perceived amount of reward offered and of the perceived degree of strength of the counterattitudinal essay. These data indicate that (1) all subjects had an accurate understanding of the amount of monetary reward they were going to receive for writing the essay, and (2) for each of the four reward conditions the subjects perceived that they had agreed to write equally strongly discrepant essays. This means that, the manipulation of differential reward being successful, the differences in attitude change cannot be seen as a function of the strength with which the subjects perceived that they had taken the discrepant stand.

It might be worthwhile to note that Cohen does not provide any objective data on the quality or length of the essays written. Nor does he give any reasons for the unusual inequality of the number of subjects used in the various conditions (6–10–6–8–14). We take it for granted that the late Cohen would not have omitted to report on this important methodological issue if the differences could have been due to differences in the frequency of subject's refusals to comply. The very fact that no reasons were offered makes it difficult, however, to defend the author when he is accused of stopping data gathering as soon as the results confirmed the predictions. A minimal self-protection of the experimenter calls indeed for a pre-determined number of subjects for each condition and a list of replacement subjects in case the results of a scheduled subject cannot be used according to clearly specified criteria of rejection.

Interpretation of the Cohen data : Festinger's cognitive dissonance theory

Cohen's experiment replicates the earlier findings of Festinger and Carlsmith (1959) which, as noted, were the first explicit confirmation of the dissonance prediction: the smaller the reward offered for counterattitudinal role playing, the larger the subsequent attitude change in the advocated direction. The Cohen data, obtained after a more elaborate counterattitudinal advocacy, and with a larger variety of monetary reward, are presented as further experimental evidence for the validity of a hypothesis derived from cognitive dissonance theory. Let us see how Festinger's theoretical framework applies to Cohen's results.

Dissonant and consonant relations Festinger's theory has to do with the organization and dynamics of the cognitive system. This system, "empty" at birth, is progressively developing as new elements of cognition add to the previously acquired ones. Any knowledge, opinion or belief about the environment, about oneself, or about one's behaviour can be defined as a cognitive element. This adding of new elements to the cognitive system however, is not to be seen as a simple accumulation but rather as an integration of cognitions. Each new cognitive element is said to establish a dynamic relation with some elements of the pre-existing system, whereas it will leave intact some other elements of the same individual cognitive system.

Festinger's theory is based on a particular conception of this cognitive integration. The dynamic relation, if any, between two cognitive elements is said to be either consonant or dissonant. The relation is dissonant if, "disregarding the other cognitive elements, the one element does not, or would not be expected to, follow from the other" (Festinger, 1957, p. 15). Thus, in Cohen's experiment, a dissonant relation is postulated between the following two elements: (*A*) "The knowledge of having a negative attitude towards the campus-riot police actions"; and (*B*) "The knowledge of having written a unilateral plea in defense of the same police actions". Cognitive element (*B*), upon entering the subject's cognitive system, is said to establish a dissonant relation with the pre-existing element (*A*), because element (*B*) does not follow from, or, "for one reason or another, does not fit together" (*ibid.*, p. 12) with element (*B*). Stating it in another way, Festinger considers the relation between (*A*) and (*B*) to be dissonant because cognitive element (*A*) psychologically implies the negation of cognitive element (*B*). As a matter of fact, if all other cognitive elements of the subject's cognitive system are disregarded, one would not expect that a student who is very much against the police action would write a pro-police essay. On the contrary, his anti-police attitude psychologically implies the negation of pro-police advocacy.

The relation between two cognitions is defined as consonant if, disregarding the other elements, the two elements under consideration for one reason or another, do fit together. Such would be the case for the relation between element (B) "The knowledge of having written a unilateral plea in defense of the police actions" and a cognitive element (C) "The knowledge of having rendered service to the experimenter who needed the essay for his research paper". The same applies for the relation between the element (B) and the cognitive elaboration of the offered reward resulting in a cognitive element (D) "The knowledge that the experimenter offered a $10.00 reward for writing the essay".

The magnitude of dissonance Dissonant or consonant relations can vary in degree of dissonance or consonance. A first determinant of the magnitude or intensity of a dissonant or consonant relation is the importance of the elements involved. The more "valued or consequential for the person" (*ibid.*, p. 16) an element is, the more weight the consonance or dissonance of the relation will have. Thus the importance of consonant element (D) "The knowledge that the experimenter offered a $10.00 reward for writing the essay" is considered to be greater than the importance of the consonant element (E) "The knowledge that the experimenter offered a $1.00 reward for writing the essay", since ten dollars can be supposed to have more value for the subject than one dollar. Consequently, the relation $(B)–(D)$ has a greater magnitude of consonance than the relation $(B)–(E)$.

When one takes into consideration all cognitive elements which are in consonant or dissonant relation with, for example, the elements (A) and (B) (concerning the private attitude and the counterattitudinal essay), one can speak of the "total dissonance" of that part of the cognitive system which is related to both these elements, or, of the total dissonance of the two clusters (A) and (B). The intensity or magnitude of this total dissonance of the cognitive clusters (A) and (B) will then not only depend on the relative importance of each of the elements involved, but will also depend on the relative proportion of dissonant and consonant relations. As Festinger states it "The total amount of dissonance that exists between two clusters of cognitive elements is a function of the weighted proportion of all . . . relations between the two clusters that are dissonant. The term "weighted proportion" is used because each . . . relation would be weighted according to the importance of the elements involved in that relation" (*ibid.*, p. 18).

Although Festinger's exposé on magnitude or intensity of dissonance is not the clearest part of his book, there is no danger of betraying his conception by applying it to the subjects of Cohen's experiment in the following way. Between the four reward conditions there is no systematic variation of the relative proportion of cognitive elements which are consonant or dissonant with the cognitive elements (A) and (B) (elements concerning attitude and counterattitudinal plea). As a matter of fact, the number of dissonant and consonant cognitive elements which are intentionally generated by the experimental situation is supposed to be identical for all four conditions. The only between condition difference which is supposed to be manipulated by the experimenter is the relative importance of the cognitive element concerning the monetary reward. This cognitive element being consonant with the knowledge of having written the essay, the intensity of the total dissonance involved will be inversely related to the importance (value, weight) of the monetary reward.

Applied to Cohen's subjects: given the fact that the subjects were against the police actions (cognitive element A) and that they complied by writing an essay in favour of the police actions (cognitive element B), the intensity of the cognitive dissonance generated by the cognitive clusters (A)–(B), all other factors being equal, will increase as the reward for having written the essay decreases: the less the weight on the consonant side of the cognitive balance, the greater the magnitude of the total dissonance.

The reduction of dissonance What about the psychological consequences of differences in magnitude of dissonance? The basic proposition of Festinger's theory states that "the existence of dissonance, being psychologically uncomfortable, will motivate the person to try to reduce the dissonance and achieve consonance. The existence of nonfitting relations among cognitions is a motivating factor in its own right and will lead to activity oriented toward dissonance reduction just as hunger leads to activity oriented toward hunger reduction" (*ibid.*, p. 3). The second proposition, linked to the former, says that "the strength of the pressure to reduce the dissonance is a direct function of the magnitude (or intensity) of the dissonance" (*ibid.*, p. 18).

From the above definitions of dissonant and consonant relations, it follows that dissonance reduction ultimately depends on a change in the *cognitive* system. Whatever overt or covert activity the subject undertakes to reduce his dissonance, this more consonant state can only be achieved through a change in the cognitive clusters under consideration.

In the case of Cohen's subjects, dissonance reduction could follow (1) either from adding new cognitions which are consonant with the compliance (e.g., the belief that the scientific study of the issue might reduce the likelihood of future police brutality) (2), or from increasing the importance of existing consonant elements (e.g., by enhancing the importance of the service rendered to the experimenter) (3), or from decreasing the importance of existing cognitive elements which are dissonant with the compliance (e.g., by diminishing the personal involvement in the riot issue) (4), or from changing the content of existing dissonant cognitions so as to make them more fitting with the cognitive element concerning the attitude (e.g., by questioning the persuasiveness and strength of the arguments elaborated in the essay); and (5) from changing the content of existing dissonant cognitions so as to make them more fitting with the cognitive element concerning the compliance (e.g., by evaluating the police actions somewhat less negatively, the cognitive element concerning the private attitude thus becoming less dissonant with the compliance).

It should be noted that Festinger introduces in this context another important notion, viz., the relative resistance to change of a cognitive element. Cognitive elements differ not only in importance but also in their resistance to change. If two dissonant cognitive elements differ in resistance to change, and if dissonance reduction is achieved by changing existing cognitive elements, it is expected that the least resistant element will change. Furthermore, "the maximum dissonance that possibly can exist between any two elements is equal to the total resistance to change of the less resistant element" (*ibid.*, p. 28).

Going back to the experiment of Cohen, one can argue that the cognitive element concerning the private attitude is less resistant to change than the cognitive element concerning the compliance. As a matter of fact, the student who has written an essay in which he purports to be strongly in favour of the police actions is confronted with the *fait accompli* of his overt behaviour and it might be more difficult for him to deny the fact that the essay was written than to change the cognitive element concerning the private attitude. Thus, Cohen expected that dissonance reduction would be more likely to occur, in his experiment, via attitude change than via any of the other enumerated possible modes.

It will be clear now that the basic strategy of dissonance research implies the experimental creation of situations resulting in magnitudes of cognitive dissonance which are systematically different between conditions and for which the dissonance reduction process is most likely to be achieved via one predictable category of adaptive reactions. This implies, in all experiments where the adding of new cognitive elements is not expected, that the experimenter is successful in tapping the change of the least resistant cognitive element.

That is precisely what Cohen, and before him Festinger and Carlsmith have tried to achieve. By varying the monetary reward for compliance, the magnitude of dissonance was supposed to be manipulated and it was hoped that the differential need for dissonance reduction would manifest itself typically via a change in the relatively less resistant cognitive element concerning the attitude towards the police actions. By finding this action somewhat more justified, the magnitude of the original dissonance created by the writing of the essay is reduced. It is worth noting that no prediction concerning other possible modes of dissonance reduction are tested in this and similar research.

Essentially then, the lack of difference between the attitude of the high reward conditions and the baseline condition is interpreted as being due to the relatively more important weight of the consonant reward element which results in a decrease of the magnitude of the cognitive dissonance. The attitude change in the advocated direction, observed in the $1.00 and $.50 conditions is attributed to the smaller importance of the consonant reward element, which thus has less effect on the magnitude of the total dissonance. This differential consonance of the cognitive reward element is seen as having such an impact on the magnitude of dissonance that even the significant difference between the $1.00 and $.50 condition is attributed to the fact that the weight of the consonant $.50 element is smaller than the weight of the consonant $1.00 reward.

Thus, the significant trend observed in the four reward conditions is presented as an experimental confirmation of the hypothesis, derived from Festinger's cognitive dissonance theory, predicting an inverse relationship between amount of reward offered for writing a counter-attitudinal essay and amount of subsequent attitude change in the advocated direction. To put it in a simple way, the cognitive dissonance hypothesis which Cohen wants to support by his findings, states that a person will begin to believe what he is saying to the extent that he is offered less important reasons for saying it.

Finally, it should be made clear that the above interpretation of the role of the reward in forced compliance research continued to be the orthodox cognitive dissonance view. J.M. Carlsmith (1968) summarizes the position of dissonance theory as follows: "A person who engages in counterattitudinal behavior holds two cognitions: 'I believe X' and 'I am engaging in behavior which implies that I believe $not-X$'. Under most circumstances these two cognitions will produce dissonance. The most obvious method of reducing dissonance is to change the belief in the direction of the behavior. Any incentive for performing the behavior produces a third cognition: 'I will receive Y for engaging in the behavior'. If the person does engage in the behavior, then *this latter (reward) cognition is consonant with the behavior and will reduce the total amount of dissonance* in the situation; it will also reduce the total amount of attitude change. *The more Y (reward), the more consonance and the less dissonance*" (p. 804, italics added).

So far, we have presented Cohen's experiment and its cognitive dissonance interpretation which, as Rosenberg (1966) states, "have received so wide attention and acceptance that, if frequent quotation by textbook writers... is a criterion of legitimation, this aspect of the work of the dissonance school has virtually attained canonical status" (p. 137–138).*

2. Rosenberg's "When dissonance fails" (1964-65)

Rosenberg was presumably the first to challenge this "canonical status" of Cohen's experiment on an empirical basis. The title of his article, paraphrasing the well-known dissonance book "When Prophecy Fails" (Festinger *et al.*, 1956), emphasizes clearly its central focus. Rosenberg's publication can, however, be seen as serving three distinct purposes. First, he shares the concern of Orne (1962), Riecken (1962) and Rosenthal (1963) who warn about experimenter-subject interaction as an uncontrolled source of bias in psychological research. Second, he expresses his scepticism about the claimed generality of the dissonance view and joins Chapanis and Chapanis (1964) when pointing to methodological and interpretational problems complicating dissonance research. Thus he will critically replicate Cohen's study in an effort to demonstrate that its results are artifactual. Third, having contributed himself both theoretically and empirically to the field of attitude organization and change (Rosenberg, 1956, 1960), he integrates the data of the Cohen replication in his own affective-cognitive consistency theory.

* For a further discussion of this controversy see Appendix, p. 223.

Our presentation of Rosenberg's article will be organized around these three points of concern. Although we can be brief about the first and third point, the second does deserve a more extensive report, since his controversy with Cohen will set the stage for the remainder of this first chapter.

Evaluation apprehension and affect arousal as research contaminants

Rosenberg devotes a substantial part of his article to a most interesting and refined phenomenological analysis of the experimental situation in which the typical research subject is volunteering to serve the theoretical purposes of the scientist. The scientist being a "psychologist", he is perceived by the undergraduate experimental subject as professionally skilled to evaluate his personality, emotional balance and other hidden characteristics of interest to psychological science. To the extent that some aspects of the experimental situation are cognitively unclear to him, the subject is likely to be more concerned about the particular basis for evaluation which the experimenter will use. More important, the typical subject being anxious to obtain a positive evaluation from the experimenter, will avoid any behaviour which is not socially desirable (Edwards, 1957) and will develop hypotheses about the kinds of responses which will be evaluated in a positive way. "Evaluation apprehension" is a constant characteristic of psychological research and an inevitable consequence of the fact that psychologists do their research on human beings who can not refrain from cognitively exploring their new research situation. Rosenberg emphasizes however, the serious interpretational problems encountered in research where evaluation apprehension might be differentially aroused between experimental conditions. If the results of an experiment are systematically affected by the differential effort to avoid negative evaluation, or to win a positive one, the relation between these results and the experimental factor, supposedly manipulated by the experimenter, might be totally obscured and the interpretation artifactual.

Rosenberg argues that Cohen's experiment is especially vulnerable to this systematic research contaminant. Arousal of evaluation apprehension is conceived to be a direct function of the size of monetary reward promised for writing the counterattitudinal plea. The higher the reward, the more the subject may come to reason somewhat as follows: "They probably want to see whether getting paid so much will affect my own attitude, whether it will influence me, whether I am the kind of person whose views can be changed by buying him off" (Rosenberg, 1965, p. 29), and the more he might become motivated *not* to manifest any attitude change. Rosenberg offers this as a basis for explaining the fact that Cohen's high reward subjects (low dissonance) did not differ from the baseline-control condition, and that the trend of attitude change between conditions was inversely related to the size of the monetary reward.

A similar attitude change suppressing effect would, according to Rosenberg, result from a second research contaminant, viz. the differentially aroused negative affect toward the experimenter. The higher the reward promised by the experimenter, the more the subject is likely to develop suspicions concerning the experimenter's possible duplicity and unrevealed purposes. This enhanced suspicion that one is going to be deceived, would generate hostility feelings toward the experimenter and the high reward subjects "may find emotional release in refusing to show the response (attitude change) that they perceive the experimenter to be after" (*ibid.*, p. 30).

Cohen's experiment is particularly vulnerable to these two posited research contaminants since the experimenter did provide cues for the response he was after. As mentioned, Cohen's experimenter invited his subjects to express their attitude in the following way: "Now that you have looked at some of the reasons for the actions of the New Haven police, we would like to get some of your reactions to the issue: *you may possibly want to look at the situation in the light of this.* So, would you please fill out this questionnaire" (*ibid.*, p. 31, italics added by Rosenberg).

The procedural aspects of Cohen's experiment, which according to Rosenberg would be most likely to contribute to the contamination of the results are: first, the fact that subject's attitude was being assessed by the experimenter in the very situation where evaluation apprehension had been differentially aroused; and second, the fact that the monetary reward was merely promised by Cohen's experimenter and only delivered after the attitude measurement had taken place. The larger the promised reward, the more suspicion and thus the more negative affect toward the experimenter.

Rosenberg's altered replication of Cohen's experiment

Guided by the above considerations, Rosenberg replicated Cohen's experiment while trying to avoid the influence of the two alleged biasing factors. It will be remembered that both biasing factors bear on the interaction between the subject, who wrote the essay, and the experimenter who presumably did arouse the evaluation apprehension and the negative affect. Since the biasing effect is considered as motivating the subject to hold back from *this* experimenter any evidence of being influenced by the rewarded essay, Rosenberg sees a first and most important step toward contaminant control in the complete *perceptual separation* between the "dissonance arousal" and the "attitude measurement" phases of the experiment. "The experiment should be organized so that it appears to the subject to be two separate, unrelated studies, conducted by investigators who have little or no relationship with each other and who are pursuing different research interests. In such a situation the evaluation apprehension and negative affect that are focused upon the dissonance-arousing experimenter would probably be lessened and, more important, they would not govern the subject's responses to the attitude measuring experimenter and to the information that he seeks from the subject" (*ibid.*, p. 32). The second step, considered to be instrumental in avoiding the arousal of suspicion and negative affect, was the actual delivery of the monetary reward, immediately upon completion of the counterattitudinal essay, and before the assessment of the subject's own attitude.

In essence then, Rosenberg's study is designed as a close replication of the Cohen experiment, with one baseline-control condition, and three experimental reward conditions ($.50; $1.00; $5.00) all three with "perceptual separation" and "actual delivery of reward". Let us summarize the Rosenberg procedure while pointing to some aspects which will become relevant for our discussion.

The 51 experimental *subjects* were male undergraduate students from an introductory psychology course. Ten were randomly assigned to each of the three experimental conditions and 21 to the baseline-control condition.

The *attitude issue* chosen was, just as Cohen's, related to an important campus issue: the possibility that the faculty council might vote against further participation of the university's football team in a nation-wide competition. The non-American reader should realize that at some American universities the football- and athletic competition issue mobilizes an incredible amount of enthusiasm and involvement among the student body.

Quoting the description given in the original article (*ibid.*, p. 33-34) . . . the *dissonance arousal phase* went as follows.

'As each experimental subject arrived at the author's [Rosenberg] office, he found him busily engaged either in writing, or in a conversation with another 'student'. The experimenter then told the subject: 'I'm sorry but I'm running late on my schedule today and I'll have to keep you waiting for about 15 or 20 minutes. Is that all right?' . . . upon the agreement of the subject, the experimenter continued: 'Oh, I've just thought of something: While you are waiting, you could participate in another little experiment that some graduate student in education is doing'. The experimenter [Rosenberg] explained that he had had a call the previous day from the 'graduate student' who needed volunteers in a hurry for 'some sort of study he's doing—I don't know what it's about exactly *except that it has to do with attitudes and that's why he called me, because my research is in a similar area as you'll see later* [italics ours]. Of course he can't give you any credit point (The usual research credit point used in American universities to keep up experimental participation rates in introductory psychology courses) but I gather they have some research funds and that they are paying people instead. So if you care to go down there you can' . . . With some show of effort and uncertainty the experimenter then recalled the name of the education graduate student and the room, actually located in the Education Department, where he could be found.

Upon reporting to the 'education graduate student' the subject received an explanation modelled word-for-word upon that used in the experiment of Cohen . . . The amount that each subject was to receive was made clear to him before he undertook to write the counterattitudinal essay (Why the university football team should not be allowed to participate in a nation-wide competition). After the subject completed the essay he was *paid* the amount that he had been promised, then thanked for his participation and dismissed. He then returned to the experimenter's office and, under the guise of participating in another study, his attitudes toward the critical competition and to various other issues were ascertained.

The attitude measurement phase of the study began by the experimenter [Rosenberg] telling the subject that the study for which his participation had originally been solicited was a continuing survey on student attitudes 'that I run every semester as a sort of Gallup poll to keep a check on opinion patterns on different university issues'. The subject then filled out an attitude questionnaire dealing with eight different issues. The critical item read: 'How would you feel if it were decided that from now on the university football team would not be allowed to participate in the Rose Bowl (nation-wide competition)'. Following the procedure in the Cohen study, the subject responded on a 31-point graphic scale, marked at every fifth point by: I think this decision would be not justified at all . . . to completely justified. The same scale form was used with the other seven issues . . . one dealt with the area of varsity athletics, the other six with non-athletic matters such as dormitory regulations, university admission policies, library rules etc.'

After these essential phases of his replication and before the usual debriefing, the subjects answered several post-experimental questions dealing with suspicion concerning "a connection between the two experiments", with the perceived strength of the essay he had agreed to write, the strength of the essay he did write, the perceived freedom in his decision to write the essay and the perception of the monetary reward.

"In distinction to the experimental subjects, each of the baseline *control subjects*, upon reporting for his appointment, was merely told that the experimenter (Rosenberg) was conducting a sort of Gallup poll on university issues and then filled out the attitude questionnaire" (*ibid.*, p. 34).

The *main results* of Rosenberg's study are very clear. In contrast with the data obtained by Cohen, the attitude change in the advocated direction is a *direct* function of the magnitude of the monetary reward. Scoring the 31-point attitude scale from 1.0 (the banning of participation in football competition would "not be justified at all") through 1.2, 1.4 . . . to 6.8, 7.0 (completely justified) the mean scores are: 1.45 for the baseline control group, 2.24 for the $.50 reward condition, 2.32 for the $1.00 and 3.24 for the $5.00 reward condition. The overall difference between groups analysed by Kruskal-Wallis test proves to be highly significant ($H = 17.89$, $p < 0.001$). Further analysis of between condition differences by Mann-Whitney rank sum test reveals that both low reward conditions, which do not differ from each other, are each significantly different from both the control and the $5 conditions. The difference between the baseilne and the $5 conditions is of very large significance ($p < 0.0001$).

Rosenberg's *conclusion* with regard to Cohen's experiment is unequivocal: "When the design of the original Cohen study is altered so as to eliminate aspects that were likely to have generated evaluation apprehension and affect arousal, the prediction that guided the present study is confirmed and the original dissonance prediction is disconfirmed" (*ibid.*, p. 37–38). "The earlier finding, in support of dissonance theory, that the degree of reward for counterattitudinal advocacy has an inverse effect upon consequent attitude change, is attributed to the operation of these contaminants (evaluation apprehension and affect arousal)" (*ibid.*, p. 28, abstract).

Paraphrasing the title of Rosenberg's paper, this conslusion states that dissonance fails when evaluation apprehension and negative affect arousal are prevented from suppressing the "normal" attitude change in high reward conditions which is predicted by Rosenberg's affective cognitive consistency theory. We should note that Rosenberg does not, of course, claim to have disproven the general value of Festinger's cognitive dissonance theory when concluding that his experiment "seems to indicate that, at least in its account of the attitude change consequences of counterattitudinal advocacy, dissonance theory has been overextended". He furthermore conjectures that probably "the kind of counterattitudinal performance that best fits the dissonance paradigm is a simple overt act that directly violates one's private attitude (e.g., eating or agreeing to eat a disliked food; expressing approval of a disliked proposal or candinate, merely committing oneself to develop counterattitudinal arguments; etc." (*ibid.*, p. 39).

Interpretation of Rosenberg's results: affective-cognitive consistency theory

Like Festinger and other balance theorists, Rosenberg postulates that inconsistency can lead to attitude change. However, the inconsistency is not seen as resulting from the presence of dissonant cognitive elements, but as a consequence of a change in either cognitions or affects. The basic postulate being that the individual strives toward consistency between the cognitive and affective components of his attitude. Any disruptive change in this equilibrium will motivate a restoration of the intra-attitudinal consistency. Thus, a subject, who feels very negatively toward police-actions, and who has been thinking up several arguments in favour of the police-action, might find himself in a state of intra-attitudinal inconsistency if he becomes convinced of the validity of the arguments produced, i.e., if his beliefs change in the direction opposite to his affect. The inconsistency-generating cognition is not "I know that I did advocate against my own position", but rather the fact of accepting the content and plausibility of arguments which do not fit together with the original feelings on the issue. The probability that such inconsistency will occur, depends upon the subject's production of new self-convincing arguments and upon other factors which enhance the impact of the newly established cognitions.

The monetary reward manipulated in counterattitudinal role playing experiments is seen as serving both functions. First, the mere promise of a reward, operates as an *incentive* which stimulates the mental activity of the subject and has a positive influence on the number and quality of new arguments generated. Second, the receipt of the monetary reward is seen to function as a *reinforcement* which fosters the acquisition or internalization of the newly developed cognitive responses. The relation

between the size of the monetary reward and its incentive and reinforcement value is considered to be positive: the higher the reward, the
better the production of new arguments will be, and the more these new
cognitions will be "internalized" and "stabilized". Also the more intra-
attitudinal inconsistency there will be between the new beliefs and the
original feelings. To the degree that these new beliefs are stabilized
(resistant to change) the generated affective-cognitive inconsistency will
be reduced via a change in the affective components of the attitude.
Thus, the more an individual is paid for counterattitudinal advocacy,
the more his attitude (in both its cognitive and affective components)
will change in the advocated direction.

Although we will refrain from a discussion of Rosenberg's theory, it
should be noted that his interpretation implies a cognitive self-persuasion
process which is not explained by the intra-attitudinal inconsistency.
As far as the double function of the reward is concerned, Rosenberg
combines the incentive (e.g., Janis and King, 1954) and the reinforcement (e.g., Scott, 1957) view in a manner which does not allow a clear
independent test of each of the posited functions. Moreover, it is not clear
what the specific meaning of the "reinforcement" concept might be in
this context which is quite different from the classical use made in the
experimental psychology of learning.

3. Our 1964 critical replication of Rosenberg's experiment

When we received the prepublication report of Rosenberg's experiment
(Rosenberg, 1964) we were in the midst of planning a critical replication
of the Festinger and Carlsmith experiment. Not thinking specifically
along the lines of experimenter-subject bias, we were more interested in
having a clear proof that the fascinating Festinger and Carlsmith results
were a function of the differential consonance weight of the monetary
reward and that the posited dissonance between private attitude and
counterattitudinal role playing was a necessary condition for the effect
to be obtained. Our main worry with dissonance research was—unlike
prevailing criticism at the time—that no convincing experimental evidence was given for the validity of the cognitive dissonance view on the
counterattitudinal role playing situation and on the precise function of
the monetary reward. That is why our experimental design would include
a *no* reward counterattitudinal and various rewarded *pro*-attitudinal role
playing conditions (see Nuttin, 1964 and 1966).

B

Rosenberg's prepublication report motivated us to extend our critical replication efforts to his own and Cohen's experiment for several reasons.

Some questions about Rosenberg's experiment

When reading the Rosenberg 1964 report, we were of course impressed by the highly significant results and their perfect fit to Rosenberg's affective-cognitive consistency theory. It was self-evident to us that the data were to become an important contribution to the field if they proved to be reliable. At the same time, however, we were puzzled by several questions (see also Nuttin, 1964).

Need for experimental manipulation of contaminants The major question is very simple: what exactly did Rosenberg prove? There is no doubt that he generated very interesting data in support of his own theory. But the full title of the report (and of the published article) reads: "When dissonance fails: on eliminating evaluation apprehension from attitude measurement". This title is indeed an appropriate label for the article which reports essentially a replication of the Cohen experiment, in which the denounced research contaminants have been eliminated. The obtained results, which are opposite to the dissonance prediction, are not only seen as corroborating Rosenberg's theory, but, and that is the central argument developed, as invalidating the Cohen experiment and its dissonance interpretation. The question which should be asked then is: what is the experimental evidence for attributing the difference between the Cohen and Rosenberg results to the procedural changes which produced "perceptual separation" and "actual delivery of reward".

Rosenberg's evidence is not convincing since his experimental design did not permit a demonstration that the Cohen type of results would be replicated *without* "perceptual separation" and "actual delivery of reward". Such a design was not necessary if the only goal had been to produce evidence for the affective-cognitive consistency theory. Generating plausible evidence for the statement that dissonance fails when evaluation apprehension is eliminated is however a quite different enterprise. The experimental situations involved are so utterly complex, and the possibly relevant differences between the Cohen and Rosenberg experiment could be so manifold that it is a very risky thing to decide that "perceptual separation" and "actual delivery of reward" are *the* only crucial factors which can account for the differences in the results obtained. Under such circumstances, the only convincing demonstration does imply an experimental manipulation of the denounced biasing factors. Let us comment briefly upon one possibly important difference between the two studies. Rosenberg rejects six subjects from the analysis of his data because it had been specified in advance that members of varsity athletic teams should not be used, "since their attitudes could be assumed to be considerably stronger, more firmly anchored than those of other students" (*ibid.*, p. 35). There is of course no objection against specifying the limits of one's research population, but the fact is that Cohen did not restrict his population to subjects with presumably less firmly anchored attitudes. One could even argue that Cohen's students might have been overall more excited or involved in the campus-riot issue, which had taken place only a few weeks before the experiment, whereas Rosenberg's study was done one year after the football-riot had taken place at a moment of "stabilization among the undergraduates of an attitude of disapproval toward any limitation upon football competition. This attitude remained salient during the period of experimentation even in the face of the fact that the faculty council, by a close vote, reversed its original decision (which had caused the riot). In general, *interested* students felt that future faculty interference with participation in football competition continued to be a real possibility" (*ibid.*, p. 33, italics added).

In this context then, one cannot but be intrigued by Rosenberg's final comment on the rejection of 11 of the 62 subjects who were originally run through the experiment. Besides the six members of varsity athletic teams, two subjects were discarded because they evidenced virtually complete and spontaneous insight into the deception (perceptual separation); one had misinterpreted the instructions and two others impressed both experimenters as showing psychotic tendencies. And Rosenberg concludes "However, when the analysis of the results is repeated with *the last three* rejected subjects included, the findings are in no wise altered" (*ibid.*, p. 35, italics added). Do we have to conclude that the findings are altered when the six rejected members with "more strongly anchored attitudes" are included? The point is that the importance or resistance to change of the attitude (or its cognitive elements) might have made a difference. And the mere possibility of such a difference seems to call for a balanced design if the point at issue is "interpreting differences between the two studies".

Other differences (which were also reported in Nuttin, 1964, and which are amply commented by Aronson, 1966, p. 123–124, and

B*

Rosenberg, 1966) are related to the social status of the three experimenters involved, and the more general characteristics of the two experimental situations, all of which do support the desirability of an experimental manipulation of the alleged biasing contaminants.

An impressive $.50 "incentive and reinforcement" effect A second question which puzzled us when reading the Rosenberg report, is the fact that his reinterpretation of the Cohen data seems to imply a truly impressive incentive and reinforcement effect of the $.50 reward (Cohen's largest attitude change), for which there is no comparable evidence in his own close replication. It will be remembered that Rosenberg attributes Cohen's inverted relationship between reward and attitude change to the change *suppressing* effect of the two biasing factors: "it would be either to avoid negative evaluation or to frustrate the experimenter, or both, that the high reward subject would hold back (from the experimenter and possibly even from himself) any evidence of having been influenced by the essay he has just completed" (*ibid.*, p. 32). This might indeed explain why there is no difference between Cohen's baseline control and the $10.00 and $5.00 conditions. But, restricting ourselves to Rosenberg's argument, the only way to account for Cohen's impressive difference ($p < 0.01$) between the $.50 and the baseline condition (4.5 versus 2.7) is by considering the half a dollar as both an incentive, stimulating new attitude-inconsistent cognitions, and a reinforcer, strengthening and stabilizing the newly established cognitions. The biasing factors being minimally activated in this lowest reward condition, the 4.5 score is indeed to be seen as a (very close to) "normal $.50" change score, normal meaning the change expected by Rosenberg's affective-cognitive consistency theory. The reader who is tempted to conjecture that the 4.5 score could be confounded with the change caused by the mere counterattitudinal plea (without any monetary reward) should however not bring this argument into Rosenberg's reasoning, because both Rosenberg and Cohen have not felt the necessity to add such a condition to their design. So there are no data in this respect, and there is nothing one can say, except that any change in attitude, both by Cohen and Rosenberg, always has been interpreted in terms of differential monetary reward.

Rosenberg states that his own $.50 condition is significantly different from the control condition ($p < .03$) and he leaves no doubt that he believes in the incentive and/or reward effect of half a dollar or even of half a dollar difference [see his analysis of the finding that the difference between the $.50 and $1.00 conditions did show up more clearly on a related attitude issue than on the crucial essay-topic (*ibid.*, p. 37)]. But his reinterpretation of Cohen's data implies such an impressive incentive and reinforcement effect of half a dollar reward, that it is hard to accept this implication.

The reader who might think that Rosenberg does not take his direct relation between activation of the biasing factors and the size of the reward so serious as to applying it, for example, to Cohen's significant difference between the $1.00 and $.50 conditions, is referred to the reply of Rosenberg (1966, p. 150) to Aronson (1966, p. 116) who rightly confronts Rosenberg's interpretation by questioning the differential effect of the research contaminants with two low reward conditions.

We should like to note that, when formulating our puzzlement with the implicit Rosenberg interpretation of the small reward Cohen effect, we are aware of the fact that one could argue that Rosenberg does not make predictions on the difference between a baseline and a $.50 reward, but on the relationship between magnitude of reward and attitude change, and furthermore that it is difficult if not completely unwarranted to transpose scores from one experiment to another even if they are close replications. These considerations taken for granted, it seems to us that within the whole context of the Rosenberg-Cohen controversy, the point raised—and the fact that no effort has been done to deal with it—cannot but add to the scepticism experienced when examining Rosenberg's reinterpretation of the complete Cohen results.

Festinger and Carlsmith elimination of contaminants There was a last major reason why we felt uncomfortable with the role attributed by Rosenberg to the absence of "perceptual separation" and "actual delivery of reward". In the dissonance study which conceptually is most closely related to the Cohen experiment, viz., the Festinger and Carlsmith (1959) experiment, the two biasing factors—as operationally defined by Rosenberg—were *not* present since the experimenters had perceptually separated the attitude measurement phase from the dissonance arousal phase and actually had delivered the monetary reward. Yet the same inverse relationship between size of monetary reward and attitude change was obtained.

Rosenberg (1965) deals with this experiment in a rather subjective way by stating that "the degree of separation may well have been insufficient. That experiment did not involve, (as did Rosenberg's) disguising the two phases as two different studies conducted in two different departments. Furthermore, the dependent variable was not a change in a previously stable social attitude but rather a momentary rating of how much the subject liked or disliked an experiment just completed" (Rosenberg, 1965, p. 32).

Rosenberg's critique is not convincing, since Festinger and Carlsmith explicitly invested considerable effort in realizing a perceptual separation and they do not report having been unsuccessful nor did they have to reject subjects (in contrast to Rosenberg) for seeing through the deception involved. Also, the implicit criterion of Rosenberg that the two studies should be run in two different departments does not seem to be a necessary condition for perceptual separation: there certainly is no great difficulty for a skilled research team to realize perceptual separation "within one single department".

Furthermore, one could argue that Festinger and Carlsmith did a better job than Rosenberg with regard to the second research contaminant. Festinger and Carlsmith actually delivered the monetary reward *before* the counterattitudinal role playing, in contrast to Rosenberg, who promised the reward before and gave it after the essay was written. According to Rosenberg's own view, the incentive function of the reward should be even more guaranteed if the reward was actually delivered before the student engaged in searching and formulating arguments in favour of the imposed attitude position.

However, as the second part of Rosenberg's quoted statement suggests, the fact that the dependent variable was not "a previously stable attitude" is also part of the argument. Does this mean that Rosenberg's theory does not apply both to attitudes which are "not previously stabilized" and to attitudes which are "previously firmly anchored"? It should indeed be remembered that Rosenberg rejected, on an *a priori* basis, the members of varsity athletic teams for the latter reason. Again then, we can ask the question if the attitudes of Cohen's subjects were sufficiently "previously stabilized" (the riot was a very recent one) and if this might not be another—non controlled—reason for the difference between the two experiments? As a matter of fact, if the attitudes of Cohen's subjects systematically are less "previously stabilized" than Rosenberg's, and if Cohen at the same time does not reject, in contrast to Rosenberg, the students with "stronger, more firmly anchored" attitudes, and if Rosenberg's theory only applies to subjects with previously stabilized but not firmly anchored attitudes, one cannot but be surprised when Rosenberg attributes the differences between his and Cohen's experiment to the elimination of the two biasing research contaminants, without manipulating experimentally these two allegedly crucial factors within his own design.

For all the above reasons, and last but not least for the very compelling reason that, apart from the controversy with Cohen, both Rosenberg's experimental data and his affective-cognitive consistency interpretation clearly do deserve a reliability test, we decided to run a critical replication of his study along with the already planned critical replication of the Festinger and Carlsmith experiment.

An experimental challenge of Rosenberg's reinterpretation

As stated earlier, our research interest was not primarily concerned with the validity of Rosenberg's assertions, but with the validity of the cognitive dissonance interpretation of Festinger and Carlsmith and Cohen's dissonance research. That is why, in our Rosenberg replication, several conditions were run which are not directly relevant to the Rosenberg–Cohen controversy. For the sake of clarity, we will break down the presentation of our research endeavour into several pieces of experimental analysis. In this section we will try to answer the following questions: (1) is there evidence for the reliability of the findings of Rosenberg, showing a direct relationship between size of reward and attitude change? (2) is there evidence for attributing an attitude change suppressing effect to the absence of "perceptual separation" and "actual delivery of the monetary reward" in high reward conditions? The results of experimental conditions which are not directly relevant to the Rosenberg–Cohen controversy will be discussed briefly in the last paragraph of this chapter.

Experiment One: The relationship between size of monetary reward for counterattitudinal advocacy and subsequent attitude change: a close replication of Rosenberg's experiment

PROBLEM AND DESIGN

The problem examined in this experiment is a very simple one: will a close replication of Rosenberg's study, carefully avoiding the alleged biases by managing perceptual separation and actually delivering the monetary reward, lead to a confirmation of the direct relationship between size of reward and attitude change as predicted by Rosenberg's

cognitive-affective consistency theory, or will the results obtained by Cohen be replicated?

In order to answer this question, five conditions from our larger 1964 design will be compared, viz., the results of four conditions in which the reward for writing a counterattitudinal essay was varied, 5 Belgian Francs (BF), 20, 100 and 500 BF, and a baseline control condition where the attitude response was emitted without previous essay writing. By using these five conditions, the design for our analysis will be quite close to the one used by Cohen and Rosenberg who also compared counterattitudinal essay-writing conditions for varying monetary rewards with a baseline control condition of mere attitude response.

As far as the incentive, reinforcement or consonance value of the Belgian Franc rewards is concerned, it should be noted that the official bank counter value of one U.S. dollar was approximately 50 BF, thus making the rewards manipulated 10 cents, 40 cents, 2 dollars and 10 dollars. 5 BF was the largest currency coin used at the time, and was just enough to buy a bar of chocolate (a glass of beer costs 6 BF); 20 BF was and still is the smallest banknote in Belgium, sufficient—at the time —to pay for a packet of 25 cigarettes plus a glass of beer; 500 BF was the second largest Belgian banknote allowing the student to pay for about 17 hot meals in the university's restaurant.

Though neither Rosenberg's nor Festinger's theory make any explicit restrictions as to where the monetary rewards should lie along the postulated psychological continuum, both theories imply a monotonic relationship between size of monetary reward and attitude change. Since Cohen as well as Rosenberg attach importance to the seemingly trivial difference between $.50 and $1.00, we can feel safe in testing both theories when using the above monetary rewards.

Apart from the reward manipulation, the various conditions were matched for the proportion of subjects who might have a "more firmly anchored attitude" as will become clear soon. All reward conditions were run, as were Rosenberg's, *with* perceptual separation between the role playing (dissonance arousal) and the attitude response phase, and *with* actual delivery of the reward.

PROCEDURE

In view of the fact that much of the theoretical debate in this area of social psychological research is based on rather subjective interpretations of what could be considered to be trivial procedural details, we are, however reluctantly, forced to give a fairly detailed description of the experimental procedure. We have amply learned that a sketchy description of the procedure can give rise to misunderstandings which seriously falsify the core of the debate (see e.g., Appendix p. 216). Moreover, we are confronted with the fact that a summary presentation of the attitude-issue and the experimental "macro-situation" would not allow sufficient understanding when the reader is not familiar with the broader social context in which the attitude and the experimental setting are contained.

Subjects The experimental subjects were students (under 25 years old) enrolled for the academic year 1964–65 in the second year of the university's Dutch-speaking Faculty of Sciences, pursuing the author's course on introductory experimental psychology. This 45 hour course is a compulsory part of the curriculum for all students who prepare a masters degree in chemistry, physics, geology, geography, biology, pharmacy and mathematics (all departments of the Faculty of Sciences). The approximately 450 students enrolled, attend the lectures simultaneously in one large auditorium. The content of the lectures deals with general and experimental psychology (psycho-physiology, learning, perception and motivation). No references are made to social psychology, nor to any deception devices used in attitude research. A few weeks before the experiment took place, all students had spent part of the lecture term to fill out a questionnaire on Walloon-Flemish attitudes, thus knowing that the author was interested in "opinion-research". At the same time, students were invited to volunteer in one of a series of psychological experiments to be run at the Psychological Institute by various graduate students preparing a Ph.D. degree. The topics of the experiment could vary from visual perception to opinion-polling and leadership studies. It was stressed that all research was "fundamental or basic research" and that none of the experiments had to do either with intelligence testing or personality assessment. With reference to the fact that the author himself might once in a while serve as an experimenter, it was made clear that participation in the experiments would have no effect whatsoever on the student-teacher evaluative relationship. Participation was encouraged by reference to the frequent use of animals in psychological research which was presented as being partly due to the easier access the researcher has to animals. The students were furthermore told that the experimenter would be happy to explain at the end of the experimental session why he was interested in the particular problem studied and that he would show how the research topic could be fitted into the general frame of the course. The Belgian university system does not use the "experimental credit points system", and, also in contrast to American laboratory customs, potential subjects are not made to expect any payment for participation in research. Special emphasis was laid upon the absolute necessity of similarity in subject's information and expectations about the experiment. Therefore, the students knew that they would have to pledge secrecy until the end of the 4-week experimentation period. Subjects were told that the average duration of the experiments would vary between 30 and 90 minutes, the absolute maximum being two hours.

Some 330 students volunteered by indicating the two hour blocks they had available. Of this population, 120 male students were used in a replication of the Festinger and Carlsmith experiment. As will become clear soon, these 120 students also provided the baseline data for the present replication of Rosenberg's study. For the other conditions of our Rosenberg research (Exp. I, II and III), 150 male and 30 female students were used. For all experiments presented in this chapter, the number of subjects is fifteen per condition. Ten subjects of each cell were randomly taken from the sub-population of students who were enrolled for the first time in the second year, the other five were sampled from the sub-population of students who were enrolled for the second time.

For the total group of 180 subjects, only two had to be replaced. For one student of Experiment II, (500 BF promised reward), it became clear during the final interview that he knew that something was wrong with the 500 BF reward. Another student explained during the same interview that he probably was a bad subject because he had been enrolled, as part of a previous curriculum, in a course of social psychology. Despite the fact that each subject went through a detailed and quite open interview (essentially similar to Rosenberg's), no other compelling reasons were found to reject data from the final analysis.

Attitude issue It will be remembered that the "importance" of the various cognitive elements is one determinant of the total magnitude of dissonance. A judgment about the importance of the attitude issue chosen, implies a minimal knowledge of the exam system operative at the time in Belgian universities, and more specifically in the Louvain Faculty of Sciences. As a rule, students of the second year in the Faculty of Sciences have 30 week courses in 7 to 12 (depending on the department) different areas. Within the same discipline (department) all these courses are exactly the same for all students enrolled. Psychology and a course on Ethics are the only "Human Science" courses of the Exact Sciences curriculum which is perceived to be among the most demanding curricula of the university. Three weeks after this thirty week period, there is a first exam session (July) during which students normally take an individual (oral and for some courses partly written) exam with the professor who taught the course. For each exam, the student is rated on a 20 point scale. If he meets the required scores on the full series of exams *as a whole*, he passes, has two months of vacation and can then enroll for the third year. If he fails, he can use the summer to study for a second exam session in September, during which he has to take again an individual exam on the *full* series of courses, even on the courses for which he had passing scores in July. It is not unusual that a student fails in September on an exam which he passed satisfactorily in the first session. If he does not meet the required scores on the full series of exams in September, he has to do the whole second year over again (bis-student), and is for all matters treated as if it were the first time he enrolled in the courses. If the bis-student fails again in both the July and September session, and still wants to continue, he might exceptionally be given a last chance within the same department and can enroll as a "tris-student". Typically a failing bis-student will enroll in a less demanding department or leave the university. These rules are identical for all students enrolled in Belgian universities at the time of our research.

The important point now is that a student who fails in the July exam sessions—this percentage varies between 50 and 60% of the students enrolled in the second year of Sciences—has to take again a complete series of exams in September, even in the courses he passed in July. It should be noted that a student can fail in July because he did very bad in one single exam (e.g., a score 5/20) or because he had two bad exams (two times 7/20 e.g.) or because he had three weak exams (3 times 9/20), or because he did not finish the full series (e.g., he was exhausted or became sick just before the last exam).

At the time of the experiment (1964) there was a rather urgent pressure to reform the university exam system. Besides the time scheduling problem, the major focus was the abolishment of the "complete exam series system" for the September session. Just the year before, some of the Human and Social Science Departments had made the quite revo-

lutionary step that a student should not have to retake a particular exam
in September if he had obtained a minimum score of 14/20 for that exam
in July (approximately 15% of exam scores reach that level in our
subject population) and fulfilled two other conditions: have taken the
full exam series in July, and have obtained a total minimum score of
50%. The students of the Faculty of Sciences, who were our experimental subjects, had not yet profited from this privileged "Human
Sciences" system, but were, for obvious reasons, very much in favour of
such a reform. At that time, however, the "university reform movement" and the influence of the student-body in the policy-making
committees of the university was practically non-existent and any change
in the desired direction could only be expected from a decision from the
tenure staff members of the Faculty of Sciences. It was very much hoped
that a favourable decision, imitating the Human and Social Sciences
example, would be taken before the first exam session to be held after
our experimentation period.

The reader is now prepared to grasp the relevance of the critical
attitude rating chosen for our experiments which was formulated as
follows: "If the committee of the Science Faculty should decide against
exam exemptions (this means that no exam, however good it might have
been in July, would be left out of the second session), I would judge this
decision not justified at all . . . completely justified". It also will have
become clear that the attitudes of the bis-students, as a group, could be
assumed to be stronger, and more firmly anchored than those of the
other experimental subjects. In fact, our bis-students can be considered
as comparable to the rejected subjects (members of varsity athletic
teams) in Rosenberg's study. As said before, 1/3 of each experimental
condition consisted of bis-students.

Experimenters For all of the eleven perceptual separation conditions
reported in this chapter, the author was the only experimenter (experimenter 1) eliciting the crucial attitude response and conducting the first,
third and fourth phase of the experiment. The second phase, in which
the subject wrote the counterattitudinal essay, was run by one of four
thoroughly trained male experimenters (experimenter 2)*.

* Thanks are due to Dirk Eeckhout who was in charge of the general organization of all
sessions and to the experimenters Karel Baeck, Erik Billiaert, Dirk Logghe and John
Rijsman.

Experimental phase 1: creation of "perceptual separation" As each subject arrived at experimenter 1's office, he offered a valid excuse for requesting the subject to wait for at least 20 minutes. Depending on the moment of the day, the subject either saw that someone was in experimenter 1's office or clearly overheard a phonecall forcing experimenter 1 "to do something very important he had forgotten". Since all subjects were invited during a two-hour free period, they could be guaranteed that even with the waiting period included, the time limits of the schedule would be respected. Experimenter 1 suggested that they could walk in the corridors, but before they had the opportunity to ask if they were allowed to leave the building, experimenter 1 said "I have just thought of something better for you while you are waiting. Now that you are here in the psychology building, you might as well have a look around. I'm sure there are some research-assistants who might welcome you as a subject for short experiments. Oh yes, as a matter of fact, there is a fellow who does short experiments and who complained only the other day that it was very difficult for him to get subjects. Let's see if he's there. Perhaps you would like to help him: this is an opportunity for you to get in contact with another section of the Psychology Department". All subjects agreed to do what was suggested.

With some show of uncertainty, experimenter 1 looked up the phone number of experimenter 2, and called him while the subject could overhear the conversation. Experimenter 2 was told that experimenter 1 just happened to have a subject who had to wait anyway 20 minutes, and that *experimenter 2 could come and pick him up if he wanted to*. It was stressed that the subject should be back in 20 minutes. Experimenter 1 continued to the subject: "So, that's O.K. I'll just help you on the right way" (and while walking with the subject some 15 metres) "It should be clear that you do not have to cooperate with that fellow to please me, but I'm sure you will find it interesting. I would even not be surprised if he had some budget for doing his research". Soon experimenter 2 showed up at the end of the corridor, thanks experimenter 1 for not having forgotten his need, and then experimenter 1 rushes back to his office. Experimenter 2 takes the subject hastily to his room, which is still at a 70 metres distance, on another floor in a part of the building opposite to where the subject had found the office of experimenter 1. While walking, experimenter 2 corroborates the perceptual separation by asking the subject if he is enrolled at the Faculty of Psychology, and when the student says that he is from the Faculty of Sciences, he says "Nuttin is a lucky man with that

big introductory course for the Sciences; he can have as many subjects as
he wants; I myself am lucky when I find two or three volunteers a day.
And that's how I have to prepare my PhD thesis!''.

Experimental phase 2: counterattitudinal advocacy As soon as they arrive in
experimenter 2's office, it is explained that experimenter 2 is preparing a
thesis on the factors contributing to success or failure in university
examinations. "There are of course one hundred reasons for failure, but I
guess that the policy of our exam committees also is quite important. I
have been interviewing members of such committees from all faculties of
the university, and I did learn quite a bit . . . you just said you are from
the Faculty of Sciences isn't it''. Experimenter 2 picks from a shelf,
among a series of files clearly bearing on their cover the name of the
various faculties, the one indicating "Sciences" and after having looked
up a particular paragraph, he continues,

> Well, when I was talking with professors of your faculty, it became clear
> for example, that they are strongly opposed to exam exemptions for
> September. They defend the point that a student who fails in July, even if he
> only fails for one bad exam, has to do over all the exams in September, even
> the ones which were excellent in July. As you probably know, we in
> Psychology and several other faculties, have since last year, a system of
> exemptions for exams with a 14/20 score. Your faculty seems to feel that
> exemptions will lower the academic standards. This problem of exemptions,
> which is a policy problem for all faculties, deserves in my opinion a thorough
> and all-round analysis and that is one of the points my thesis is focussing on.
> As you might or might not know, it has been proven that one of the better
> techniques to get relevant arguments on all sides of an issue, is to ask people
> to write essays favouring only one—the pro or contra side. Since I do have
> already plenty of arguments against the complete exam series system, in
> favour of exemptions, I would like you to write down all arguments you can
> in favour of the severe exam policy. I know that it is not an enjoyable job to
> write a plea which runs contrary to your private conviction, but you must
> understand that this is important for my work.

After having searched again in some files, experimenter 2 finds a blank
sheet entitled "Plea in favour of a severe exam policy: arguments *against*
exemptions of courses which were passed successfully in July". Handing
over the sheet, experimenter 2 invites the subject to write "the strongest,
most forceful, most creative and thoughtful essay you can, in favour of
this severe exam policy. Thus you should use all arguments you can *against*
exam exemptions for the September session".

The reward manipulation was then introduced: "I should add that I have been receiving financial support for my research from the National Institute for Scientific Research (a fictitious name). I am paying the students who help me a—BF reward. Of course, I do not want to force you to write the essay, but you certainly would do me a favour . . . and if you are yourself interested in the results, I'll be happy to inform you, because after all the exam system is a quite important issue for you too isn't it?" Experimenter 2 paused for the subject's reaction, and upon compliance of the subject with the request, he says "Why don't you think first a few minutes and then start writing. Wow! we only have about 15 minutes left. Please do not be concerned with style and grammar, the only thing which matters is that you do present a strong and convincing plea against your own position and in favour of the severe exam policy with regard to exemptions". After 5 minutes, experimenter 2 interrupts the subject by reminding him that he should only give arguments in favour of the severe exam policy. After 20 minutes of essay writing, experimenter 2 says: "I think we have to stop. I would not like to have Nuttin waiting too long otherwise he might never send me a student anymore". At this moment, experimenter 2 *delivers* the monetary reward to the subject who signs a receipt "for bookkeeping purposes". Since the subject would have great difficulty in finding the way back to the office of experimenter 1, experimenter 2 accompanies the subject while thanking him for his cooperation. When delivering the subject back experimenter 2 says "Thank you very much, professor, if you ever have another student who has to wait, please think of me again!".

Experimental phase 3: attitude measurement Experimenter 1 (the author) who is now conducting the experiment, explains to the subject that social psychology is his major area of research interest. He points to the Walloon-Flemish questionnaire which the student answered the day he had volunteered for the experiment. The experimenter explains that he is quite interested in long term opinion change, that the same Walloon-Flemish questionnaire had already been administered 8 years earlier (which is true) and that it is quite interesting to see how opinions change or remain constant over such a long period of time. The experimenter continues by asking the subject if he would be willing to be interviewed on a variety of student problems. Emphasis is laid upon the fact that an interview is not an exam, that there are no answers which are right or wrong, but that the only answers which are of interest to the experimenter are the ones which are sincere and straightforward. "If you prefer not to answer one or another question which might seem to you to be rather indelicate, I would appreciate your refusal much more than an insincere answer". Upon agreement of the subject, the experimenter continued: "As a first start on the interview, which I want to keep somewhat standardized, I would like you to answer a few short questions, which I would invite you to read aloud before checking off your own position on this type of scale which we often use in opinion-research". The student was given a booklet of 19 pages, one item per page.

The first items had to do with various topics of university policy: absenteism in courses, student marriages, student-professor relations, commuting students, etc. The fifth item, which elicited the crucial attitude response, read "If my faculty committee should decide against exam exemptions (this means that no exam, however good it might have been in July, would be left out of the second session), I would judge this decision . . .". The student could then respond on a 31-point scale, marked at every fifth point by the following labels: "I think this decision would be not justified at all, very little justified, little justified, slightly justified, rather justified, very justified and completely justified". This scale form, identical to the ones Rosenberg and Cohen used, was the same for all 8 items. For each rating, the experimenter read aloud in a neutral way the subject's response, e.g., "so you think . . . is somewhat between very and completely justified". The items being answered in a relaxed way, the subject usually stuggled a bit with the fifth item which was the first to be formulated in a negative form, so that they had to think over how correctly to express their opinion on the matter. By repeating aloud the checked answer, the experimenter made certain that no error in interpretation occurred. If a student, exceptionally, said "I happen to have had a similar topic while I was waiting", the experimenter said indifferently "Is that right" and let the subject continue the next three filler questions.

As soon as the eighth item was answered, the experimenter interrupted the subject by asking "was there any question which struck you until now? A question which made you react for instance: how come this question is being asked here?" After the subject's comments, which were almost invariably of the type "they all are pretty interesting issues", the experimenter went back to the page with the critical item and applied all his skills in probing the subject for possible suspicion concerning the two-experiment disguise. Despite this almost suggestive opportunity offered to the subject to show off his insight in the deception used, not a single student indicated having seen through it and all appeared quite surprised when told that experimenter 1 and experimenter 2 had each conducted part of the same experiment. The experimenter told the subject that he would soon explain everything more in detail, but that he would appreciate if the subject would be willing to answer the rest of the items in the booklet, which had to do with the essay he just had written in the office of experimenter 2. The last questions were similar to the ones asked by Rosenberg except for the fact that a very detailed assessment was made of the evaluation of different sizes of monetary reward given for participation in psychological experiments.

Experimental phase 4: debriefing As soon as the subject had filled out the questionnaire, the author explained the purpose of the experiment and commented in detail upon the reasons forcing social psychologists to use deception for the study of some types of problem. Before the student was thanked and dismissed, they all gave a formal promise not to talk to other people about any features of the experiment. The monetary reward subjects were told that no funds whatsoever were available for paying subjects (which was very true indeed) and were invited to return the money. Since some subjects were paid 500 BF (as was explained to all subjects) it seemed appropriate to give a standard non-monetary reward to all participants. It should be noted that, after the full experimentation period was over, this non-monetary reward given individually to all subjects during the debriefing, was extended to all students, even those who did not volunteer, because "they must have had some personal reason not to participate, maybe because they did not trust themselves enough for keeping their mouth shut and that should also be considered as a fair cooperation to the research projects involved". This was done in order to avoid the creation of an expectation that participation in psychological experiments would normally lead to individual rewards. The non-monetary reward which consisted of allowing the student, who wished to do so, to participate in a written exam on part of the course immediately after the Easter vacation, was highly appreciated since almost every student profited from this opportunity to reduce his final examload. The effort invested from the author's side in this extra-exam duty, was justified by his interest in "gathering data on the performance of students in a relaxed as compared to a more tense exam atmosphere".

Procedure for subjects of baseline condition Data for the baseline condition, directly comparable to the Rosenberg and Cohen baseline conditions, were collected individually from 120 students, randomly taken from the same subject pool as the subjects for our Rosenberg replication (cf. supra, p. 25). These subjects had been participants in one of the eight conditions of our replication of the Festinger and Carlsmith experiment where the very last item they had to answer in the attitude measurement phase of the experiment was identical to the crucial item of our Rosenberg replication. It should be noted that the replication of the Festinger and Carlsmith experiment was run concurrently with the replication of Rosenberg's experiment, during the same four week experimentation period. The experimental treatment of the subjects used for our baseline condition was of course not related at all to any university policy attitude issue. Therefore, these responses can be taken as a basis ($N = 120$) for an estimation of the pre-experimental attitude response of the subjects used in the various experimental conditions of the Rosenberg replication.

Summary of procedure and design Sixty male students were induced to write a 20 minute essay strongly in favour of a policy that was clearly opposite to their own attitude. They were paid either 5, 20, 100, or 500 BF for doing so. After this "forced compliance", their attitude change towards the same issue was assessed by comparison with the attitude responses given by 120 subjects who had not been previously invited to cognitively elaborate the attitude issue. Procedure and design are a close replication of Rosenberg's experiment, with special emphasis on the elimination of the alleged attitude change suppressing research contaminants (perceptual separation and actual delivery of reward).

RESULTS AND DISCUSSION

The average attitude responses given on the critical item "how justified the faculty decision against exam exemption would be" are presented in Table 1. As in the Cohen and Rosenberg studies, the ratings were scored from 1.00 (not justified at all) through 1.2, 1.4 . . . to 6.8, 7.0 (completely justified).

Looking at Fig. 1, it becomes clear that our results confirm the Cohen data and are exactly opposite to Rosenberg's. Taking the baseline condition as a dependable ($N = 120$) estimation of the pre-experimental attitude response of the subjects, the obtained changes in the advocated

TABLE 1

Mean attitude response towards complete exam sessions as a
function of differentially rewarded counterattitudinal advocacy

Baseline	Monetary Reward			
	500 BF	100 BF	20 BF	5 BF
2.6	3.0	3.5	3.7	4.1

Note. 15 subjects per experimental condition and 120 subjects in
the baseline condition. The higher the mean, the more
positive the attitude toward complete exam-sessions. Highest
value 7·0, lowest value 1.0.

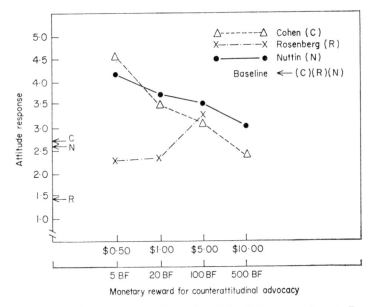

Fig. 1 Comparison between the main results of the Cohen experiment, Rosenberg's
replication of Cohen and our own replication of Rosenberg (Experiment 1).

direction are indeed an inverse function of the magnitude of the monetary
reward.

Statistical analyses of the data (Table 2, 3 and 4) reveal that the
attitude change in the advocated direction is very significant and that the
relation between size of reward and attitude change is inverse and linear,
as predicted by cognitive dissonance theory.

Although the effect of the monetary reward, reflected in the deviation from the baseline score (2.6) was found to be very significant, it is shown in Table 3 that this only applies for the 5 BF and 20 BF reward conditions (4.1 and 3.7).

TABLE 2
Analysis of variance for data of Table 1

Source	SS	df	MS	F
Treatments	45.94	4	11.48	4.16*
Within treatments	483.22	175		
Total	529.16	179		

$*p < 0.01$ (All p values reported throughout the monograph are two-tailed unless specified otherwise.)

TABLE 3
Test for significance of linear regression for the four reward conditions of Table 1

Source	SS	df	MS	F
Linear regression	9.90	1	9.90	4.63*
Deviation	0.25	2	0.13	
Within treatments	119.77	56	2.14	
Total	129.92	59		

$*p < 0.05$

TABLE 4
Summary of t values for differences between the mean attitude responses of Table 1

Conditions and Means	100 BF (3.5)	500 BF (3.0)	Baseline (2.6)
5 BF (4.1)	1.12n.s.	2.11*	3.14†
20 BF (3.7)		1.42n.s.	2.23*
100 BF (3.5)			1.83n.s.
500 BF (3.0)			0.76n.s.

n.s. = not significant.
$*p < 0.05$
$†p < 0.01$

As far as the effect of the intensity of the pre-experimental attitude towards the exam reform is concerned, an analysis of variance for the attitude response as a function of reward and the belonging to the category of bis-students (whose attitudes could be assumed to be stronger and more firmly anchored) failed to confirm any differential prediction based on this criterion.

CONCLUSION

The above findings lead us to the following conclusions:

1. Rosenberg's thesis with regard to the attitude change suppressing effect of evaluation apprehension and/or hostility toward the experimenter in Cohen's experiment, has received no support. The Cohen results were replicated, notwithstanding the fact that the two biasing factors, as operationally defined by Rosenberg, were very carefully eliminated.

2. The predictive value of Rosenberg's affective-cognitive theory is not confirmed within the present experimental situation.

3. The reliability of the Cohen results and the predictive value of the cognitive dissonance hypothesis concerning the inverted relationship between size of reward for counterattitudinal advocacy and subsequent attitude change are corroborated.

Experiment Two: Experimental test of Rosenberg's attitude change suppressing research contaminants

PROBLEM AND DESIGN

We have already amply commented on the fact that Rosenberg (1964–65) did attribute the absence of attitude change in Cohen's high reward conditions to the suppressing effect of two data biasing research contaminants, identified as "absence of perceptual separation" and "mere promise as opposed to actual delivery of the monetary reward". Although the results of our replication do not support the importance attributed by Rosenberg to the procedural changes of his altered replication, an experimental manipulation of these very procedural aspects which are supposed to arouse evaluation apprehension and negative affect toward the experimenter is the only way to determine whether, in fact, they produce a suppression of attitude change.

Since these biasing factors are considered by Rosenberg to be maximally operative in the high reward conditions, we decided to replicate our own 500 BF condition while altering the experimental treatment only by eliminating one or the other of the two crucial aspects. The three conditions to be compared in the present experiment thus will be: (1) the 500 BF reward of Experiment One (with perceptual separation and delivery of reward); (2) a 500 BF reward without perceptual separation (and with delivery of reward); (3) a 500 BF reward with mere promise of reward (and with perceptual separation). No other baseline or control conditions are necessary for the present purpose, the only question being the following: will conditions 2 and 3, compared to condition 1 manifest less attitude change, as a result of the change suppressing effect of one or the other alleged contaminant?

PROCEDURE

The subjects for Experiment Two were randomly taken from the same pool as the subjects of the first experiment (see p. 25). The two new conditions were run at the same time (in random sequence) with the other conditions previously discussed. The only procedural differences with the 500 BF reward condition of Experiment One, are the following:

(1) *Without perceptual separation:* experimental phase 1 "creation of perceptual separation" is dropped completely. Experimental phase 2 starts with experimenter 2 picking up the subject in a waiting room, because it would be too difficult for the subject to find the office by himself. For the rest, the treatment of phase 2 remains unchanged, except of course for the "I would not like to have Nuttin *waiting* etc." comments. Upon reception of the reward, the subject is invited to answer a few questionnaire items, "which all have to do with university topics which are more or less closely related to my thesis interest". Instructions and questionnaires are identical to experimental phase 3 (attitude measurement) of Experiment One, except of course for the probing as to subject's insight into the two-experiment disguise. Upon termination of the attitude measurement phase, experimenter 2 explains to the subject that experimenter 1 would like to talk briefly to him, and brings him to the office of the author, who conducts the debriefing. Just before starting the debriefing, the subject is invited to answer once again the critical attitude item thus suggesting to the subject that his answer on that particular item was the most important question of the experiment.

(2) *With mere promise of reward:* this condition differs from the highest

reward condition of Experiment One only in so far that there was no actual delivery of the monetary reward. Before leaving the room of experimenter 2, the subject was told that the reward would be mailed by the Administration of the Institute.

RESULTS AND DISCUSSION

It will be remembered that the 500 BF reward condition of our replication of the Rosenberg experiment did produce the smallest attitude change of all reward conditions, the average attitude score being 3.0 which was not significantly different from the baseline (2.6). When there is no perceptual separation whatsoever between the "evaluation apprehension and negative affect arousing" essay-writing phase and the "attitude measurement phase", the results are almost identical: 3.2. The difference, if any, lies in the direction opposite to Rosenberg's expectations.

It might be worth noticing that the mean attitude score was 3.3 when these same subjects were invited by experimenter 1 (at the beginning of the debriefing phase) to answer once more this critical item. If anything, the subjects should have been maximally suspicious at that moment since it became clear that the experimenter's focus was on his own attitude towards the issue. Although the high monetary reward was, to be sure, in the subject's wallet, "there must be something wrong with it, since I couldn't just go home after having completed the experiment with experimenter 2". We see that under these circumstances of enhanced suspicion, the attitude responses do not differ from the condition with complete perceptual separation. It should be conceded however, that there might be other factors—to be discussed in the final chapter of this monograph—which could be responsible for the stability of the attitude responses tapped from the same subjects.

In the "mere promise of 500 BF reward" condition the average attitude score becomes 3.9 which differs at the 0.05 level from both "delivery of 500 BF reward" conditions (3.0 and 3.2). The difference however is again in the direction opposite to Rosenberg's interpretation of the Cohen results. As a matter of fact, the attitude change in the advocated direction is not suppressed but enhanced when the reward is merely promised, and not actually delivered. So again, the data for this source of bias do not confirm the attitude change suppressing effects claimed by Rosenberg.

With regard to the latter results, dissonance theorists might be tempted to consider the 3.0–3.9 difference as consistent with the dissonance theory prediction. The importance (value) and resistance to change of the consonant relation between the cognitive element concerning "promised 500 BF" and "counterattitudinal essay writing" can be seen to be smaller than with an "actually delivered 500 BF reward". A high reward in the air might indeed be less valued than the same reward in the wallet. This speculation is however free-floating since we do not have any other promised-delivered reward comparisons available. Moreover, the result is rather disturbing when we remember that Cohen did not have any attitude change effect for his "merely promised" $10.00 and $5.00 reward conditions.

CONCLUSION

The absence of perceptual separation or actual delivery of reward under conditions close to the original Cohen experiment, do not lead to a suppression of attitude change. The results of an experimental manipulation of both research contaminants, do not support Rosenberg's thesis with regard to the identification of the artifactual nature of Cohen's results.

Despite the clarity of the evidence offered in our Experiments One and Two, Rosenberg in several papers, (Feldman, 1966, Abelson et al., 1968) has claimed that our replication does not bear on his critique of Cohen and does not seriously challenge the conclusions drawn from his study. Basically his defence consists of an attack on the validity of our replication. His extensive critique however, is so riddled with blatant errors of fact and interpretation that we decided to devote an appendix to a rather detailed presentation of his argument and our counterargument. The interested reader who shares some fundamental ethical publication standards might find it instructive to be confronted with Milton Rosenberg's unusual example of polemical backbiting (see Appendix). Suffice it here to point to the fact that quite recently Rosenberg (1970) published an extensive discussion of Cohen's and his own 1964 experiment without even mentioning our critical replication of his study.

4. Inconclusive evidence about the dissonance effect

The data from our 1964 research project presented so far are clearly in support of Festinger's cognitive dissonance theory. However, they cover only 7 of the 21 conditions upon which our 1964 mimeographed report was based. In this last section of the chapter on our earlier research, we will briefly present some additional data and formulate several questions which were raised with regard to the experimental foundation of cognitive dissonance theory. None of the questions which will be put forward here will be treated in detail, since Chapter Two deals with them in a more extensive way.

Experiment Three: Partial replication of Experiment One on female subjects

PROBLEM, DESIGN AND PROCEDURE

It will be remembered that Experiment One did confirm the dissonance predicted inverted trend between size of monetary reward and attitude change. The largest difference between reward conditions was found, as expected, between the 5 BF and the 500 BF conditions, for which the average attitude scores were 4.1 and 3, the two intermediate reward conditions (20 BF and 100 BF) lying in between these scores (3.7 and 3.5). However beautiful the trend was, the very fact that these intermediate reward conditions were not significantly different from each other, and that the maximum difference obtained for a centuple of the small reward was only 1 scalar unit (change from "little" to "somewhat" justified), did raise some scepticism about the strength of the dissonance effect. Of course, the effect was there, and was impressive when considering the fact that the attitude chosen could be assumed to be particularly resistant to change for all subjects and quite firmly anchored for at least one third of each condition (bis-students). Still, it was felt that the reliability and external validity of the dissonance effect could gain from a replication of our smallest and largest reward condition (5 BF and 500 BF). That is why, at the end of the experimental period the latter two cells were refilled each with 15 subjects taken at random from the same population except for the fact that they all were female students.

It should be noted that there is no reason to think that the attitude issue is less important for female students. This might be the case for some girl students of one or another Department in Human Sciences, but it is very unlikely that the girl students enrolled at the quite demanding Faculty of Sciences would be less motivated to succeed in their exams than their male study fellows. It might also be worthwhile to point to the fact that for all experiments referred to so far (Festinger and Carlsmith, Cohen, Rosenberg) only male subjects were run. Especially for the two latter studies, this probably is related to the nature of the attitude issue chosen. The fact that the two experimental conditions reported in this section are the only cells of this monograph for which we called upon female students, is simply a consequence of the relatively small proportion of female students in the Science Faculty. Since sex homogeneity within designs can be considered as part of common practice in our research area, and since male students are by far more numerous in our subject population, it should not be surprising that all our experiments, except Experiment Three, are based on an all-male design.

The experimental situation and treatment for the subjects of Experiment Three is in all respects identical to the 5 BF and 500 BF condition of Experiment One (with "perceptual separation and delivery of reward").

RESULTS

The results for this identical replication on female students are rather discouraging. The average attitude response for the smallest (5 BF) reward condition is 4.1, whereas the largest reward (500 BF) results in an average of 3.9. The difference, which lies in the dissonance predicted direction is obviously trivial. It should be noted that for both conditions there is presumably a significant change from the baseline, since both conditions are at the level of the male 5 BF condition. Being only interested in a confirmation of the difference between a 5 and 500 BF reward manipulation, we did not collect baseline data for female students.

CONCLUSION

The external validity and reliability of the dissonance effect obtained on male students proved to be very weak. In an effort to replicate the effect on female students of the same population, no significant difference was found between the smallest and largest reward condition of Experiment One. The difference between a very small and very high reward does not seem to offer a valid basis for predicting differential attitude change. The dissonance theory derived hypothesis on the inverted relation between size of monetary reward and attitude is not supported, nor are the rivalling theories predicting a direct function between the two same variables. Most likely the very small and very high reward both had a significant attitude change effect in the advocated direction. The absence of a female baseline group prevents us from drawing this conclusion with the usual assurance.

Experiment Four: Counter- versus pro-attitudinal re-warded advocacy

PROBLEM AND DESIGN

Our basic concern with the Festinger and Carlsmith and Cohen support for cognitive dissonance theory had to do with the fact that the experimental designs used did not seem to provide sufficient guarantee for the validity of the crucial concepts postulated in the cognitive consistency view of the studied phenomenon.

"*Central dissonance*" It will be clear by now that in the Cohen experiment, as well as in the Festinger and Carlsmith study, where students were differentially rewarded for a short counterattitudinal oral role playing (tell a waiting stooge that boring tasks were interesting and enjoyable), the crucial supposition made by dissonance psychologists is that cognitive dissonance was generated between the cognitive element concerning the private attitude and the cognitive element concerning the overt counter-attitudinal role playing (see e.g., Festinger and Carlsmith, 1959, p. 253: "the knowledge that he believes 'X' " and "the knowledge that he has publicly stated that he believes 'not X' "). The theoretical interpretation of the subsequent attitude change is based on the posited experimental creation of cognitive dissonance between these two cognitive elements which form the conceptual centre or nucleus of the experiment and which we call, for the sake of clarity, the "*central dissonance*".

It should however, be emphasized that this conceptual structure is a label imposed on only two of a most complex set of cognitions which were generated by the experimental situation and treatment. The difficult point now is that there is no way of checking that this "central dissonance" is really crucial for the interpretation of the attitude change, except by *experimentally manipulating* this aspect of subject's cognitive system. On what basis can Festinger and Carlsmith and Cohen prove that this central dissonance was a necessary condition for the effect to be obtained? The experimental designs used, had a small and large reward *counter*attitudinal advocacy condition and the only control group was a baseline without any form of advocacy or reward. Since the effects of both counter- and pro-attitudinal rewarded advocacy upon attitude change are not yet sufficiently established, it seemed to us that an experimental manipulation of the posited central dissonance was quite appropriate. It could indeed be that the experimental subjects perceived the reward as simply given for helping the experimenter who was in an emergency situation, and that there was no such cognition as "I was paid *for telling a lie*, or for writing an essay *against* my own attitude". There was for example, no guarantee that the subjects would think that their colleagues who supposedly had already been helping Cohen by writing a *pro-attitudinal* essay would have been paid differently "for their cooperation". So it might be that the counterattitudinal nature of the help needed was of so peripheral importance that the posited relevant relation between the cognitive element concerning the reward and the one concerning the counterattitudinal role playing as such was not established at all.

"Forced compliance" We also were dissatisfied with the subjective interpretation of the small consonant reward as a "minimal force" for compliance. Although we will deal with this question in more detail in Experiment Six, we would like to point to the fact that Festinger (1957) sees the manipulated small monetary reward as *"just enough reward to elicit the overt compliance"* (p. 95, original italics) or as Festinger and Carlsmith (1959) put it "the dissonance is maximized if the promised reward . . . is just *barely sufficient* to induce the person to say 'not X' " (p. 204) and "the greater the reward (beyond what was *necessary* to elicit the behaviour) the smaller the effect" (p. 208, italics added). We agree, of course, that the reward *can* be seen as one of the forces which induce the subject to comply with the experimenter's request, and can be seen as consonant with the compliance, but in none of the dissonance experiments is there sufficient evidence that the money offered does have a "coercive" function as a pressure element for the compliance. Festinger and Aronson (1960) go even so far as defining the forced compliance as a situation in which "the subject makes a public statement which is dissonant with his beliefs *in order to* receive a small reward" (p. 225, italics added).

It seems to us that this is an interpretative description of what *could* have been the cognitive elaboration of the subject. Again, no evidence is offered that the subject would be less likely to comply if no monetary force—*ceteris paribus*—would be used. Since money is the only force manipulated in the research under discussion, and since we are hesitant to subscribe to the above interpretation of this force, we prefer to label the compliance merely as a *rewarded* (instead of "forced"), compliance. Thus we felt that the interpretative unclarity of the "minimal force" and "minimal consonance weight" of the low reward condition would profit from the insertion of a not-rewarded compliance condition in the conventional design.

On the basis of the above considerations, the following conditions were run concurrently with those of Experiments One and Two:

1. A counterattitudinal advocacy condition without monetary reward. In this condition, the supposedly consonant cognitive element concerning the monetary reward was not created, and the total cognitive dissonance of the system presumably should be somewhat greater than in the small reward condition (see e.g., supra p. 9). At the same time, Festinger's interpretative description of the small monetary reward as "barely sufficient to elicit the compliance" was also tested, since this conception would mean that a relatively higher proportion of subjects of the no reward condition would refuse to comply with the request of the experimenter. It is clear that the above reasoning implies that all other external forces or cognitive elements consonant with the compliance are held constant between conditions. The briefing of the experimenters was very strict in this respect.

2. Three pro-attitudinal advocacy conditions, in which the subjects were invited to give arguments in favour of their *own position* with regard to the attitude issue. In these conditions, all factors of the experimental situation and treatment are kept constant, except for the "central dissonance" which is turned into a "central consonance" or absence of central dissonance. The three (consonant) pro-attitudinal "compliance" or "cooperation with experimenter" conditions only differ *qua* monetary reward which is either zero, 5 BF or 500 BF.

These new conditions combined with the small and high reward condition of Experiment One, do result in a 2×3 factorial design, whereby a first factor of cognitive nature is varied at two levels (presence or absence of central dissonance) and a second reward factor with three levels, zero, 20 and 500 BF.

PROCEDURE

The subjects were all sampled from the same male student pool as the ones of Experiment One and Two. As said before, all conditions of the experiments reported in this chapter (except for the replication on female subjects in Experiment Three) were simultaneously run in random sequence until the criteria of 10 normal and 5 bis-students were reached.

The differences in experimental situation and treatment were as follows:

The zero reward counterattitudinal advocacy condition is in all respects identical to the reward conditions of Experiment One except for the fact that no monetary reward is ever promised or delivered by the essay-eliciting experimenter. There might however be some ambiguity in the operationalization of the "zero reward" in this experiment, which could impede an unambiguous interpretation of the results. As a matter of fact, following closely the instructions of Rosenberg, the subject in all con-ditions (with perceptual separation) of our Rosenberg-Cohen research was told by the first experimenter (the author), that the essay-eliciting experimenter "might have some budget for doing his research" (cf. supra, p. 29). Since the first experimenter—who also did elicit the attitude response—was always blind with regard to the specific experimental treatment of the subject, this possible creation of an expectation of a reward was kept constant. In this sense, the zero reward conditions of this experiment (counter- and pro-attitudinal plea) might actually have re-sulted in mild "disconfirmation of expectation" conditions. The fact that our perceptual separation manipulation was not performed for a zero reward condition does not allow us to use any direct reference data for the solution of this problem.

The *pro-attitudinal advocacy conditions* are identical in all respects to the counterattitudinal condition of Experiment One, except that the essay-eliciting experimenter invites the subject to only write arguments in defence of his own attitude. After 5 minutes of essay writing, the subject is reminded that he should restrict his essay to those arguments which are in favour of his own position.

RESULTS AND DISCUSSION

The mean attitude responses for the six conditions analyzed in the present experiment are presented in Table 5.

An analysis of variance (see Table 6) shows that neither reward nor presence or absence of "central dissonance" do have a significant main

TABLE 5

Mean attitude response towards complete exam sessions
as a function of monetary reward and pro- or counterattitudinal
nature of advocacy

Advocacy	Monetary Reward		
	Zero	5 BF	500 BF
Counterattitudinal	3.7	4.1	3.0
Pro-attitudinal	2.7	2.9	3.7

Note. 15 subjects per condition.

TABLE 6
Analysis of variance for data of Table 5

Source	SS	df	MS	F
Advocacy (A)	5.77	1	5.77	$2.02^{n.s.}$
Reward (R)	1.83	2	0.92	
A × R	16.62	2	8.31	$2.91^{n.s.}$
Within treatments	239.63	84	2.85	
Total	263.84	89		

n.s. = not significant.

effect, nor is there a significant interaction between the two variables manipulated. Also no systematic differences were obtained between normal and bis-students.

Whatever one might be tempted to conclude from the above data, we would like to emphasize the main implications of the lack of significance of main effects and/or interaction. There can be no doubt that the classical cognitive dissonance interpretation of the data obtained in Experiment One is based upon the "central dissonance" generated by the inconsistency between the cognitive elements concerning attitude and advocacy and upon the dissonance reducing function of the monetary reward received for engaging in the counterattitudinal advocacy. If this theoretical frame is to have any specific explanatory power for the assessed attitude change, one has to expect, it seems to us, that attitude responses emitted after differentially rewarded counterattitudinal advocacy will be systematically different from attitude responses emitted after equally rewarded pro-attitudinal advocacy, where there is no reason to postulate cognitive dissonance between the crucial cognitive elements concerning attitude and advocacy. The data of the present experiment however, do not foster this specific explanatory function of Festinger's theory: the only safe conclusion warranted by the above analysis of variance is that one should not reject the null hypothesis which holds that the attitude responses given by subjects after either pro- or counterattitudinal essay and with high, low or no reward, all are drawn from the same attitude response population. Although this straightforward data analysis does not allow for any further valid comparison between a posteriori selected conditions, it might be worthwhile to briefly speculate upon the observed new data of this experiment.

First, we would like to point to the fact that within the counterattitudinal advocacy conditions, the attitude change obtained for the zero reward condition (3.7) is not superior to the small 5 BF reward condition (4.1), as one should expect on the basis of dissonance theory. The difference from the baseline (2.6) however is significant. We have already mentioned that the possible creation of a "disconfirmed expectation" might interfere with an unambiguous check of the effect of a complete absence of any consonant reward element. Still one would—on the basis of a cognitive dissonance analysis of the situation—feel entitled to consider a disconfirmed reward expectation as enhancing the total magnitude of dissonance, and thus as leading to an attitude change which is somewhat greater than in the case of a very low reward (5 BF). Since the classical dissonance literature predicts linear trends in attitude change for seemingly trivial differences in monetary reward one would indeed predict that zero reward and/or mild disconfirmation of reward expectancy would produce increasingly more attitude change than a 5 or 20 BF reward. The present data do not confirm these predictions: the attitude change assessed in the zero reward (or mild disconfirmation of reward expectancy) condition is identical to the one obtained in the 20 BF condition of Experiment One (3.7) and smaller (although not significantly so) than the one obtained in the 5 BF condition (4.1).

Also in this context it is worth noting that not a single subject did refuse to write the essay under zero reward conditions, although no extra force was applied to elicit the compliance. It thus becomes difficult to accept Festinger's interpretation of the minimal reward as a force "just barely sufficient to elicit the compliance". The absence of a comparable no-reward condition in the relevant literature adds to our scepticism that this "minimal pressure" condition ever has been realized.

As far as the pro-attitudinal essay conditions are concerned, our data suggest that the delivery of a 500 BF does produce attitude change. The average attitude response for this condition (3.7) is identical to the one obtained in the counterattitudinal zero and 20 BF reward condition. Since the students were merely invited to write an essay in defence of their own attitude position, there is no reason to consider the attitude change as restoring a cognitive equilibrium between pre-experimental attitude and advocacy. Nor can the change be interpreted along the lines of Rosenberg and other defendants of a positive relationship between reward for advocacy and attitude change: the more one is paid for pleading in favour of exam reform, the less one should consider the faculty decision against exam exemptions as justified. The observed data show that the higher reward for cognitively elaborating the subject's own position does not lead to an intensification or greater extremity of the attitude response but rather to a moderation of the original attitude.

The puzzling attitude change, found in the pro-attitudinal high reward condition, clearly is responsible for the lack of significance of the horizontal main effect of the presented analysis of variance. If the experimental design of Experiment Four is restricted to the zero and 5 BF reward manipulation, the main effect of the "central dissonance" becomes very significant ($F = 7.08$) and could be considered as a (partial) confirmation of the cognitive dissonance hypothesis.

Also, if the zero and 5 BF reward conditions are pooled and compared with the high reward condition, the interaction between reward and "central dissonance" becomes significant ($F = 2.91$). One possible way of interpreting this interaction could then be to consider the discrepancy between reward and costs invested in the advocacy as crucial for the production of dissonance. It does indeed seem plausible to accept that this discrepancy is especially high in the counterattitudinal zero and 5 BF and the pro-attitudinal 500 BF conditions. Still, such a reformulation of the conceptual variables involved would remain in need of a theoretical explanation of the attitude change assessed. Why would overpayment for a pro-attitudinal essay lead to a moderation in the attitude position? It is difficult to suggest any sensible answer, especially when considering the circumstance that to receive 500 BF for writing a 20 minute counterattitudinal essay also looks pretty well overpaid. The data obtained in the other 500 BF conditions of the experiments so far reported do not seem to shed much light upon the problem. The average attitude responses obtained in our 500 BF conditions indeed cover almost the entire range between very small (4.1) and very high (3) reward treatment of the first experiment: 3.9 for the 500 BF counterattitudinal plea condition for female students and for 500 BF promised reward counterattitudinal plea male students; 3.7 for 500 BF pro-attitudinal plea; 3.2 for 500 BF reward in the no perceptual separation condition and 3.0 in the original high reward condition of the first experiment. Clearly, the effect of a 500 BF reward is not easily predictable under the present circumstances.

Conclusion of chapter one

At the end of this introductory chapter on our unpublished 1964 research, there are only two conclusions which can be drawn with a considerable degree of confidence. First, there has been no support for any theoretical view which predicts a direct relationship between size of monetary reward for (pro- or counterattitudinal) advocacy and attitude change in the advocated direction. Notwithstanding the fact that Experiment One was designed as a very close replication of the Rosenberg study, the reliability of the latter findings seems to be questionable. Second, we have presented experimental evidence against the validity of Rosenberg's thesis attributing Cohen's results to the artifactual attitude change suppressing effect of his operationally defined sources of "evaluation apprehension" and "negative affect arousal".

With regard to the cognitive dissonance view on the inverted relationship between size of monetary reward for counterattitudinal advocacy and subsequent attitude change in the advocated direction, the evidence seems to be rather inconclusive. Although the classical Cohen study was successfully replicated in Experiment One, we were unable to reproduce the effect in an identical setting for female students. Moreover, the attitude change assessed in various rewarded counterattitudinal advocacy conditions does not prove to be significantly different from the attitude change obtained in pro-attitudinal advocacy conditions for which Festinger's theoretical framework does not apply.

It should be noted that our failure to demonstrate the crucial impact of the "central dissonance" is not restricted to the above presented research endeavour. In our published replication of the Festinger and Carlsmith experiment (Nuttin, 1966), the attitude change effect, predicted by cognitive dissonance theory, *was relatively stronger in the conditions where the posited central dissonance was absent* than in the replicated conditions of the original experiment. As a matter of fact, the *inverted* relationship between reward and attitude change was particularly striking for the conditions in which the subjects had been telling the waiting stooge that the boring tasks were *boring* (pro-attitudinal role playing). Also, an analysis of the perceived appropriateness of the high 500 BF reward gave rather strong support for the interpretation that an (embarrassing?) high reward might itself be dissonance enhancing instead of functioning as a cognitive element which is consonant with the compliance.

Leon Festinger, who participated in the discussion at the working conference where our 1964 research was presented, reacted with the following basic criticism: it might be that the experimental situation in which the counterattitudinal essay-writing has been elicited, was not enough dissonance arousing, so that the clarity and uniqueness of the effect could not sufficiently show up. One might of course criticize this comment by pointing to the weakness of a position which could imply that "dissonance is sufficiently aroused if the data confirm the dissonance predictions", but after all, this question is a basic one for a theory which does not offer precise instruments or criteria to check upon the absence or presence of the posited independent variable. Festinger has indeed never claimed to have given an exhaustive list of the necessary and sufficient conditions for the arousal of a particular magnitude of dissonance leading to a particular type of attitude change.

This difficult position with which dissonance theorists are confronted, has in the mean time been amply commented upon (see e. g., Carlsmith, 1968) and gave rise to multiple research efforts focusing on the realization of optimally dissonance-arousing experimental conditions. In the following chapter, it will be shown that, five years later, we have renewed our dissonance research effort, while taking into account all procedural elements, which according to various authors had proved to enhance the arousal of cognitive dissonance.

2

An Experimental Challenge of the Interpretation of a Cognitive Dissonance Effect

Our 1964 effort to critically replicate the classical Festinger and Carl-smith and Cohen studies had led to inconclusive results and, if anything, had shown that it is not easy to produce a clear-cut dissonance effect which would contrast neatly with the attitude change obtained under differentially rewarded pro-attitudinal or "no-compliance" conditions. We became even more discouraged after having invested much energy in unsuccessful replications of the equally provocative Aronson and Carl-smith (1963) and Turner and Wright (1965) dissonance experiments on the effect of mild versus severe threat of punishment upon attitude change (see Mertens, 1967 and Cré, 1970). Thus our research interest turned away from cognitive dissonance theory, until we were restimulated by the truly impressive data published by Helmreich and Collins (1968). These authors, who had chosen a fairly stabilized and firmly anchored attitude (government control on family size), asked students who all very strongly disagreed with such control, to present a counterattitudinal public plea under conditions in which the advocate was clearly *identifiable* (class room videotape). In the $.50 reward condition the mean attitude response changed from extreme anti to the positive side of the continuum (from 1–19 on a 31 point scale) in contrast with a $2.50 reward condition and in contrast with both small and high reward *anonymous* public advocacy conditions (class room audiotape) whose average attitude change scores ranged between 7 and 11. The latter two anynomous conditions showed a (non-significant) positive relationship between amount of reward and attitude change. The dissonance effect obtained for the $.50 identified condition was so dramatically strong that it did look as if finally an important source for a reliable operationalization of cognitive dissonance arousal had been identified. It was at this stage of the development of the dissonance debate that, in close collaboration with Annie Beckers (1969), a second series of investigations was planned and executed.

But undertaking research on this problem in 1969 was quite different than in 1964. Five years had passed in vigorous experimental attempts to uncover various factors which would produce dissonance. As said before, Festinger in his original formulation had not attempted to exhaustively categorize the conditions under which cognitive dissonance would occur. The theoretical concepts considered as related to magnitude of dissonance, e.g., the relative importance of cognitive elements, had no one to one relationship with particular specifiable and realizable conditions and investigations made the most of the opportunity for "creative operationalization" of the central theoretical variables. Zajonc (1968, p. 360) characterized the research of this period as an effort to determine the "extra-theoretical assumptions" of dissonance theory. Since Festinger's theoretical variables appear broad enough to encompass a wide variety of specifications we rather prefer to characterize the research as oriented toward "*intra-theoretical explicitations*". The study of the role of volitional commitment (Brehm and Cohen, 1962) in the production of dissonance can, in our opinion, be considered as an explicitation of one of the many possible determinants of the "importance" or "consequentiality" of the cognitive elements involved in a dissonant relationship. The same could apply for other specifications such as decision freedom (Linder *et al.*, 1967), and identified or anonymous character of the role playing (Helmreich and Collins, 1968), since all these can be seen as determinants of what Festinger in 1957 called—with a very general term—the "importance" or "consequentiality for the self" of a cognitive element.

These efforts at explicitation and extension of the theory were further stimulated by the fact that in some instances Rosenberg's direct (instead of inverse), relationship between reward and attitude change was replicated. Since classical dissonance experiments manipulated a reward variable, it was not surprising that the phenomena also caught the attention of psychologists who, ever since the pioneering work of Hovland, Janis and Kelley (1953) had been studying the effect of reward contingencies upon attitude change in a learning-theoretical framework.

c

Gradually as the controversial research progressed it became more and more clear that dissonance theory was not alone in predicting reward effects upon attitude change after counterattitudinal advocacy. The empirical and theoretical controversy crystallized itself into two camps typically identified as the "dissonance" versus the "incentive" camps (see e.g., Elms, 1967). We would like to underscore the fact that the latter labelling is somewhat misleading.

The common link of the "incentive camp" is not at all a communality in theoretical explanation but merely a consensus in the prediction of a direct relationship between reward and attitude change. The controversy might better be characterized as between a "dissonance" and an "anti-dissonance" or a "direct" versus "indirect" relationship camp since the experimental evidence for an established direct relation between reward and attitude change is interpreted by various authors along quite different theoretical lines. Some authors (see e.g., Janis and Gilmore, 1965) stress the *incentive* function of the reward, which motivates the subject to engage in a biased scanning of the arguments against his own position. The more important the reward, the more likely the subject will generate and consider new arguments which ultimately will influence his attitude position. A theoretically quite different view on the function of the reward is that, if a subject is confronted with new arguments (either coming from another source or as a result of his own cognitive elaboration of the issue) the mere contingency of an extrinsic or intrinsic reward will have a *reinforcement* effect, thus enhancing the probability that the reinforced arguments will become more important determinants of subsequent attitude responses (see e.g., Scott, 1959). We did already express our scepticism with regard to the adaptation of the reinforcement concept whose classical use does not seem to be warranted in this attitude change context. A third clearly distinct process is the *generalization* effect of the reward. If subjects receive an appreciated monetary reward for (counterattitudinal) role playing, some of their research irrelevant needs might become satisfied, so as to put them in a good mood. When generalized to the task which was contingent with the delivery of the reward, their attitude towards the task might change in a more favourable direction (see e.g., Carlsmith, Collins and Helmreich (1966, p. 13) when explaining the positive relationship between reward and attitude change for the essay conditions). A fourth theoretical interpretation offered for the same direct relationship is the affective-cognitive consistency theory of Rosenberg (cf. supra, p. 16) where *both the incentive and reinforcement* concepts are used together with the essential assumption of the change motivating intra-attitudinal *inconsistency* caused by alterations in the cognitive attitude component.

So, the heterogeneity *qua* theoretical explanation of the sometimes observed direct relationship between size of reward and attitude change leaves no doubt that the researchers from the anti-dissonance camp have not yet bridged the gap between "experimental psychology of learning" and the effect of reward for counterattitudinal advocacy upon the subsequent attitude response. Moreover, whatever the merits of the direct relation research have been, it also is clear that thus far only dissonance theory could easily account for some "minimal reward" effects like the one previously referred to (Helmreich and Collins, 1968).

But we would unduly digress by reciting, at this time, further details of a theoretical debate upon which our own research bears. Our major purpose in citing the controversy is to clarify somewhat the differing contexts of our earlier investigations and the research to be described in this chapter. In 1964 only a few studies had been done and the conditions which might or might not produce dissonance were poorly understood. In 1969 we still had little unambiguous evidence about dissonance arousal but there was a large number of variables which had been identified by one or another investigator as likely candidates. The most promising steps in the delimitation of the phenomena which called for a cognitive dissonance interpretation were made in a few research efforts where, within one single experimental design, it was shown that under some conditions an inverse, and under other conditions, a direct relation between reward and attitude change was obtained. We will refrain from giving a systematic account of all relevant research efforts for the simple reason that Zajonc (1968) has written an excellent and comprehensive review of the area for the new edition of the "Handbook of Social Psychology". As will become clear, we have planned our own research while making maximum use of the recommendations, inferred from the existing literature, for the production of a powerful cognitive dissonance effect. Along with the description of our experimental procedure we will take the opportunity to refer to those studies which affected our own research strategy.

Since all experiments of our 1969 programme have many procedural features in common, and since the rationale for the procedure used should be given in detail, we decided to organize this chapter in such a way that a first section deals exclusively with general features and rationale of procedure, whereas the remaining sections will be devoted to the presentation of the various experiments in chronological order.

1. Some common procedural features of our 1969 research and their rationale

"Subjects" : One quite distinctive characteristic of the experiments to be reported in this chapter is that *no subjects* in the classical sense of the term were run. All data were gathered on students who did not realize that they were participating in psychological or social research; the situation in which the counterattitudinal advocacy and the attitudinal responses were elicited was experienced as "real life"—to use a label cherished by some anti-laboratory minded students of psychology. To distinguish the subjects and experimenter in these "real life" situations from the usual subjects and experimenters (as, e.g., those of Chapter One) the terms subject and experimenter will be put between inverted comma's whenever the subject is prevented from accurately perceiving his own and the experimenter's role. Some of the implications of this procedural feature will be commented upon in the remainder of this section (see "decision freedom" and "elimination of suspicion and other biasing factors").

The students were selected from the same pool of male second year Science students (1969) as for our 1964 research, except that the status of bis-students was no longer used as a criterion for sampling. Approximately four-fifths of the potential subjects volunteered under circumstances similar to those described in Chapter One (cf. p. 25). In the individual letter of invitation signed by the author, special emphasis was laid upon the fact that all students volunteering for any of the research projects would be expected to formally pledge secrecy for a specified period of time, at the end of which all students—volunteering or not—would individually receive a summary presentation of the experiments run. As usual, the students were not to expect any credit points or individual rewards. It might also be noted that the sampled Science student pool had never been used in psychological research organized by the Department of Psychology.

Eleven "subjects" were randomly assigned to each condition of all the experiments to be reported.

Attitude issue The major dependent variable chosen was again the attitude response towards the reform of the exam system. Since our 1964 research, examination exemptions for September had become part of the new policy in all departments. One of the more recent victories of the exam reform movement was that the 14/20 criterion for exemption was significantly mitigated by reducing the minimum score to twelve points out of twenty. Although the other criteria (50 % of points in total exam series score, etc.) were maintained, this liberalization of the exam policy thus became even more important, also for the weaker students, since the probability of obtaining a minimum of 12/20 for any course in July was much higher than the probability of fulfilling the earlier criterion of 14/20. The new focus of student demands had shifted in the mean time toward a temporal spread of the exams over a much longer period of time. Therefore, the attitude issue for our 1969 research was redefined so as to make it maximally relevant for the subject population involved. In order to illustrate how salient the issue was, we refer to the fact that the student representatives, who since May 1968 had been gaining in status and power, did for example, demand that the final exam on the psychology course the author had been teaching during the first semester, be programmed at the end of the first semester or around Easter vacation, so as to diminish the exam burden of the official exam sessions. This and similar urgent requests could however not be granted, national rules restricting all final exams to the short official exam sessions of July and/or September. Since all experiments to be reported in this chapter were run during the second semester at this very period of conflicting positions of academic authorities and student masses, it will be clear that a plea against wider temporal spread of exams was a quite salient counterattitudinal position to be advocated by our student-"subjects".

In an effort to enhance even more the reluctance of our "subjects" to advocate against university reform, it was decided to also incorporate within the position to be defended the abolition of the recently acquired exam exemptions. The counterattitudinal nature of this advocacy has been amply commented upon in Chapter One (cf. p. 26). There is no doubt that any official threat of revocation of the exam exemption procedure would immediately cause a most severe outburst of student protest. Thus, the counterattitudinal position to be defended by our "subjects" was not simply "in favour of the traditional exam system", but explicitly defined as (1) against a wide temporal spread of exams and (2) against exam exemptions. Also the attitude response to be tapped as the main dependent variable of our research, consisted of a self-rating expressing *how much in favour the "subject" was of the traditional exam system*, *restrictively defined as a system with minimal spread* (all exams scheduled in a very short time period) *and without exam exemptions* (in case of failure in July session, the full series of exams has to be taken again in September).

Obviously, the choice of the above described attitude issue provides us with a source of highly important cognitive elements, whose consequentiality for the self favourably compares to most of the attitude issues chosen in similar research. Convincing evidence on the homogeneity of the student population with regard to the pre-experimental attitude position, will be offered at various occasions throughout the remainder of the monograph.

Nature of advocacy It will be recalled that our 1964 subjects were invited to write, during a 20 minute period, a short essay in defence of the requested position. In view of the fact that the manipulation of the public or private nature of the advocacy became part of our new research programme, we substituted for the written essay an *oral plea*. Moreover, both the resistance to change of the newly developed cognition concerning the counter-attitudinal plea, and the internalization of the generated counter-attitudinal arguments were fostered by the fact that each "subject" was exposed *three times* to the outcomes of his own biased scanning of the issue.

The student was first asked to prepare, in solitary conditions, during a fifteen minute period, the oral plea. He was allowed to make a written outline of what he felt were the strongest, most forceful, creative and thoughtful arguments against a wider spread of exams and against exam exemptions. After this preparation phase, the "subject" was invited by the "experimenter" to give an oral presentation of his plea which lasted an average of six minutes. During this second self-exposure phase, the student was urged to focus on the argumentation proper and not on matters of style and rhetoric. The third confrontation with his counter-attitudinal arguments was given when the "experimenter" "wanted to check with the 'subject' if the plea was properly recorded". After this careful rehearsal of his own plea, there was no doubt that the student had been thoroughly exposed to the content and the *fait accompli* of his own argumentation.

We should point out that no arguments were offered by the "experimenter", this in contrast with, e.g., the Helmreich and Collins study (1968), there the subject was merely required to state four arguments prepared in written form by the experimenter. Although the latter subjects were allowed to give additional arguments, it seems to us that a fair test of the incentive effect of the monetary reward is impeded when the student restricts his role to the mere statement and/or elaboration of arguments which he did not have to generate himself. One could however argue that the improvization procedure is at a disadvantage for the ascertainment of the so-called reinforcement effect when one cannot be sure that the amount and content of arguments proferred is constant across conditions. As said before these points are in need of appropriate research.

It should also be noted that the required advocacy was not only imbedded in a complex and very important social reality but also allowed for various pro- and contra-arguments. The students being deeply involved in the attitude topic—all of them had experienced a minimum of one university exam session—could be assumed to know very well what they were talking about. The nature of the advocacy required in our study is in this respect quite different from, e.g., the role playing in the classical Janis and King study, where college students actively or passively were exposed to communications concerning the number of cinemas, the national supply of meat and the prospects of an effective cure for the common cold. The difference is not only one of personal involvement, which was not required for the purposes of Janis and King, but also in terms of possible cognitive elaboration and self-persuasion.

This leads us to a consideration of Rosenberg's thesis with regard to the relevance of cognitive dissonance theory for rewarded counterattitudinal performance. In various writings (Rosenberg, 1968, p. 106; 1970, p. 195) a position already suggested in the discussed 1965 article is further documented. Rosenberg distinguishes between "simple counterattitudinal *assertion*", where the subject merely makes a counterattitudinal statement (such as telling a waiting stooge that boring tasks were enjoyable and exciting, Festinger and Carlsmith, 1959) and counterattitudinal *advocacy* which implies "the elaboration of new, if only roleplayed, improvised cognitive structures and arguments supporting them". He concedes that cognitive dissonance theory may be useful in explaining the consequences of inadequately elicited, simple counterattitudinal assertions, but holds that, under conditions of more complex elaboration the intra-attitudinal cognitive-affective inconsistency generating dynamics will be operating so as to produce a direct relationship between attitude change and size of monetary reward. Although it may not always be easy to decide when role playing is a simple assertion and when it is a true advocacy, the task of our "subjects" clearly belongs to the latter category, since Rosenberg and Finkelstein manipulated the "assertion-advocacy" nature of the role playing by allowing one and a half versus six minutes for performing the counterattitudinal task (Rosenberg, 1970, p. 196).

In view of the fact that cognitive dissonance theorists never have proposed any restriction with regard to this aspect of the counterattitudinal behaviour, and that we wanted to give another fair chance to Rosenberg and other defenders of a "direct relationship" view, we consider the policy adopted as quite appropriate for the present purposes.

Decision freedom Brehm and Cohen (1962) were the first to stress the role of behavioural commitment for the understanding of post-compliance attitude change. They argue that the mere confrontation of discrepant information ("I believe A" and "I advocate not-A") does not necessarily produce dissonance. Commitment, resulting from a free decision actively to engage in counterattitudinal behaviour (advocating not-A) is considered to be the crucial point at which cognitive dissonance occurs. Although commitment, which is closely linked to the notion of volition, is in our opinion but one way in which the perceived importance or consequentiality of the cognitions relevant for the self might differ, there is no doubt that Brehm and Cohen's specification serves as an important contribution to Festinger's vague and general treatment of factors affecting the total magnitude of cognitive dissonance. Clearly commitment is not a pure cognitive process, but neither is Festinger's dimension of "importance or consequentiality for the self" of the cognitive elements.

Various studies (Cohen and Latané *in* Brehm and Cohen, 1962, p. 88–91; Brock, 1962; Davis and Jones, 1960) support the hypothesis that greater perceived choice in deciding to engage in an attitude-discrepant act will lead to more attitude change in the advocated direction. In an often quoted experiment, Linder, Cooper and Jones (1967) showed that the dissonance effect obtains if the subject remains relatively free to decide against compliance after he has been fully informed about the reward, whereas the relation between reward and attitude change is a direct one if this freedom is reduced and if the incentive is announced only after the subject commits himself to compliance (as was the case in the procedure used by Rosenberg, 1965).

In our own 1969 research we deliberately invested considerable effort in trying to maximize the perceived decision freedom. This was realized in both a direct and an indirect way. As was the case in the Linder *et al.*

study, the "experimenter" made it clear to the "subject" that he should feel completely free to engage or not in the discrepant behaviour and that he should refrain from any decision until he was fully informed about all aspects of the task. Probably more important however, decision freedom was assured in a more indirect way, by carefully avoiding any form of prior commitment from the student with regard to an implicit demand of the "experimenter". The typical "free-decision" subject, it seems to us, is already committed, prior to his final decision, to the role of a subject who is prepared to volunteer for almost anything the experimenter might ask or suggest. He came for an appointment with a psychologist, and volunteers at the latter's suggestion for another little experiment run by another psychologist. Typically the subject who is confronted with a delay in the start of the scheduled experiment, has a choice between either waiting some 20 minutes or participating in another experiment for which he is made to expect some monetary reward. Under such circumstances the effect of the verbal assurance "that he should feel completely free to decide" until the second experimenter has explained the task might indeed be impeded by the overall prior commitment of the subject to volunteer for any research suggested by "his" experimenter.

That is why our "subjects", in addition to the usual explicit assurance, about freedom of choice, were approached by an "experimenter" who skillfully avoided being perceived in a research role. Furthermore, because of the sequence of experimental phases, the "experimenter" could not possibly force the "subject" on the basis of his volunteering status, since the latter had already fulfilled his obligation to serve in an experiment. As will become clear in the description of the procedure used for Experiment Five, the real experiment did not start until the "subject" had gone completely through a pseudoexperiment (debriefing included) which he perceived to be *the* experiment for which he volunteered. It was only "by accident" that he met the real "experimenter" who thus had set the stage for a decision which supposedly was free of any prior commitment.

Upon completion of the pseudoexperiment, all "subjects" were randomly reassigned to the different conditions of the real experiment, so as to control for possible effects of the preceding experience.

Attractiveness of the "experimenter" Ever since Zimbardo (1960), social psychologists have examined the dissonance view that perceived attractiveness of the compliance inducing agent (the experimenter) could be a source of cognitive elements which systematically affect the total magnitude of dissonance. The cognition that the counterattitudinal behaviour was emitted at the request of a quite attractive experimenter is indeed consonant with the compliance, whereas the cognition that the experimenter was dull and unattractive would be either relatively less consonant or even dissonant with the compliance. Since total magnitude of dissonance is a function of the weighted proportion of all relevant cognitive elements involved, the dissonance hypothesis states that post-compliance attitude change will be greater when the inducing agent is unattractive. This hypothesis, derived from Festinger's general theoretical statement, is intriguing because it is contrary to common sense practice and expectations, and exciting, since it offers an opportunity to deal with truly social antecedents of behavioural change.

Recent research by Baron (1968) and Kelman et al. (1969) suggests that there might be various limiting conditions for the above hypothesis to be confirmed. These promising research endeavours did not directly affect our own research strategy. However, we did make an effort to keep this possibly important factor constant. Throughout all the experiments to be reported, the same experimenter, Annie Beckers, was the only person used for inducing compliance and eliciting the attitude responses. It must be conceded that a semantic differential approach of her perceived attractiveness, obtained under conditions of rigorous anonymity, was quite flattering. If anything the assessed attractiveness should reduce rather than enhance the total magnitude of post-compliance dissonance. The important point however is that our "experimenter" made a deliberate effort to keep constant under all conditions all non-verbal communication and appearance cues so as to not systematically generate new consonant or dissonant elements in the cognitive system of the experimental "subjects".

It is obvious that an attractive, ingratiating and appealing experimenter might at the same time affect the proportion of subjects who do comply with her request, but it will be understood that this issue is not directly relevant for the dissonance hypothesis under investigation.

Consequences for self and audience In his original formulation, Festinger (1957) considered the importance or consequentiality of the cognitive elements involved in a dissonant relation as a major determinant of the magnitude of dissonance. In recent research (Aronson, 1968, 1969; Bramel, 1968; Collins, 1969) an attempt has been made to specify the role of the consequentiality to the self-concept and/or the audience of the counterattitudinal role playing. The discrepancy between the self-concept and the consequences of the counterattitudinal behaviour is seen as the crucial source of dissonance: "I am a decent, truthful human being" versus "I have misled a person" (Aronson, 1968, p. 24). Although we will later present data bearing on this and similar revised versions of cognitive dissonance theory, it is appropriate to point out here that, for all our public conditions, one safely can assume that we produced a quite strong discrepancy between self-concept and consequences for the audience. The audience for the counterattitudinal behaviour was extremely large and heterogeneous *qua* attitude and commitment. Also, in view of the general salience of the debated issue, there is no doubt that the forceful counterattitudinal plea might be successful in convincing at least part of the audience. In this respect, our public conditions correspond to the specifications made by Nel, Helmreich and Aronson (1969), who demonstrated that the persuasibility of the audience contributes to the arousal of dissonance.

Elimination of suspicion and other biasing factors Much of the research in psychology, and especially research inspired by the Festinger tradition of complex and inventive experimental procedures, has been criticized for its vulnerability *qua* arousal of subject's suspicion. Taking into account the impressive number of experiments which make use of elaborate and sophisticated deception devices, and the fact that the real experimental purpose in most instances is afterwards revealed to the student-subjects, one could argue that quite a few subject pools are so profoundly polluted that the external validity of various findings applies only to the universe of sophisticated student-subjects. Although we have already commented upon this aspect, we would like to stress the point that throughout our programme the utmost care has been given to this quite difficult aspect of research strategy.

Let us briefly point to some features which should reassure the critical reader in this respect. As mentioned before, the students used in our 1969 research were not aware of their role as subject, nor of the role of the experimenter. The fact that their counterattitudinal advocacy was thus part of a real life situation should eliminate an important source of experimenter-subject bias and other demand characteristics of the usual experimental situation. As will become clear from the detailed description of procedure, the rationale used for eliciting compliance was imbedded in a most plausible and realistic macro-situation, which did not offer any reasons for suspicion. None of the subjects ever gave any evidence of suspicion or perspicacity notwithstanding the fact that a post-experimental interview offered ample opportunity to show off in this respect. The information about the monetary reward was given, as all other relevant information, before the "subject" could make his decision, and the actual amount was delivered before enacting the counter-attitudinal behaviour. Although Rosenberg's criticism with regard to the mere promise of a reward was not confirmed in our 1964 research, this procedural aspect was maintained since Freedman (1963) had shown that the fact that minimal justification was given before instead of after engaging in a boring task seemed to be critical for a successful arousal of dissonance.

Finally, the "experimenter" was quite conscious of the theoretical imperatives concerning a rigorous standardization of the external pressure exerted upon the "subject" before his decision to comply. In this respect, "forced compliance" research can be considered as a most demanding and exhausting practice for any experimenter. Not only should the decision freedom be maintained at a comparable level across conditions, but also any other systematic administration of subtle pressures for compliance must be avoided. An unskilled experimenter might quite easily be tempted to compensate for a low reward with extra verbal or non-verbal pressures, which could generate new cognitive elements consonant with the compliance. In this case, the total magnitude of dissonance across conditions would not solely be determined by differences in manipulated monetary reward, but also by systematic differences in non-monetary "consonant forces". Thus the pressure for dissonance reduction could become equalized across reward conditions or even become directly related to the size of the monetary reward. Careful pilot experimentation with full recording and evaluation of the subject-experimenter inter-actions clearly is a prerequisite for any valid research in this area. The very fact that this seemingly self-evident feature of the practice of dissonance research is never commented upon in the literature, served as a source of primary concern in our own dealing with the issue.

Temporal sequence of experimentation In our 1964 programme we ran simultaneously and in random sequence all of the twenty experimental conditions (except for the replication on females) of our Rosenberg and Festinger and Carlsmith replications. For reasons of research economy, we decided not to have such a complex multi-factorial design and choose instead a step-by-step analysis of restricted clusters of experimental conditions. In view of the nebulous state of the problem area, this research strategy seemed to be much more appropriate, since it allowed for a flexible development of enquiry, whose direction could be determined by the promising data of the preceding step.

All experiments for our 1969, and also for the subsequent 1970 and 1971 programmes were run in immediate temporal sequence, without any interruption and with an average of 6 sessions per day. Within each cluster of (minimally two) experimental conditions, the "subjects" were randomly assigned to each condition, whereas the individual sessions were held in random sequence across conditions. The reader will be informed whenever the actual temporal sequence of clusters might be different from the order of presentation in the monograph, and also whenever two different clusters of conditions are combined for the presentation of one single experiment. This is, e.g., the case for Experiment Six, where the combined results are presented of two successive clusters of conditions.

So far we have given a summary description and justification of some common procedural features of our 1969 research. It is hoped that the reader is now prepared for a more routine report of the various experiments performed.

2. Experiment Five: The effect of the anonymity of public counterattitudinal advocacy upon subsequent attitude responses (television and radio)

PROBLEM AND DESIGN

In 1966, Carlsmith, Collins and Helmreich, a team composed of psychologists coming from the "dissonance" as well as from the "anti-dissonance" camp succeeded in obtaining—within one single experimental design—an indirect relationship between size of reward and attitude change under conditions of face-to-face role playing and a direct relationship under conditions of anonymous essay-writing. Although this study did not allow for an unequivocal specification of the crucial conceptual difference between "face-to-face" and "anonymous" advocacy, it clearly set the stage for a renewed effort in pinning down the necessary and sufficient conditions for a cognitive dissonance effect. Face-to-face confrontation between the advocate and the recipient of his counterattitudinal message, combined with the fact that the former had no means to set the misled audience straight, was interpreted as an instance of high commitment (see also Aronson, 1966). It seemed as if the "face-to-face" versus "anonymous" manipulation promised to be a smooth and flexible operationalization of the psychological commitment variable, whose importance had been stressed ever since Brehm and Cohen (1962).

After five failing efforts (Collins, 1968a, 1968b; Collins and Helm-reich, 1966; Hornbeck, 1967), Helmreich and Collins (1968) obtained the strongest cognitive dissonance effect ever reported in the literature, by manipulating the anonymity of a counterattitudinal plea in favour of government control on family size. As mentioned in the introduction to this chapter, it was this study which encouraged us to resume our own critical analysis of the dissonance effect. It will be recalled that Helm-reich and Collins invited their "subjects" to record a counterattitudinal presentation of arguments, on videotape (identified) or on audiotape (anonymous). The "subjects", who received either $.50 or $2.50 for complying with the request, were told that the tapes would serve as stimulus material in an attitude change experiment to be conducted in a large psychology class. Although the design was more complex than the above summary suggests, the main results were that the relation between size of reward and attitude change was inverse for the identified, high commitment, essays ($p < \cdot 001$ with 11 "subjects" in each cell), whereas this relation was positive (although not significantly so) for the anonymous, low commitment conditions. The most impressive difference was between the anonymous and identified low reward conditions: the identified videotape advocacy, combined with a $.50 reward, seemed to create a tremendous need for dissonance reduction via attitude change in the advocated direction (from extremely anti to slightly in favour of government control), whereas the low reward anonymous argumentation resulted in an attitude change which was comparable to the high reward identified condition.

Since our first objective was the production of a clear-cut dissonance effect, whose constituent factors would then progressively be analyzed, it was decided to begin with a simple design in which maximum use would be made of the Helmreich and Collins paradigm for the production of cognitive dissonance. In an effort to carry the identified high commitment condition of Helmreich and Collins to a maximum level, for the class-room videotape we substituted a very realistic nation-wide television appearance, with full identity of the advocate, whereas the anonymous audiotape was substituted for by a nation-wide radio-speech under full guarantee of anonymity (see procedure, infra). As far as the monetary reward was concerned, it did not seem justified to start the programme with a comparison between high and low rewards. The Helmreich and Collins study had shown that half a dollar did produce a highly significant effect under conditions of identifiability of the advocate (videotape). As long as we did not succeed in reproducing a sizable attitude change under low reward, it was indeed useless to waste high monetary rewards, especially when considering the circumstance that, in view of the planned assessment of the long term persistency of the predicted attitude change, we could not any longer ask the "subjects" to return the money.

The choice for a specific amount of the low monetary reward to be used, was guided by the conjecture based on our 1964 research, that both the defenders of an indirect and a direct relationship between reward and attitude change might be wrong in assuming its monotonic nature. As suggested earlier (Nuttin, 1966, p. 56–57) it is very probable that, in the experimental situation under study, the relationship between the absolute monetary size of a reward and its "utility"—or consonance, incentive and/or reinforcement value—is a curvilinear one. Also it did seem to us that the reactions of the forced compliance subjects might rather be related to the discrepancy between a "reasonable" or "equitable" reward and the reward actually offered for performing the counterattitudinal task. Thus we decided to administer a truly trivial if not insultingly low monetary reward. It will become clear from the description of the quite demanding "real life" task that a 20 BF (40 cents) reward could serve this purpose. It should be stressed that such a very low reward still fits the conceptual requirements of an experimental test of the cognitive dissonance view. When discussing the "size" of manipulated monetary rewards, Aronson (1966, p. 122) refers to an experiment of Lependorf (1964) who found more attitude change following a bribe of 5 cents than following one of half a dollar. Since these data are presented as a confirmation of Festinger's hypothesis, one can indeed take for granted that dissonance theory does not put any practicable limit to the operationalization of the manipulated "cognitive elements consonant with the compliance".

The first step of our 1969 project was thus restricted to the following three cell design: (1) a very low reward (20 BF) identified television condition; (2) a very low reward (20 BF) anonymous radio condition; and (3) a baseline condition (mere attitude responses without any previous advocacy). In essence, we simply wanted to know, (1) if we would succeed at all in affecting the nature of the attitude response by engaging the "subjects" freely, for very low monetary justification, in a counter-attitudinal advocacy destined to be broadcast to a vast and influencible public, and (2) if this effect would be enhanced when the advocate's identity was made maximally visible. On the basis of the findings of the Helmreich and Collins experiment it was expected, (1) that the identified advocacy would result in an attitude change which would be significantly more in the advocated direction than for the anonymous condition; and (2) that both conditions would manifest a change in the advocated direction as compared to the baseline data. The latter expectation, which by itself is not crucial for dissonance theory, refers to the fact that all experimental conditions of the Helmreich and Collins experiment did indeed affect the pre-experimental attitude response of the "subjects". Although no exact information is given in this respect, the average baseline data are situated around 1—with almost no variability—whereas the lowest cell mean is somewhat above 5 on a scale from 0–31.

It should be noted that Festinger's classical formulation of cognitive dissonance theory predicts a sizable effect for both, identified and un-identified low reward conditions, and that his vague definition of "importance or consequentiality for the self" and "total magnitude of dissonance" also would allow for the prediction of a relative greater change in the identified condition. Although an important development marked by the Helmreich and Collins study at first sight seems to be the prediction of a direct relationship between reward and attitude when the advocate's identity is withheld from the audience, one should not forget that the positive relationship obtained for their anonymous audio condition does not even approach significance (Helmreich and Collins, 1968, p. 78). Thus the essential contribution of the latter study might amount to the enhanced confidence about the reproducibility of a sizable dissonance effect under conditions of identifiability of the advocate. The fact that they were not successful in producing a dissonance effect with the anonymous classroom audiotape simply points in the direction of some minimal requirements for the arousal of a sufficient amount of dissonance. Our planned research project ultimately could contribute to the specification of such necessary and sufficient conditions. The main objective however, was the experimental validation of Festinger's theoretical interpretation and this enterprise was of course conditioned by the successful production of a clear-cut attitude change effect under conditions which fulfilled the basic conceptual requirements of Festinger's theory.

PROCEDURE*

As said before, the experiment was conducted in two separate phases. In order to elicit the TV or radio advocacy against the reform of the exam-system in a way that would be valid and not create suspicion, we had to be sure that each "subject" believed that he was one of a very small number of university students who were invited to participate in the programme. To achieve this and also to enhance decision freedom, all "subjects" participated in an irrelevant experiment considered by them as the real study for which they had volunteered. As will become clear later on, the pseudo experiment was also useful in providing a cover-story which did not jeopardize the assessment of long term effects of our experimental manipulations. Following this experiment, the subjects were dismissed and while leaving the laboratory, were intercepted by the "experimenter" and "spontaneously" requested to do her a favour. The true experiment was conducted during this latter phase.

The pseudo experiment

The pseudo experiment was a critical replication of a study by Freedman (1963) on the effect of the time at which justification for performing a boring task is given upon the attitude towards the task. Although this experiment clearly is relevant for the dissonance controversy, we will refrain from reporting it, since Freedman did not use any counter-attitudinal role playing or advocacy, which is the focus of the present monograph. We nevertheless should give a summary description of the subject's treatment, so that the reader can ascertain how the triple function of the pseudo experiment was fulfilled.

Upon his arrival in the laboratory, the subject is told by a male experimenter† that he is interested in a comparative study between human and computer random output. The subject's task consists in randomly writing down digits between 0 and 9 as fast as he can, while avoiding any thinking or systematization. The independent variables are (1) high versus low justification for doing the task ("your cooperation is very useful" versus "almost of no use any more"); and (2) the moment at which justification is offered: before or immediately after performing the 20 minutes lasting task. After the evaluation of various task characteristics (dependent variable), the experimenter gives all subjects an identical and

* The reader is supposed to be familiar with section 1 of this chapter (p. 56-65).
† Thanks are due to Jos Feys for his precious collaboration.

quite detailed but fictitious description of the experiment which essentially amounts to the following:

> This research project has to do with the role of chemical and psycho-
> logical components of motivation. You belong to a control condition*, which
> is fortunate in that the experiment lasts only one third of the time needed for
> the experimental conditions. The subjects of the drug conditions start as you
> did with 20 minutes random digits, but then have to take a mild (real or
> placebo) stimulant or tranquillizer, and—after a waiting period for absorp-
> tion—have to produce a second series of random digits. Together with this
> chemical manipulation, we have a balanced treatment with a conscious
> task motivation factor by telling them—as we did also in the control
> condition you were in—how important and useful the collaboration is for us.
> I myself am basically interested in the emission of so-called dominant digital
> responses like 7, 3, 5, as a function of these variables. In the long run, this
> type of research might be helpful for a comparative study between computer
> and human output systems.

After this debriefing, the subject was reminded of his formal commitment to secrecy, thanked for his cooperation and dismissed. It should be
noted that our Science students all seemed quite interested and satisfied
with the rationale offered, so that we can assume that their overall mood,
when "leaving the laboratory" was quite homogenized across conditions.
As mentioned before all subjects were randomly reassigned to the
conditions of the real experiment.

The real experiment: Procedure for identified public advocacy (TV) condition

The procedure in both public conditions (television and radio) is, with
some exceptions, almost identical. We will first describe in detail the
procedure of the TV condition and then point to the modifications in the
radio condition. In view of the confusion in some publications with regard
to the use of the terms "public", "face-to-face" and "anonymous", we
would like to point out that in the present experiment, both advocacy
conditions are public, that is, perceived by the advocate to be used to
influence an audience. The terms "identified" or "anonymous" simply
refer to the fact that the "subject" knows that the audience does or does
not have information about his identity. In the TV condition, the "subject" is not only carefully introduced to the public, but also his face is
being focused upon by the camera during his presentation. In the
anonymous radio condition none of this information is given.

---

* It will be remembered that all subjects were familiar with basic notions of experimentation and theory in the field of motivation.

Eliciting the counterattitudinal advocacy The subject of the pseudo experiment, who had volunteered for a two hour period, but who was fortunate to be dismissed after only half an hour, was surprised when approached in the corridor by Annie Beckers, whose academic position was unknown to the 1969 "subjects". Having alluded to the fact that he might have some spare time, she invited him to consider if he could do her a favour. "If you don't mind coming with me, I'd briefly explain what precisely I'd like to ask you. Afterwards you should feel completely free to say yes or no." Upon agreement of the "subject" (no refusals were registered), they both went to a small room which was arranged as an improvised and rather disorderly TV studio.

When seated, the "subject" sees his own face focused upon a TV screen and on a control monitor across the table. A professional TV camera and videotape—all plugged into a mobile set—completed the picture of an ambulant TV unit.

In a quite direct and informal style, the "experimenter" then tries to elicit the "subject's" compliance by use of the following standardized instructions.

I'd like to first explain what favour you could do for me, and let me emphasize again that afterwards you should feel completely free to accept or refuse my proposal. Well, as you might or might not know, the BRT* will devote the months of June and July† to a series of well-documented programmes on current hot problems, such as birth control, celibacy of the clergy and university reform. For each of these programmes, several experts have been invited to help in the preparation of this rather demanding enterprise. Professor Nuttin was asked to sponsor the preparation of part of a programme dealing with university reform. As a psychologist he is especially interested in the problem of student evaluation and more precisely in the reform of the university exam system‡. He has accepted to help take care of the two programmes which will be devoted to the university exam system.

The general plan of the exam reform programme is to present first some relevant information concerning American and Russian exam systems, and

---

* Belgian Radio and Television. There are only two TV networks in Belgium, the BRT, destined for the Dutch speaking (approximately six million Flemish citizens) and the RTB for the French speaking part of the country. It should be noted that the prestige of a TV appearance is quite high. Not only are there no local stations, but telecast is restricted to evening periods and no commercials are allowed.

† The experiment was run in early spring; June and July is the period of the first official exam session.

‡ All "subjects" knew this to be true since they had cooperated in an elaborated survey which the author had organized on this topic several weeks before the experiment.

confront this with various statistical data on the Belgian situation. Further-more, one would like to give the floor to a few individual students expressing their own opinions on the issue, and that is precisely the part of the pro-gramme Nuttin asked me to take care of. You might wonder why I am bothering you with this, and why we do not proceed via the official student representatives. Well, although these bodies will also be approached for obvious reasons, we on purpose want to have the collaboration of a few randomly chosen individual students, because this, we hope, will give the programme a less official and more real life character. Since you happened to be around today, I thought that it might be worthwhile to sound you on your willingness to cooperate in the programme.

I must tell you that some students have already agreed to my proposal and have built a very strong case in favour of the reform of the exam system. Their special point of concern seemed to be a much larger temporal spread of exams and a greater flexibility with regard to the exam exemptions for the September session. Since all interviewed students until now have defended a quite similar point of view, it would be appreciated to see now the opposite point of view being defended for a change, so that the discussion at the end of the programme does not turn out to be too monotonous. That is why we can only accept your collaboration if you agree to present arguments in favour of the traditional exam system. So what I'd ask you to do is to present over TV for a few minutes, a forceful and convincing plea *against* a larger temporal spread of the exams and *against* exam exemptions for September. It is self-evident that you can prepare a written statement and use this at your convenience. You don't have to worry about style and rhetorics, the only thing that matters is that you attack the reform of the exam system, and present the most convincing and persuasive arguments against a longer spread of exams and against exam exemptions for September. If you should stammer or interrupt yourself do not feel embarrassed, because we can cut this afterwards, during the editing of the videotape.

Now, for your information, I also have to tell you that Cas Goossens* would introduce you as a defender of the traditional exam system, whereafter I would briefly introduce you to the public by asking your name, the place where you live, and what you are studying. I also should inform you that the BRT would pay you 20 BF for your cooperation. Well, do you comply with my request?

The "experimenter" on purpose avoided noticing any reaction from the "subject" until all information relevant for his decision had been transmitted. In case the "subject" hesitated to commit himself, she was allowed to offer two neutral types of comments, (1) the fact that some

---

* Cas Goossens is the BRT broadcasting reporter specialized in the presentation of hot topics. His very typical voice is easily recognized by Louvain students, since he was a most appreciated commentator during the long-lasting riots of 1968. We are highly indebted to his invaluable help.

people do call in question the benefits of exam reform proves that there are arguments against it; and (2) the discussion at the end of the programme will certainly profit from it and become more animated. In the event of a "subject" refusing to cooperate, the "experimenter" immediately started the full debriefing phase, with an additional inquiry as to the reasons for the refusal (for data on number of refusals, see p. 183).

If the "subject" complied with the request, the "experimenter" continued in the following way. "Let me first give you the twenty BF. Would you please sign this receipt (she hands over a printed receipt, on which she writes the exact amount of the monetary reward). Let me show you now how far we are in our registered programme, so that you realize better where your speech is to be situated." The "experimenter" starts the replay videotape so that the TV screen shows the face of Cas Goosens who, in a truly professional way, says "Ladies and gentlemen (viewers)* we just saw some students who made a dead set at the traditional exam system, and who were fervent advocates of a radical reform of this system. Now we'll give the floor to a few other students who are holding a perhaps equally strong plea in favour of the positive sides of the traditional exam system. Here they are." The "experimenter" stops the videorecorder. "So, that is where your speech should follow. Now I will let you alone for a quarter of an hour or so. Here you have paper and pencil. Let me write down the two points you should concentrate on: no spread of exams and no exam exemptions for September. The only thing which matters is that you present the most convincing arguments in favour of the traditional exam system, and that you attack both exam spread and exam exemptions."

After 15 minutes, the "experimenter" returns to the TV studio. "I guess you have prepared something. Remember, it should not be a real speech, you need only talk in defence of the traditional exam system. Try to speak into the camera so that your face is focused on the screen. Do not worry if anything goes wrong, we can cut whatever we want during the editing of the tape. Whenever you feel you are through, we will stop". The "experimenter" flashes a spotlight, zooms the lens, starts the video-recorder and introduces the "subject" to the TV audience: "May I ask your name please? . . . where are you from? . . . what are you studying?" Then the "subject" presents his arguments while seeing his face filling the

* The Dutch term "kijkers" (viewers) makes it immediately clear that the message is addressed to the largest possible audience one can get in Belgium, viz., the public of the nation-wide BRT Television programme.

TV and monitor screen. As soon as the "subject" says that he is through, the "experimenter" stops the videorecorder and says: "Well, you did a good job, let's play back the tape and look again so that we can be sure that it was properly recorded". Without any comments, the "experimenter" confronts the "subject" with the *fait accompli* of his video-recorded plea, which from now on is in the hands of the BRT. No "subject" did ask to destroy or change the tape.

By way of *summary* we can state that, during the experimental phase just described, a deliberate effort was made to induce a very high amount of dissonance in the cognitive system of "subject's" attitude toward the reform of the university exams. As a matter of fact, a student who on valid grounds can be supposed to have entered the TV studio as a strong opponent of the traditional exam system, is confronted with a series of new cognitive elements, which clearly fulfill the theoretical requirements of classical and revised versions of the dissonance hypothesis under investigation. The relevant cognitions can be summarized as follows: (1) I am very much opposed to the traditional exam system; (2) I just have made a strong plea in favour of the traditional exam system; (3) For doing this I have accepted a paltry sum of 20 BF; (4) There is no doubt that my plea will reach a very large and influencible audience; (5) I clearly was in a position which allowed me to refuse my cooperation; (6) I never will be able to deny the fact that it was me who made the plea.

Eliciting the attitude response The procedure for this very short, but most important phase of the experiment was quite simple and straightforward. Since the only imperative was that the evaluative characteristics of the attitude response be maximally situation-free, the utmost care was exerted to avoid the "subject" suddenly understanding or suspecting his own or the "experimenter's" true role. Various pilot runs and skillful post-experimental probing provided ample guarantee for the validity of the following procedure.

As soon as the play back of the videotape was over, the "experimenter" continued in a spontaneous, relaxed and direct way:

> I wonder if you'd have two more minutes left, because I'd enjoy discussing with you some more points, but before doing so I'd like to ask you this: (she takes a piece of scratch paper and draws a horizontal line while saying), When I draw here a line, and here I put "very strongly anti", here "strongly anti" — "anti" — "rather anti" — "neutral" — "rather pro" — "pro" — "strongly pro" and "very strongly pro" (these labels are rather hastily

written with abbreviations at equal intervals of $\pm$ one inch with intermediate marks in between*, where would you place yourself if I ask you *your
own* personal attitude towards the traditional exam system seen as a system
with a minimum spread and without exemptions? Where would you mark
off your own position?

The "experimenter" hands her pencil over to the "subject" and as soon as
he gives his answer, she interprets the rating by reading aloud in a neutral
fashion "So you yourself are . . . (e.g., strongly anti, between rather anti and
neutral) the traditional exam system". This verbal description of the rating
is made in order to make sure that the "subject" did not commit a technical
lapse when marking off his attitude position.

So, the crucial dependent datum of this and all subsequent experiments is
the attitude response with regard to the traditional exam system, obtained
by means of the above described self-rating with 17 categories. "Subject's"
attitude score was then the numerical value obtained by the following transformation of the category scale into an ordinal scale† :

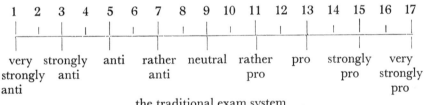

| 1 | 2 | 3 | 4 | 5 | 6 | 7 | 8 | 9 | 10 | 11 | 12 | 13 | 14 | 15 | 16 | 17 |

very   strongly   anti   rather   neutral   rather   pro   strongly   very
strongly   anti   anti   pro   pro   strongly
anti   pro

the traditional exam system

Post-experimental ratings The "experimenter" continued "Would you mind
answering some final questions? Afterwards we can discuss at ease whatever
you wish". She hands over a small mimeographed booklet, and page after
page, the "experimenter" reads aloud each of the following questions, while
inviting the subject to mark off his answer. (1) Try to estimate how the average
televiewer would judge your own opinion concerning the traditional exam
system, if he bases his judgment only on your recorded plea. I think the
average viewer will judge that I am . . . (very strongly anti . . . very strongly
pro) the traditional exam system (17 point rating identical to the one used for
the assessment of 'subject's' attitude response); (2) Suppose that your best
study-friend, without any prior warning from your side, would be confronted with your TV plea in favour of the traditional exam system. What
would he think about you? (open answer) How would he judge your
opinion on the basis of your plea? (identical 17 point rating); (3) If yesterday
I had been asking your best study-friend about your attitude towards the

* The rating-scales used in the pseudo experiment were of a quite different nature and
format, so as to avoid any resemblance and suspicion.
† As far as the statistical treatment of these ordinal data is concerned, we saw no
reasons to deviate from the common practice in the field which is to treat the data as if it
were reflecting an interval scale. The reader will be warned whenever a non-parametric
treatment would lead to different conclusions.

traditional exam system, how would he have rated you? (identical 17 point rating); (4) How much effort did you exert during the preparation of your plea in order to find arguments in favour of the traditional exam system? (very much . . . not at all, 21 point scale); (5) Did you find the preparation of the plea to be difficult or easy? (very difficult . . . very easy, 26 point scale); (6) How pleasant did you find your cooperation? (very pleasant . . . very unpleasant, 26 point scale); (7) How much did you hesitate before complying with the request? (very much . . . not at all, 26 point scale); (8) I had the impression that I could have refused my cooperation. (very easily . . . very difficultly, 26 point scale); (9) Would it have been easier to hold a plea in favour of the reform of the exam system? (much easier . . . much more difficult, 26 point scale); (10) Do you think you could have used many more arguments? (many more . . . no more, 21 point scale); (11) Did you make yourself any considerations during your cooperation? Which ones? When? (open answer); (12) Did you feel sleepy? (very much so . . . not at all, 26 point scale); (13) Do you feel that the interviewer had forced you to cooperate? (strongly so . . . not at all, 26 point scale); (14) What about your feeling of fitness (the Dutch term "fit" has a connotation of excitement) during your cooperation. (very "fit" . . . not at all, 26 point scale); (15) Would you be willing to join, within a couple of months, a panel-discussion, where you would defend the same position with regard to the traditional exam system? (with much pleasure . . . not at all, 26 point scale).

When filling out these ratings, the "subject" was still left with uncertainty concerning the rationale of these questions. As expected however, the post-experimental interview revealed that "subjects" became aware or at least suspicious of their own and "experimenter's" role during this third phase of the real experiment.

Provisional debriefing As said before, not a single "subject" ever manifested the slightest suspicion during the compliance and attitude measurement phase. Moreover, the "experimenter" had been witnessing numerous non-verbal symptoms of real conflict and commitment from the "subject", who was fully convinced of the social reality of his publicly identified advocacy. On mere ethical grounds, we were bound to give a detailed and fully reassuring debriefing to each individual student before he left the TV room. Since the experimenter knew that the student was under no time pressure (he had volunteered for a block of two hours), this ethically quite important and delicate final phase of the experiment got all the time it deserved.

Since we planned to assess, several weeks after the experiment proper, the long term persistency of the experimental effect (see infra, p. 157), there were however, constraints other than ethical, for the concrete debriefing strategy. In an effort to dismiss each subject with the reassurance that his plea would not serve any other than a strictly scientific purpose, while still diverting his attention from the real attitude-focus of the experiment, we were forced to have recourse to a debriefing which was not a true description of the scientific problem under investigation, but which was so plausible and close to the real manipulation that we did judge it as a justified solution for the ethical and scientific problems involved. It should be noted that the fact that the students became aware of their subject role did not at all imply that they grasped the import of the casual question concerning their own attitude position. The post-experimental questions and cover-story were deliberately designed so as to mask the interest in the crucial attitude response.

The experimenter started the debriefing phase by carefully probing the subject's perception of the whole experimental situation. She then went back to the post-experimental ratings 12 and 14 (how sleepy and how excited did you feel?) and asked if the subject could not see through the rationale of these questions. As a matter of fact, these ratings were introduced as a means for a smooth transition to the provisional debriefing. She explained that the whole TV advocacy was nothing but a second panel of an experiment which had started with the male experimenter of the pseudo experiment. "You will remember that the other fellow invited you to produce random numbers under various chemical and psychological incentive conditions. What you have been doing here is basically the same, except that the simple digit-responses have been substituted by the thinking up of arguments whereas the motivation manipulation was enhanced by making you believe that your plea would serve for a TV programme, and that you were also offered a monetary reward. The reason why we asked you to advocate against exam reform is simply because such a task implies some real creative thinking since you are used to hearing arguments in the opposite direction. Now you will remember from your course on motivation that the effect of arousal might be a function of the difficulty of the task, and that is precisely one of the problems we are interested in at the moment." So far a summary description of the debriefing which lasted an average of twenty minutes per subject.

The experimenter answered within the same framework any further questions the subject might ask. When there were no more doubts that he was fully relieved and reconciled to the experimental disguise, she finally underlined the absolute necessity of the subject's secrecy, until he would receive around mid-May a clearance letter from the author*. When the student had signed his formal pledge to secrecy, he was thanked for his help and dismissed.

Procedure for anonymous public advocacy (radio) condition

Most of the differences between the radio and the television condition are self-evident. The treatment of the "subject" throughout all phases (including the pseudo experiment) was identical except that he was informed that the audience of the advocacy would be reached through the nation-wide broadcasting service and, most important, that the subject's anonymity was fully guaranteed. The TV studio room is replaced by a similar office room with a professional reporter's recorder and an all-weather microphone on the desk. The introduction made by the BRT reporter Cas Goossens is of course only an audio-presentation, but the typical and well known pitch of his professional voice ensures the credibility of the situation. Needless to say that, in contrast to the TV condition, the "experimenter" does not invite the "subject" to give his name or any other information which could facilitate his identification by the audience. Before the "subject" complies with the request he is informed that his identity will never be revealed and this is again stressed just before he starts his plea. In summary, all new relevant cognitions listed on p. 74 are included, except the last one: "I never will be able to deny the fact that it was me who made the plea".

Procedure for the baseline condition

The initial treatment for the baseline condition was the same as for the radio condition. Upon arriving in the radio-office, the "experimenter" says: "Please sit down, I will explain to you what you could do for me in a moment, but first I would like to ask you one question." She then elicits the attitude response in the same way as was done for the two preceding conditions. The only difference being that the term "traditional exam system" is briefly explained so as to be sure that the meaning of the attitude-issue be comparable to the other conditions where a rather detailed description was given during the "eliciting of compliance

---

* As usual, the successful maintenance of secrecy was thoroughly checked in various direct and indirect ways. The students of the Science Faculty have always been truly remarkable for their understanding of this essential research imperative.

phase". The subsequent treatment of the subjects of this baseline condition will be reported later on.

The attitude response thus obtained should serve as a baseline from which the effect of the experimental treatment can be measured. It offers a valid estimation of the attitude response which the experimental "subjects" of the TV and radio conditions would have emitted if they had not been exposed first to the experimental treatment.

Summary of procedure

Eleven male students, randomly assigned to each of three conditions, emit an attitude response concerning the very important and salient issue of exam reform. In the first two conditions, they do so after having freely complied, in a real life situation, under remuneration of a trivial sum of 20 BF, with an attractive female interviewer's request to hold a strong plea against this much desired reform, before a nation-wide TV or radio audience. After fifteen minutes of solitary preparation, the plea is recorded and hereafter played back to the "subject". The "subjects" of the TV condition are fully identifiable whereas anonymity has been guaranteed in the radio condition. In the third, baseline condition, the attitude response is not preceded by any experimental manipulation except for the pseudo-experimental treatment and the attitude response eliciting question which are kept constant across conditions.

RESULTS AND DISCUSSION

The mean attitude response towards the traditional exam system for the three conditions of Experiment Five are given in Table 7. It will be recalled that a score of 1 represents the most extreme anti- and 17 the most extreme pro-traditional exam system attitude position; a score of 9 indicates a neutral attitude response (see p. 75).

TABLE 7
Mean attitude response towards traditional exam system for baseline, anonymous and identified public counterattitudinal advocacy conditions (20 BF reward)

Baseline	Public Counterattitudinal Advocacy, 20 BF	
	Anonymous (Radio)	Identified (TV)
2.3	6.6	6.1

Note. The higher the mean, the more *pro* the attitude.

The data for the baseline condition confirm the adequacy of the topic chosen for the counterattitudinal advocacy. Not only is the mean attitude response situated at the extreme anti-side of the continuum (between very strongly and strongly anti the traditional exam system), but equally important, the variability of these pre-advocacy attitude responses is remarkably small. The eleven attitude responses are distributed as follows: very strongly anti: 4; between very strongly and strongly anti: 2; strongly anti: 3; between strongly anti and anti: 2. It was indeed highly unlikely to find a single student who would not spontaneously reject the traditional exam system characterized by absence of a decent temporal spread and exemptions for the September session.

As far as the public advocacy conditions are concerned, contrary to the expectations based on the Helmreich and Collins study, the observed attitude change is somewhat smaller for the identified TV (6.1) than for the anonymous radio (6.6) condition. This difference however does not even approach significance ($t = 0.38; 0.70 < p < 0.80$).

Although the identifiability of the advocate did not produce any effect, there is no doubt that the experimental treatment, common to both rewarded public counterattitudinal advocacy conditions, did have a quite strong influence on the attitude response: the differences between baseline and radio- and between baseline and TV-condition are both highly significant ($t = 4.72; p < 0.001$ and $t = 3.95; p < 0.01$). As

TABLE 8

Distribution of attitude responses for the experimental conditions of Table 7

Conditions	Attitude Responses						
	very strongly anti	strongly anti	anti	rather anti	neutral	rather pro	pro
Baseline	6	5	—	—	—	—	—
Radio 20 BF	1	1	1	6	—	2	—
TV 20 BF	2	—	3	4	1	1	—

shown in Table 8, there are, for each of the public advocacy conditions, only two "subjects" who emit an attitude response which falls within the range of the baseline condition. For the combined advocacy conditions, there are not less than 10 students who consider themselves as only "rather anti", one as "neutral" and three who even score at the positive side of the continuum. Clearly one does not need a sophisticated statistical analysis to infer a real change in the attitude expressed by our TV and radio advocates.

It should be noted that the proportion of subjects who refused to comply with the "experimenter's" request was so small that self-selection of the "subjects" could not account for the data obtained (for more information on refusals, see p. 183).

The similarity of the attitude responses emitted after anonymous (radio) and identified (TV) advocacy clearly does not strengthen the validity of any interpretation of the dissonance effect which implies the identifiability of the advocate to his audience. Whatever the nature of our experimental effect might be, the identifiability of the advocate cannot be considered as a necessary condition for an impressive attitude change to be produced.

With regard to our operationalization of the identifiability it is clear from the description of the procedure that the anonymity manipulation was not an all or nothing dichotomy. Whereas the TV condition did approach the maximum of identifiability of the advocate, one might object that the anonymous radio condition still left the subject with the fear that one or another listener might recognize his voice. One should however, consider the fact that this was also true in the Helmreich and Collins experiment and that, even if identifiability of the radio condition is not at an absolute zero level, it is definitely at a maximum level in the TV condition, where no subject ever could deny that he was the one who had been advocating against the reform of the exam system.

Of course, the possibility of a *ceiling effect* for either or both the independent and the dependent variable is left open as an explanation for the disconfirmation of the Helmreich and Collins findings. It might be that "commitment", which was the conceptual variable underlying the anonymous-identified manipulation of Helmreich and Collins, was already pushed to its effective maximum in our anonymous radio condition. If we confront the latter condition and the anonymous audiotape condition of Helmreich and Collins with, e.g., some of the criteria for commitment advanced by Kiesler and Sakumara (1966, p. 350), viz., importance of act, how public the act was, degree of irrevocability of act, degree of perceived volition, one could argue that our anonymous condition implies much more commitment that the one of Helmreich and Collins, and it might be that the added identifiability of the advocate simply did not lead to an effective increase of commitment.

Also it could be that the dependent variable did not allow for any stronger effect. In view of the intensity of the pre-advocacy attitude position and the importance of the attitude issue, one can expect both a very strong resistance to change and a narrow latitude of change of the attitude, so that the maximum possible effect might already be obtained in the anonymous treatment. As will become clear later on, our further research invalidates this interpretation.

Another possible explanation for the absence of any difference between TV and radio conditions could be that the mere prospect of an appearance on a nation-wide TV screen was so rewarding and thus consonant with the compliance that it compensated for the dissonance produced by identifiability. One then could argue that the intrinsic reward of the identified communication was much smaller in the Helmreich and Collins experiment, whereas in our study the total magnitude of dissonance was more equalized between the two conditions. Although a comparison between identified and anonymous radio advocacy would help us in pinning down the precise role of identifiability of the advocate, we have not conducted such a study since our research interest was not focusing on this variable. It will become clear that the next steps of our research project bypass the difficulties related to the unknown differential reward nature of a TV versus radio speech. As said before, we were not interested in the effect upon subsequent attitude responses of a counterattitudinal TV or radio speech as such. The only reason why we chose for a replication of the Helmreich and Collins paradigm, was because their low reward video-speech manipulation promised to be a dependable one for the arousal of cognitive dissonance. Since our manipulation had been quite effective in producing attitude change, we felt that the main objective of the first experiment of our 1969 research had been reached. Although its design, for obvious reasons, did not allow for any interpretation beyond the anonymity factor, the stage was set for a systematic analysis of the determinants of the observed attitude change.

As far as the theoretical conclusions with regard to the identifiability of the advocate are concerned, we prefer at this point not to discuss possible implications of our negative findings. Clearly, one instance of no difference is a weak platform for any conclusion. It should be recalled however that Collins and Helmreich also report several failures when manipulating anonymity (cf. supra, p. 66).

The remainder of this chapter will be devoted to a progressive examination of various factors which might have contributed to the demonstrated attitude change effect. We will concentrate successively upon the role of the monetary reward, the counterattitudinal and the public nature of the advocacy.

3. Experiment Six: The effect of monetary reward for public counterattitudinal advocacy upon subsequent attitude responses

PROBLEM AND DESIGN

In the first chapter of the present monograph, it was pointed out that the manipulation of the magnitude of a monetary reward offered for compliance, has served as the classical device for an experimental confrontation between the controversial theories concerning the effect of counterattitudinal advocacy upon attitude change. In the experiment just reported, one of the crucial features of the "subject's" treatment—crucial at least in the intention of the researcher—consisted of the administration of a very low and trivial 20 BF monetary reward. In the present experiment, an effort will be made to clarify somewhat the role of this reward as a possible determinant of the attitude change observed in the anonymous public (radio) counterattitudinal advocacy condition. As a consequence of Experiment Five, it was decided to abandon the technically more complicated TV advocacy, and to pursue the analysis with the equally effective anonymous public advocacy. An analysis of the post-experimental questions did not offer any arguments against this decision.

Guided by our 1964 research, we will not restrict ourselves to the classical low-high reward comparison, but add several conditions which should allow a more rigorous test of the major theoretical assumptions involved. Let us briefly comment on the rationale for each of the new conditions of Experiment Six, whose design also will include the baseline and anonymous low reward data obtained in Experiment Five.

High reward (200 BF) condition The rationale for this 200 BF reward treatment hardly needs any comment since a comparison with the 20 BF reward condition of the previous experiment enables the classical test of the positive or negative relationship between reward and attitude change. It is obvious that the impressive effect already produced in the low reward radio condition does not necessarily imply that an inverse function between reward and attitude change will be obtained. For the time being it is equally plausible to attribute the observed effect to the various non-monetary incentive characteristics of the public advocacy situation and it remains an empirical question if decupling the low monetary reward will enhance or reduce the attitude change effect. On the basis of one of the main conclusions from our 1964 Cohen-Rosenberg replication, where no evidence was found in favour of a positive relationship, we do of course predict that the attitude change effect will be smaller in the 200 BF than in the 20 BF condition.

It should be noted that a 200 BF reward is a quite plausible remuneration for cooperation with the Belgian broadcasting service. It will be understood that we do not attach much importance to the fact that the absolute magnitude of our high reward is comparable to the high ($5) rewards used by Rosenberg (1965), Carlsmith, Collins and Helmreich (1966) and Helmreich and Collins (1968). As said before, we were more concerned about comparing an inappropriately low with a plausible high reward. It is only on the basis of budgetary considerations that we refrained from administering abnormally high monetary rewards. As will become clear later on we will eventually manipulate disproportionally high non-monetary rewards.

The zero reward condition The rationale for this condition has already been commented upon in Experiment Four. It will be recalled however, that a straightforward interpretation of the results was somewhat hindered by a possible effect of a "disconfirmation of expectancies" contaminant (see p. 46). The replication of a zero reward (anonymous public counter-attitudinal advocacy) condition in the present experiment—where no financial payment was expected—should enable us to further test the conceptual role of the monetary reward either as a cognitive element consonant with the compliance or as an incentive and/or reinforcer for self-persuasion. Together with the next condition, it also allows for an indirect check upon Festinger's conception of the low reward as a "minimal" force for compliance (see p. 44).

The relative deprivation condition In this anonymous public counterattitudinal advocacy condition, the "experimenter" tells the "subject" that the usual BRT funds unfortunately were given out and apologizes for the fact that he, unlike previous collaborating students, will not receive any monetary reward for his participation in the programme. Although the "subjects" did not expect to be paid for their compliance, this condition should make

the students feel deprived of an appropriate but unspecified monetary
reward which they believed has been paid to their predecessors, who
collaborated by performing the much less demanding task of making a
plea in favour of exam reform.

By introducing this relative deprivation treatment, we wanted to create
a cognitive *reward* element which would be clearly *dissonant* with the
compliance, and whose effect could be compared, using the zero reward
as a baseline, with that of the "consonance" of the small and high reward.
As said before, we had become sensitive to the possibly dissonance enhancing characteristics of an inequitable or unusual reward. The present
design would enable us to study the effect of two different inappropriate
or unusual reward conditions: a paltry sum of 20 BF, and an unspecified
relative deprivation. The basic hypothesis being that Festinger's low
reward effect is not a function of the *low consonance* of the reward, but of the
dissonance producing inappropriateness of the reward. The further implications
of this hypothesis will be considered more thoroughly in the discussion
section of this and several subsequent experiments.

Zero reward pro-attitudinal advocacy Finally, we again introduced a condition which we consider as a more appropriate control condition for the
assessment of any effect of counterattitudinal advocacy, viz., a situation in
which all factors are kept constant except for the counterattitudinal
nature of the advocacy. The findings of our 1964 research, where the
importance of a control for the "central dissonance" was demonstrated,
called for another test of this crucial supposition of the experimental
foundation of cognitive dissonance theory. As said before, we have always
regretted the absence of a pro-attitudinal advocacy control condition in
the relevant literature. The comparison of a counterattitudinal advocacy
effect with a pre-advocacy baseline condition clearly does not allow for
any firm conclusion which is based upon the posited but completely
uncontrolled "central dissonance" generated by the counterattitudinal
compliance.

The treatment of the "subjects" of this condition was in all respects
identical to that of the students of the zero reward anonymous public
counterattitudinal advocacy condition, except that they were asked to
hold a strong plea *in favour* of exam reform, i.e., longer temporal spread of
exams and exemptions for the September session.

To summarize, the design of Experiment Six consists of six conditions:
besides the classical baseline plus low and high reward counterattitudinal

D

advocacy, there is a no reward and a relative deprivation counter-attitudinal advocacy condition. In addition a no reward pro-attitudinal advocacy condition supplements the control function of the classical baseline which is essentially both a no reward and no advocacy condition.

PROCEDURE*

As far as the temporal sequence of the experimentation is concerned it should be noted that one day after the completion of Experiment Five, a first cluster with the high and no reward counterattitudinal conditions was run, immediately followed by a second cluster with the two remaining conditions. It will be recalled that all data, discussed in Experiment Six (the baseline and low reward condition included), have been gathered within a period of approximately two weeks.

The procedure for the four new conditions of Experiment Six was in all respects identical to that of the anonymous public condition of Experiment Five, except for the self-evident modifications which will be pointed out very briefly.

High reward condition The 20 BF of the low reward anonymous condition are replaced by two banknotes of one hundred francs. In view of the assessment of the long term persistency of the experimental effect, the students were not asked to return the monetary reward.

Zero reward condition The "experimenter" simply did not allude to any monetary reward.

Relative deprivation condition At the very moment that the "subjects" of the reward conditions are informed about the payment (before the decision for compliance is taken), the "experimenter" says: "I should add that the students who until now did collaborate in our radio-programme have been paid for their cooperation. Unfortunately, the funds which were provided for the full series of hot-topic programmes are given out, so that I cannot pay you". Just before leaving the "subject" alone for the solitary preparation of his plea, she repeats in a quite natural and incidental manner "Again, I'm sorry that there is no money left to pay you".

Zero reward pro-attitudinal advocacy The "subjects" are asked, in terms exactly analoguous to the ones used in the counterattitudinal condition, to present arguments exclusively in favour of the reform of the exam

* The reader is supposed to be familiar with section 1 of this chapter (p. 56-65).

system. The introduction by the BRT reporter Cas Goossens is also identical except for the appropriate reversals. It is obvious that the provisional debriefing was slightly adapted to the pro-attitudinal nature of the advocacy.

RESULTS AND DISCUSSION

The mean attitude responses for each of the conditions of Experiment Six are given in Table 9. As said before, the baseline and low reward data are taken from Experiment Five.

TABLE 9

Mean attitude response towards the traditional exam
system as a function of monetary reward

| | | Anonymous Public Advocacy | | | |
| | Pro-attitudinal | | Counterattitudinal | | |
Baseline	Zero BF	Zero BF	200 BF	20 BF	Rel. Depr.
2.3	4.2	4.9	4.8	6.6	7.1

Let us discuss the theoretical implications for the results obtained in each of the new conditions.

High versus low reward If we restrict ourselves to an inspection of the data for the classical low and high reward conditions, there is no doubt that the relation between magnitude of monetary reward and attitude change is not a direct but an inverse one, 6.6 (20 BF) being a greater change in the advocated direction than 4.8 (200 BF). The difference is significant at the 0.07 level (one-tailed $t = 1.62$). As expected on the basis of the first conclusion of Chapter One (see p. 49), there is no confirmation of predictions made by incentive, reinforcement or cognitive-affective consistency theories. Again the thesis of Rosenberg concerning the distinction between "mere assertion" and "true advocacy" does not receive empirical support. The data are in line with the results produced in the classical dissonance experiments. It might be worthwhile to summarize once more the interpretation offered by dissonance theorists for the assessed inverted relationship between size of reward and magnitude of post-compliance attitude change. Basically they hold that the greater attitude change for the low reward is due to the fact that the cognitive element concerning the 20 BF reward is relatively less important and less consonant with the compliance than that of the 200 BF reward. This leads to a greater total magnitude of dissonance in the cognitive clusters concerning examreform (attitude and counterattitudinal public behaviour) and to a stronger manifestation of dissonance reduction via attitude change. Festinger and his school also put it in other, negative relationship, terms: the greater attitude change in the low reward condition is due to the fact that the compliance was *less justified* in the low than in the high reward condition. By becoming less anti-traditional exam system, greater (*although far from perfect*) consonance is achieved within the cognitive system concerning the attitude and the overt compliance.

Zero reward for counterattitudinal advocacy Thus far we have seen that, if we restrict our discussion to an inspection of the classical dissonance design (baseline, low and high reward for discrepant advocacy) we do have a replication of a cognitive dissonance effect and a confirmation of Festinger's thesis. The validity of the classical interpretation of the observed dissonance effect seems however once more to be challenged by the results obtained in the zero reward counterattitudinal condition, for which the attitude change (4.9) is almost identical to the change observed in the high reward condition (4.8), and which differs from the low reward condition (6.6) at the 0.6 level (one-tailed $t = 1.64$) (at the $p < 0.05$ level by median test (Fisher)).

When applying Festinger's conceptual framework to the no and high reward conditions, we have to conclude that there is no evidence that the posited consonance of the high reward does reduce the total magnitude of cognitive dissonance. According to dissonance theory, the zero and 200 BF reward treatments do generate identical clusters of cognitive elements, except for the cognition concerning the monetary reward. For obvious reasons, there is no consonant reward cognition which could influence the total magnitude of dissonance in the zero reward condition whereas such a cognition is claimed to fulfill an important dissonance reducing role in the high reward condition via its consonance with the compliance. Given the identity of the central dissonance and the crucial conceptual difference in the consonance of the reward, the total magnitude of dissonance should be larger in the no reward than in the high reward condition, and so should be the attitude change. Since the attitude responses of both the zero and 200 BF conditions do not evidence any differential need for dissonance reduction, it becomes difficult to maintain the basic dissonance assumption that the high reward, as an important justification for the counterattitudinal advocacy, reduces the magnitude of the total dissonance.

At the same time, we see that the attitude change in the advocated direction is substantially greater in the low than in the no reward condition. Since "no monetary justification" is less than a "small or minimal monetary justification", the attitude change should, if anything, be greater in the no reward condition. The argument that in a zero reward condition the "subject" might have recourse to other, non-monetary, sources of justification is perfectly plausible but in our opinion not relevant since the experimental demonstration of the dissonance effect implies by design that all non-monetary reward elements, which might be consonant with the compliance, are equalized across conditions. We see no compelling reason why this would apply for the comparison between a low and high reward treatment and not for the comparison between "minimal" and "no monetary justification" conditions.

On the basis of these considerations, and in line with our 1966 *a posteriori* interpretation, we propose the following conclusions, while for the time being, making maximal use of the cognitive dissonance conceptual framework.

(1) The very low and trivial 20 BF reward is not to be seen as a weak or minimal justification for the compliance but as a reward which is *dissonant* with the counterattitudinal advocacy and thus enhances the total dissonance. The student's cognition that he signs a receipt for a twenty franc "reward" "does *not* fit"—is dissonant—with the cognition that he makes a nation-wide plea against his profound conviction. Betraying a firm standpoint for a package of cigarettes creates more conflict than if there were no reward. The dissonant reward *adds* to the total dissonance and thus motivates a greater change in the attitude.

(2) The perfectly plausible 200 BF remuneration for collaborating in a BRT programme is not to be seen as an important justification which inhibits the attitude change asked for by the "central dissonance". If this were the case, there should have been a differential effect between the high and no reward condition. We would argue that the 200 BF is an *irrelevant* cognitive element, which does not affect the central dissonance, at least not in its hypothesized manifestations. The subject might think that a 200 BF remuneration is what everyone gets for whatever cooperation of this sort. This cognition can be considered as "simply having nothing to do with" the counterattitudinal nature of the compliance (Festinger, 1957, p. 11). We do not want to discuss the technical meaning of "irrelevant relation" which, in Festinger's terms is actually identical with "no relation in terms of consonance or dissonance". The main point

we wish to make, is that there are good reasons to abandon the classical dissonance conception of a monotonic, consonant reward variable. Instead we should distinguish between inappropriate, embarrassing, not fitting, *dissonant* rewards and rewards which are irrelevant and possibly also rewards which indeed might be truly consonant.

(3) A third conclusion derived from the comparison of the discussed data, and to which we will come back later on, is that both an appropriate and a no reward counterattitudinal advocacy treatment have a significant effect upon the attitude. As a matter of fact, the attitude responses of both conditions (4.8 and 4.9) are very significantly less extreme than the base-line data $(2.3)(t = 4.26; p < 0.001)$. These data suggest that an anonymous counterattitudinal plea by itself tempers the extreme attitude position which the student had before engaging in his advocacy. The precise determinants of this effect (counterattitudinal and/or public nature of the plea) will be examined further.

Relative deprivation Further support for our provisional interpretation of the low reward effect is offered by the results of the relative deprivation condition. The induced cognitive element concerning the monetary reward "I am not getting paid whereas other students were paid for doing a similar (or much less demanding) job", clearly is *dissonant* with the compliance. The effect of this relative deprivation upon the attitude responses (7.1) is essentially similar to that of the 20 BF reward (6.6), and significantly different from the zero (4.9) and high (4.8) reward conditions $(t = 2.12; p < 0.05)$.

Taking into account the similarity of the zero and high reward effects and the similarity of the relative deprivation and low reward effects, and given that the relative deprivation treatment by definition does generate a cognitive element which is dissonant with the compliance, we would argue that the latter effects are both related to the dissonance *enhancing* characteristics of an inappropriate reward for the compliance. This conception of a dissonance enhancing reward (see also Nuttin, 1966) contrasts with the monotonic functions which are tested in both the dissonance and anti-dissonance camp where monetary reward is manipulated and conceptualized along a purely quantitative continuum determining varying degrees of consonance, incentive and/or reinforcement.

As will become clear later on, this proposed redefinition of the inappropriate reward, implies more than the apparent trivial correction in the conceptual interpretation of classical "forced compliance" research.

"*Minimal force for compliance*" Before looking at the data of the pro-attitudinal advocacy condition, we apologize for briefly digressing on another aspect of Festinger's conception of forced compliance research. It will be recalled that Festinger considers the low reward treatment in the classical dissonance experiments as situations in which "just enough reward is given to elicit the overt compliance" (cf. supra, p. 44). The data for our zero reward and relative deprivation conditions corroborate our earlier conclusion with regard to this interpretational definition of the "minimal reward". Notwithstanding the fact that all external pressures, except for reward, were kept maximally constant and that a blind analysis of the "experimenter"-"subject" interactions did not reveal any systematic differences in this respect* the number of "subjects" who refused to comply was not larger in the no reward, or relative deprivation condition, than in the conditions with low or high reward (cf. infra, p. 183). However appealing Festinger's conception of a "minimal force" might be, we see again that there is no evidence whatsoever that this subtle manipulation —for which the relevant literature lacks adequate control conditions— has ever been realized. Clearly there are many other, non-monetary forces, which induce the subject to comply. We might even argue that a low inappropriate reward functions as a negative force for compliance, rather than as a weak or minimal positive force. We are sceptical therefore with regard to the experimental foundation of Festinger's thesis, which has been the leitmotif of much research ever since, viz., "If one wanted to obtain private change in addition to mere public compliance, the best way to do this would be *to offer just enough reward or punishment to elicit the overt compliance* (Festinger, 1957, p. 95, original italics). Not only do we lack convincing evidence for the above thesis and its conceptual infra-structure, but there obviously is an even less expensive way to obtain private change, namely by merely saying: "Sorry, there is no more money left for you". Our major concern in this respect however, is not to show that a relative deprivation does have a similar effect as a "minimal" reward, but to challenge the pretended confirmation of sweeping inter-pretational statements which are offered to the public as based on "experimental facts" and for which there is no compelling evidence whatsoever. Long before social psychologists tried to study the phenomena of minimal justification, one must have been aware of the fact that there was more conflict and attempts at conflict resolution when

* Thanks are due to Mrs Suzanne Willock who performed all blind-analyses reported in this volume.

counterattitudinal behaviour is induced by minimal forces. To pretend that the classical forced compliance research has given an experimental demonstration of this subtle process, is in our opinion, an overstatement made by scientists who, understandably so, are frustrated by the gap between rigorous experimentation and complex psychological reality.

Pro-attitudinal control condition Although the data hitherto presented raise serious doubts about the validity of Festinger's hypothesis concerning both the relative consonance of the monetary reward and the "minimal force" characteristics of a very low reward, they do not mean that the general framework of Festinger's theory with regard to counterattitudinal advocacy cannot be applied. As a matter of fact, we have argued that the central dissonance (between the pre-experimental attitude and the counterattitudinal advocacy) is not affected by normal or irrelevant reward features (no reward or 200 BF), but that the magnitude of dissonance is enhanced whenever the reward is unusual, embarrassing, exceptionally low, or *does not fit* with other relevant reward cognitions or expectations of the subject. Since such rewards "which do not fit" can be considered to create new cognitions which are dissonant with the cognitions concerning the service rendered to the BRT, or concerning the payment deserved by self and/or gained by other collaborators, we simply called them *dissonant rewards*. Since they are added to the central dissonance generated by the counterattitudinal advocacy, there is no problem in applying cognitive dissonance theory to account for the difference in attitude change obtained.

The adequacy of the cognitive dissonance interpretation for attitude change after counterattitudinal advocacy, is however, challenged in a quite fundamental way by the results of our pro-attitudinal advocacy control condition. These new facts can be summarized as follows: (1) the effect of *pro*-attitudinal anonymous public advocacy is quite similar to that of *counter*attitudinal advocacy under normal reward conditions (zero and 200 BF), the means being respectively 4.2, 4.9 and 4.8 (difference between 4.2 and 4.9 is not significant, $t = 1.00$; the same applies for the difference between 4.2 and 4.8, $t = 0.69$); (2) the attitude responses after pro-attitudinal advocacy (4.2) are significantly different from the pre-advocacy baseline condition (2.3) ($t = 3.67$, $p < 0.01$). Let us consider some of the implications of these findings.

The striking similarity between the attitude responses tapped after pro- and counterattitudinal advocacy seriously questions the claims made by cognitive dissonance theory to account for the inverse relation between magnitude of reward and attitude change after "forced compliance". It will be recalled that the dissonance interpretation essentially holds that the monetary reward reduces the magnitude of cognitive dissonance generated by the discrepancy between attitude and counterattitudinal advocacy (central dissonance), and that the smaller the reward, the less this central dissonance will be reduced by the consonant reward element.

We have already shown that there is no evidence for the dissonance reducing function of the reward. Now we are faced with the fact that the results for our pro-attitudinal control condition, which are similar to those obtained in the counterattitudinal condition, fail to provide us with evidence for the dissonance generating nature of the counterattitudinal advocacy proper. We are of course bound to restrict the meaning of "cognitive dissonance" to its operational definition of a tension which motivates observable attitude change in the direction of the attitude discrepant behaviour. In other words, our data do not confirm the fundamental assumption that attitude discrepant advocacy creates cognitive dissonance—and this, it should be stressed, in an experimental situation which allowed us to reproduce the classical dissonance effect.

We are not prone to accept the common defence strategy of dissonance theorists who argue that the dissonance aroused in the rewarded and non rewarded counterattitudinal conditions might be reduced via different avenues, or that dissonance theory does not make predictions about attitude change after pro-attitudinal advocacy. To the first objection, we would answer that our low and high reward counterattitudinal conditions did produce a dissonance effect which is in all respects comparable to the large body of evidence on which the theory is based, and that there is no theoretical reason why the postulated dissonance should motivate attitude change in our rewarded advocacy conditions, and not motivate attitude change in our non rewarded counterattitudinal advocacy conditions. The second objection is one which was frequently made by defenders of dissonance theory with whom we discussed our data. They argued that the observed change after counterattitudinal advocacy can be caused by cognitive dissonance, whereas a quite similar change observed after pro-attitudinal advocacy might be caused by other factors which are only operative in pro-attitudinal advocacy. Since cognitive dissonance theory does not pretend to make any predictions concerning attitude change after pro-attitudinal advocacy, and since the effects of pro-attitudinal advocacy upon attitude change are not well known, it is bad strategy—so the argument goes—to use a pro-attitudinal advocacy treatment as a control condition for the analysis of the dissonance effect. That would be the main reason why pro-attitudinal advocacy conditions are never used as a control condition in the relevant literature.

It seems to us that this position is defensable only from a purely formalistic point of view. We all know that to disprove a theory is a quite different enterprise than to prove the plausibility of a statement. The basic question however which we would like to formulate is the following: what can be the value of a theory if its empirical foundation does not allow for a control over its most crucial assumption? Since this central assumption is that cognitive dissonance is generated by the simultaneous presence of the knowledge that one says "not X", and the knowledge that one really believes "X", we argue that an appropriate control for this assumption is to compare the effect of the simultaneous presence of the knowledge that one says "X", and the knowledge that one really believes "X". If both effects are similar, there is in our opinion no support for the validity of the assumption made. The conventional control conditions used in all relevant experiments in the literature, which are mere baseline estimations of the pre-advocacy attitude responses, we believe, can only serve as a control for the assessment of attitude change and its direction. They cannot be used as a control for all aspects of the experimental treatment, since this treatment is usually so utterly complex that one cannot have any confidence in the precise nature of the factors manipulated as long as one does not check with a treatment which is identical in all respects except for the element on which the interpretation is based.

This is precisely what we have tried to accomplish. We were successful in replicating the classical dissonance effect, but the adding of a zero reward pro- and counterattitudinal advocacy condition confronted us with the fact that giving a 200 BF reward or no reward does not make any difference, and that holding a counter- or pro-attitudinal plea does not make any clear-cut difference either. There obviously was a significant attitude change effect in *both* the pro- and counterattitudinal conditions, since the pre-advocacy (baseline) attitude responses are much more extreme, but it does not seem justified anymore to call for an explanation which is based on the posited dissonant nature of the relations between the cognitive elements generated by the pre-experimental attitude and the public counterattitudinal behaviour.

As a consequence, we hold that there should be a more economical interpretation not only for the observed attitude change after the not rewarded pro- and counterattitudinal advocacy and the 200 BF reward counterattitudinal advocacy, but also for the 20 BF and relative deprivation effects, for which a modified cognitive dissonance interpretation no longer seems in order. It would indeed not be justified to continue to force the phenomena under study in a cognitive dissonance frame if none of its basic theoretical assumptions prove to be necessary to account for the experimental effects obtained.

Our search for a more economical interpretation will be guided by the hypothesis that it is the embarrassing, unusual, upsetting or "dissonant" nature of the reward treatment that produces the impressive attitude change effect, and indeed, makes it distinctly superior to the effect obtained in both counter- and pro-attitudinal advocacy conditions with normal or irrelevant reward features.

The fact that we continue using the term "dissonant" for qualifying the 20 BF and relative deprivation reward treatment should not confuse the reader who might think that we are still working within a *cognitive* dissonance framework. As we have said before, we abandoned Festinger's cognitive dissonance interpretation which is based upon the restoration of an equilibrium between cognitions concerning attitude and attitude discrepant behaviour in which the reward functions as a dissonance *reducing* element. Since the inconsistency between attitude and attitude discrepant behaviour did not prove to be important, there is no basis anymore for a cognitive dissonance interpretation of the equilibrium restoring attitude change. Nevertheless, the fact remains that receiving 20 BF or getting relatively deprived from a reward does produce a dramatic attitude change effect. Since we have reasons to think that this effect is linked to the unusual and upsetting nature of the reward treatment, but do not as yet want to speculate about the underlying process, we simply call the reward "dissonant", hereby implying nothing else but a reward which "*does not fit*" with the requested compliance.

For the time being, it seems justified to dichotomize the discussed 1969 post-advocacy data as follows:
"dissonant" reward: TV, 20 BF; radio 20 BF and radio relative deprivation—(all counterattitudinal):
normal or irrelevant reward: zero BF, pro- and counterattitudinal and 200 BF—counterattitudinal (all radio).

The mean attitude responses for these pooled data are respectively 6.6 and 4.6. The difference between the two clusters of conditions is very significant ($t = 3.03$; $p < 0.01$). Clearly also both these means are very different from the pre-advocacy baseline attitude response (2.3); for the dissonant reward conditions, $t = 7.47$ ($p < 0.001$); for the normal reward conditions, $t = 4.70$ ($p < 0.001$).

We therefore propose to distinguish between three families of attitude responses: (1) the baseline attitude response (2.3), emitted prior to any experimental treatment; (2) the normal reward post-advocacy response (4.6), obtained after the "subject" engaged in pro- or counterattitudinal advocacy under normal reward treatment (zero or 200 BF); (3) the "dissonant" reward post-advocacy response (6.6), obtained after the "subject" presented a counterattitudinal plea (identified or anonymous) under unusual, embarrassing or "dissonant" reward conditions (20 BF, relative deprivation).

Before pursuing more explicitly the "dissonant" reward issue (Chapter Three), we will examine the role of two other major features of our experimental situation. Whatever the mechanism behind the "dissonant" reward effect might be, it seems worthwhile to first check if the counter-attitudinal and/or the public nature of the advocacy were necessary conditions for the "dissonant" reward effect to be obtained. These questions will be treated briefly in the next two sections.

4. Experiment Seven: "Dissonant" reward and counter-attitudinal nature of anonymous public advocacy

PROBLEM, DESIGN AND PROCEDURE*

In our 1964 replication of the Cohen and Rosenberg studies, we did not find any clear evidence for the conceptual importance attributed to the counterattitudinal nature of differentially rewarded advocacy. More-over, in the experiment just reported, the attitude change obtained after pro- and after counterattitudinal advocacy (without reward) was almost identical and was significantly different from the pre-advocacy baseline data. It seemed worthwhile to examine if the "dissonant" reward effect assessed in the previous experiment would be maintained after pro-attitudinal advocacy. Thus it was decided to run a low (20 BF) reward and a relative deprivation condition while inviting the students to hold an anonymous plea before the nation-wide radio audience in defence of the exam reform. A comparison of these two new conditions with the two "dissonant" reward treatments of Experiment Six should enable us

---

* The reader is supposed to be familiar with section 1 of this chapter (p. 56-65).

to answer the question if the counterattitudinal nature of the advocacy was a necessary condition for the impressive "dissonant" reward effect to be obtained.

It should be conceded that the decision to run these conditions—one day after the collection of the previous data—was not very well documented and was rather of an heuristic nature. We are indeed somewhat at a loss when making predictions which are based on, for example, the appropriateness or embarrassing nature of the monetary reward, especially since the intrinsic reward of having the opportunity to defend one's *own* position before a nation-wide audience might change completely the relevance and meaning of the monetary reward features involved. We did not include any retrospective questions concerning the perception of the monetary reward, because these very answers might be in part determined by the specific treatment of "subjects" who are suddenly made aware of their role as a subject.

The procedure for Experiment Seven is exactly the same as that employed in Experiment Six for the pro- and counterattitudinal anonymous public advocacy conditions (radio). The administration of the low reward and the relative deprivation is of course identical for pro- and counterattitudinal advocacy conditions.

RESULTS AND DISCUSSION

In Table 10, the data obtained for the two new pro-attitudinal "dissonant" reward conditions are compared with the corresponding counterattitudinal data of Experiment Six.

TABLE 10
Mean attitude response towards the traditional exam system as a function of attitude discrepant nature of advocacy

| | Monetary Reward | |
Anonymous Public Advocacy	20 BF	Relative Deprivation
Counterattitudinal	6.6	7.1
Pro-attitudinal	4.0	4.4

Note. Baseline mean is 2.3

When recalling that the mean attitude response in the no-reward pro-attitudinal condition of Experiment Six was 4.2, it becomes clear that there is no "dissonant" reward effect whatsoever if the students are asked to hold a strong plea in defence of their own position and are paid either 20 BF (4.0) or undergo the relative deprivation treatment (4.4). These data contrast with the "dissonant" reward effects obtained after counter-attitudinal advocacy (6.6 and 7.1). Table 11 presents the results of a two-way analysis of variance showing a very significant main effect of the pro- or counterattitudinal nature of the plea ($F = 10.62$; $df = 1/40$; $p < 0.01$). The type of "dissonant" reward does not have a significant effect upon the attitude response nor is there an interaction between the two factors studied.

TABLE 11
Analysis of variance for data of Table 10

Source	SS	df	MS	F
Advocacy (A)	79.11	1	79.11	10.62*
Reward (R)	1.84	1	1.84	
A×R	0.09	1	0.09	
Within treatments	297.86	40	7.45	
Total	378.90	43		

* $p < 0.01$

It also should be pointed out that each of the new pro-attitudinal conditions leads to an attitude response which is significantly less extreme than the 2.3 pre-advocacy baseline (for 20 BF: $t = 2.54$; $p < 0.01$; for relative deprivation: $t = 3.72$; $p < 0.01$).

What can we conclude from these new data? Disregarding the various control conditions of the previous experiment, they seem indeed to corroborate the cognitive dissonance view which predicts maximum attitude change after minimally justified counterattitudinal advocacy. We should not however, forget that the data of Experiment Six induced us to abandon the crucial cognitive dissonance assumptions for interpreting the obtained "dissonant" reward effects. In view of this we must, on an a posteriori basis, make the assumption that the administration of a 20 BF reward or a relative deprivation of and by itself is not a sufficient condition to produce the "dissonant" reward effect for the simple reason that the "dissonant" nature of any reward feature is a function of the contingent rewarded behaviour. Receiving 20 BF or being told that no money is left, may become quite irrelevant if the situation allows the "subject" to defend his *own* strong attitudinal position before a nation-wide audience. The crucial difference between the pro- and counter-attitudinal advocacy situation might indeed not be a function of the mere cognitive consonance or dissonance with the private attitude, but might lie in its intrinsic reward-cost structure which affects the meaning or relevance of any additional reward information brought into the situation. What we are saying is that to receive a paltry sum or to get deprived of a normal reward might be quite upsetting when the task is one of the last things one would wish to do whatever the reward might be, viz., make a public plea against one's own profound conviction; whereas an identical reward treatment might be completely irrelevant if it is offered contingent upon a unique opportunity to win adherents for one's own firm standpoint on university reform.

Although it hardly needs any argument to accept the proposition that our counterattitudinal advocacy was a much less rewarding task than the pro-attitudinal plea, we might briefly illustrate this point by referring to the answers given on post-experimental question 15: "Would you be willing to join, within a couple of months, a panel-discussion, where you would defend the same position with regard to the traditional exam system: with much pleasure ... not at all". As expected, the reactions of the pro- and counterattitudinal advocates are concentrated on the opposite poles of the continuum, the counterattitudinal "subjects" not being prepared at all to defend the same position once again. The same applies for post-experimental question 9: "Would it have been easier to hold a plea in favour (or against) the reform of the exam system?" The students of the counterattitudinal treatment all quite strongly expressed the opinion that it would have been much easier to hold a pro-attitudinal plea, whereas the pro-attitudinal advocates say that it would have been much more difficult for them to hold a counterattitudinal plea. Again, the distributions hardly overlap and concentrate on opposite sides of the continuum.

These data, combined with the fact that counter- and pro-attitudinal advocates do not seem to differ in terms of subjective effort invested during the preparation of their plea (post-experimental question 4)—which for all subjects was quite high—documents it seems to us, our conjecture that the 20 BF and relative deprivation was much more inappropriate or "dissonant" in the counter- than in the pro-attitudinal conditions.

The main point we wish to make then is that the absence of a "dissonant" reward effect in the pro-attitudinal advocacy conditions does not necessarily force us into an interpretation which centres around the consonant or dissonant nature of the relations between the cognitive elements concerning attitude and advocacy. Since we have seen, in the previous experiment, that the latter cognitive characteristics do not affect by themselves the attitude response in any significant way, it seems more plausible to attribute the absence of the "dissonant" reward effect in the pro-attitudinal condition to the fact that the intrinsic reward structure of the pro-attitudinal advocacy might have been so totally different that the additional "dissonant" reward simply turned into an irrelevant feature of the experimental treatment. Who cares to be deprived from a normal reward, or to receive a trivial sum of money, if one gets a unique opportunity to express and make others share one's views on the most important topic of exam reform?

We are fully aware of the *a posteriori* nature of these comments, whose validity will have to be tested out in a more appropriate way. The reader might be warned that a similar restriction will apply to the next experiment which, it should be remembered, was run in immediate temporal contiguity, in order to complete a first analysis of the three major characteristics of our 1969 point of departure in which "subjects" received a monetary *reward* for holding a *counter*attitudinal plea before a nation-wide *public*.

Let us now see if the public nature of the advocacy was a necessary condition for the production of the "dissonant" reward effect.

5. Experiment Eight: "Dissonant" reward and public or private nature of the counterattitudinal advocacy

PROBLEM AND DESIGN

In the first paragraph of this chapter, we have documented why we decided to invite our "subjects" to hold a counterattitudinal plea, which was perceived as being addressed to a very large and susceptible audience, unaware of the advocate's true position on the debated issue. In the present experiment we will simply examine if the public character of the plea constitutes a necessary condition for obtaining the "dissonant" reward effect. We wanted indeed, for the two last days of our 1969 experimentation phase, to just forget about all recent literature on the importance of commitment, consequences to self-esteem and perceived aversive consequences for the audience, while turning the clock back to the early sixties where Cohen obtained his classical dissonance effect under conditions which were very close to a private production of counterattitudinal arguments. The question was an important one, since the theoretical implications of the necessity of the advocacy to be public might lead us in quite different research directions than if a similar effect were obtained under private conditions. Needless to say that, after all the energy invested in realizing a truly public advocacy condition, we expected that the attitude change effect would not show up under the much simpler private instructions. Before planning new experiments we wanted however to be sure that the ethically and technically rather imposing radio cover-story was still justified. So we decided to replicate three crucial counterattitudinal radio conditions, zero reward, 20 BF reward and relative deprivation, while removing the public character of the plea. A comparison between these three private conditions and the corresponding three public conditions of Experiment Six should then allow for an assessment of the role of this aspect of our initial experimental situation.

As will become clear from the description of the procedure, private advocacy is defined as the production of a plea which is not perceived by the advocate to be directed towards an audience. The subject is merely invited to help a Ph.D. student, who needs an inventory of arguments pro and contra the reform of the exam system. As was the case in our radio condition, the subject is guaranteed that nobody, except the experimenter, will ever know that he is the source of the arguments proferred. Also of course, the subject knows that the experimenter does not consider him as being against exam reform (a circumstance kept constant throughout all experiments).

The reader will have noticed that the term "subject" is not any longer put between inverted commas. Although almost everything is kept constant between public and private conditions, it should be understood that the student in the private advocacy condition is fully aware of the fact that he is "helping a Ph.D. student". Since this situation is very comparable to an interview situation, it is no longer justified to consider the student as not being aware of his role as a social research subject. In this respect, our private conditions are again quite similar to the classical Cohen study.

PROCEDURE FOR PRIVATE ADVOCACY*

After having induced decision freedom as usual, the experimenter proceeds as follows:

* The reader is supposed to be familiar with section 1 of this chapter (p. 56-65).

I am working on my doctoral thesis which is about university reform and more precisely about the exam system. For the moment I am collecting arguments in favour and against the traditional exam system, my present focus being the spread of exams and the exemptions for September. You will understand that this is an important problem, if you realize that most professors, and especially those of the Faculty of Sciences, some two years ago strongly defended the position that spread and exemptions are totally undesirable at the university. I myself found it worthwhile to make a thorough study of this reform problem. As you might or might not know, it has been proven that one of the better techniques to get relevant arguments on all sides of an issue is to ask people to give arguments favouring only one, the pro *or* contra side of this issue. I must tell you that I have already interviewed a sufficient number of students who gave arguments exclusively in favour of exam reform. So what I need now are arguments in favour of the traditional exam system, and more precisely against a larger spread of exams and against exam exemptions, or in other words, no exams at all during the academic year, all exams being taken during a very short session, and no exemption in September for exams how ever good they might have been in July. So what I would like to ask you, whatever your own personal opinion might be, is to hold a strong plea in favour of the old traditional exam system. I want to emphasize that your collaboration is completely anonymous and that nobody except myself will ever know what you say or how you formulate your arguments. If you do not mind, I would prefer to record your plea for the simple reason that this facilitates my work.

The main reason is of course that the experimenter always exposes the subject once more to the full advocacy just before the attitude response is elicited.

Then follows the usual information concerning the solitary fifteen minutes preparation of the plea and the administration of rewards. Just before the subject starts with the oral presentation of his advocacy, he is once more reminded of the private and anonymous nature of his unilateral plea in favour of the traditional exam system.

The rest of the experimental and post-experimental procedure is strictly similar to the treatment in the public conditions, but of course adapted to the demands of the private nature of the collaboration. The joint rehearsing of the plea—which was obvious for the public conditions—is here motivated as a means for checking if the student has said all he wanted to say. The experimenter who also listens carefully refrains as usual from any comment. Needless to say that several post-experimental ratings were not presented. Special care was taken in order to continue safeguarding the study of the long term persistency of the experimental effects.

RESULTS AND DISCUSSION

Table 12 presents us with the surprising result that the relative deprivation treatment under private conditions leads to an attitude change which is equally dramatic as the one obtained under public radio advocacy (for both conditions 7.1). The data for the 20 BF reward are however much less impressive in the private (5.1) than in the public (6.6) condition, and do not seem to differ from the zero reward public (4.9) and private (4.5) advocacy.

TABLE 12

Mean attitude response towards the traditional exam system as a function of public and private character of differentially rewarded advocacy

Anonymous Counterattitudinal Advocacy	Monetary Reward		Relative Deprivation
	Zero BF	20 BF	
Public	4.9	6.6	7.1
Private	4.5	5.1	7.1

Note. Baseline mean is 2.3

TABLE 13

Analysis of variance for data of Table 12

Source	SS	df	MS	F
Public-Private (P)	8.02	1	8.02	1.19n.s.
Reward (R)	65.07	2	32.53	4.82*
P×R	6.55	2	3.28	<1
Within treatments	404.82	60	6.75	
Total	484.45	65		

n.s.=not significant.
*$p < 0.025$

A 2×3 analysis of variance produces a significant main effect for reward at the 0.01 level. Table 14 reports the significance of the differences between the various means of Table 12. The difference between the two zero reward conditions is not significant. All means still differ at the 0.01 level or better from the baseline mean (2.3). There are two differences between public and private conditions. First, the difference between 0 BF public (counterattitudinal) advocacy and relative deprivation condition for a private plea (4.9 v. 7.1; $t = 2.44$, $p < 0.05$) and second, the difference between 20 BF public and 0 BF private advocacy conditions (6.6 v. 4.5; $t = 2.14$, $p < 0.05$). Within the private conditions, 7.1 (relative deprivation condition) is significantly different from both 4.5 (zero BF) and 5.1 (20 BF) ($t = 3.10$, $p < 0.01$, and $t = 2.28$, $p < 0.05$). Those differences contributed most to the reward effect found in the analysis of variance.

TABLE 14
Summary of t values for differences between
mean attitude responses of Table 12

Conditions and Means	Baseline (2.3)	Public Zero BF (4.9)	Public 20 BF (6.6)	Public Rel. Depr. (7.1)	Private Zero BF (4.5)	Private 20 BF (5.1)	Private Rel. Depr. (7.1)
Baseline (2.3) Public	—	3.66‡	4.71§	3.89‡	3.27‡	4.24§	6.57§
Zero BF (4.9)		—	1.63n.s.	1.65n.s.	0.54n.s.	0.27n.s.	2.44†
20 BF (6.6) Rel.			—	0.34n.s.	2.14†	1.46n.s.	0.43n.s.
Depr. (7.1) Private				—	2.03n.s.*	1.51n.s.	0.03n.s.
Zero BF (4.5)					—	0.85n.s.	3.10‡
20 BF (5.1) Rel.						—	2.28†
Depr. (7.1)							—

* This t value is significant at 0.05 level when tested one-tailed.
† $p < 0.05$
‡ $p < 0.01$
§ $p < 0.001$

The main conclusion to be drawn from these new data is that the public nature (anonymous radio) of the advocacy is not a necessary condition for the replication of our "dissonant" reward effect, at least if the treatment consists of the relative deprivation of an unspecified monetary reward. One cannot but be puzzled and impressed with this substantial change in the attitude response, when considering the fact that this was achieved by a simple private counterattitudinal plea without any apparent commitment or consequentiality. Taking into account that the attitude issue was of paramount importance to the subjects and presumably very resistant to change, it is quite surprising to see that the effect of the private treatment is as strong as the maximum effects obtained a few days earlier, after real life TV and radio advocacy, under otherwise identical circumstances. What could be the underlying process which explains this sudden and drastic change in the attitude response tapped under conditions identical for all reported treatments?

Of course, Festinger's cognitive dissonance theory fits beautifully for the relative deprivation data, if we consider deprivation as a cognitive element dissonant with compliance. We have however, explained why we cannot support any longer his conceptualization of the phenomena under study. The data for our zero reward private condition add to this scepticism, since they are almost identical to the results of the various pro-attitudinal advocacy conditions run in the previous experiments, notwithstanding the crucial difference *qua* inconsistency between attitude and behaviour. Also the absence of a difference between pro- and counterattitudinal zero reward advocacy, shows that the discrepancy between behaviour and attitude cannot play the role posited by Festinger. Moreover, for both public and private conditions, the 20 BF change is larger than the zero reward change despite the fact that the consonance of 20 BF (as defined by Festinger) is undoubtedly greater than the consonance of the zero reward treatment.

Clearly, the present experiment cannot help us much in explaining the exciting results. Still, the data continue to suggest that it might be the unusual or "dissonant" nature of the reward treatment which triggers the attitude change effect. As a matter of fact, it seems plausible to state that the 20 BF reward of the *private* condition is not perceived as an embarrassing, "dissonant" treatment. We should realize that the shift from public (radio) to private advocacy again could be accompanied by a thorough change in the meaning of the 20 BF reward. This amount of money undoubtedly is trivial, if not insulting, when paid by the National Broadcast Service for betraying publicly one's firm conviction. The same amount of money could however be quite acceptable if it is given by a Ph.D. student—who does not refer to research funds—for helping her in her search for arguments against exam reform.

By the same token, however, these considerations make us wonder even more why a relative deprivation persists in producing such an effect, if it is only a Ph.D. student and not the BRT, who apologizes for being out of funds. Is the subject embarrassed by the repeated excuses of the experimenter, who should not pay anyway for half an hour help in her interesting Ph.D. thesis? Is he puzzled by the fact that he does not know how much other subjects were paid for a similar task? Is he frustrated and angry for not getting a deserved fee, especially after having collaborated in the pseudo experiment where the experimenter did not even mention that he paid his subjects? And if puzzled, embarrassed or angry, why should this make him change his attitude? Evaluation apprehension or negative affect arousal, according to Rosenberg, should induce the subject to withhold any symptoms of attitude change, which is exactly the opposite of what is being observed here. Or is the subject just being friendly to an ingratiating experimenter, who excused herself twice for not being able to pay him? Friendly, by showing that after all it was an easy job to do since he has a rather critical attitude towards the reform of the exam system? There certainly are other plausible speculations. Obviously, new experiments are needed to set the stage for an alternative explanation of the overall results of the research thus far presented.

Finally, we wish to emphasize the fact that the replication of the relative deprivation effect in the private advocacy condition has several implications which are relevant for the various theoretical considerations which led us to the production of the complex *public* advocacy situation, and which were commented upon in the first paragraph of this chapter. It is self-evident that our private and public conditions do differ quite strongly in terms of commitment, perceived consequences to self and/or audience and overall importance of the counterattitudinal behaviour. The fact that an identical attitude change effect was obtained notwithstanding these profound differences between the private and public conditions, also allows us to feel comfortable when pursuing our research efforts with the so much simpler private advocacy situation.

Conclusion of chapter two

Our primary concern at the outset of the present chapter was to prepare the stage for the production and a progressive experimental analysis of a classical cognitive dissonance effect. Stimulated by the successful Helmreich and Collins paradigm, and taking into account various recommendations of the recent forced compliance literature, we succeeded in obtaining a quite dramatic change in attitude responses of students who, unaware of their subject role and in a "real life" situation, had complied under conditions of high decision freedom with an attractive "experimenter's" request to hold a strong plea before a nation-wide audience against a much desired reform of the exam system.

The principal ideas guiding the research stemmed from our scepticism with regard to the experimental foundation of Festinger's theoretical interpretation of the inverse relation between size of reward and magnitude of attitude change after counterattitudinal advocacy. The deficiency of the classical experimental designs and the inconclusive results of our 1964 attempts incited us to challenge the validity of the postulated cognitive equilibrium restoring model for the assessed attitude change. Appropriate experimental comparisons were performed in order to test the theoretical assumptions concerning the monotonic consonance function of the monetary reward and concerning the cognitive dissonance generated by the discrepancy between attitude and counterattitudinal advocacy.

The main conclusions can be summarized as follows: (1) The observed inverse relationship between reward and attitude change cannot be attributed to the decrease of the total magnitude of cognitive dissonance as a function of the increase in importance of the consonant reward element. (2) There is no compelling evidence that the attitude change can be explained by referring to the postulated cognitive dissonance generated by the discrepancy between the pre-experimental attitude position and the public counterattitudinal behaviour. (3) The above conclusions, which amount to an invalidation of the cognitive dissonance interpretation of the phenomenon under study, call for an alternative interpretation of the assessed attitude change. The results of several experimental comparisons advise against searching for interpretations which imply theoretical concepts related to the identifiability of the advocate or the public nature of the plea. It should be noted that the same negative conclusion applies for the interpretation proposed by Bem (1965): several interpersonal replications of successful experimental treatments presented in this chapter failed to confirm Bem's predictions (see Dumez, 1970). (4) The available evidence warrants the conjecture that the impressive attitude change effects are tied up with the unusual, upsetting or "dissonant" nature of the trivial or embarrassing low reward and relative deprivation treatments.

In the next chapter, an effort will be made to substantiate the "dissonant" reward effect and to narrow down the potential avenues for an interpretation of the underlying process.

3

Evidence for an A-Cognitive "Dissonant" View

The challenge of our (1969) research to the cognitive dissonance interpretation of post-compliance attitude change centred around the thesis
that the theoretical assumptions made by the classical view on the role of
minimal or insufficient justification for attitude discrepant behaviour, do
not withstand empirical testing; namely, the importance attributed to the
consonance of the reward and to the cognitive dissonance produced by
the discrepancy between attitude and counterattitudinal behaviour.
Although the overall evidence thus far presented does not allow yet for an
alternative interpretation, it was argued that the sizable attitude change
effects obtained in the relative deprivation treatments and in both the
20 BF public advocacy conditions (radio and TV) could not be interpreted within the framework of cognitive dissonance theory. Our
data suggest instead that the observed change in the attitude responses
should be linked in a more direct way to the rather disturbing, unusual or
"dissonant" nature of the reward treatment via one or another "a-
cognitive" process, by which we simply refer to a process which is independent of the posited cognitive equilibrium restoring or cognitive dissonance reducing effect of the reward and even from the cognitive dissonance or inconsistency postulated on the basis of the simultaneous
presence of two not-fitting important cognitive elements concerning the
pre-experimental attitude and the counterattitudinal advocacy.

1. Experiment Nine: The effect of a "dissonant" but highly appreciated non-monetary reward upon post-advocacy attitude change (1970 research)

PROBLEM

As a first step towards further consolidation of our conjecture concerning the effect of a strange, novel or unusual "dissonant" reward, we decided to design an experiment in which we would offer a very important and valued reward for engaging in private counterattitudinal advocacy, while at the same time making the reward unusual, novel or "dissonant". The basic idea guiding the present experiment was quite simple: if we are right in assuming that the "dissonant" reward effect, produced in the low reward and relative deprivation conditions of Experiment Six, should be attributed independently from a cognitive equilibrium process, to the "dissonant" features of the reward treatment itself, then we ought to be able to reproduce a similar attitude change effect when administering a very important reward, provided that the latter also could be considered to be "dissonant" in the sense of not fitting with one or another aspect of the situation in which the compliance is elicited. Thus we planned to invite students to engage in private advocacy against exam reform while giving them a very important but "dissonant" non-monetary justification for doing so. The prediction was that the attitude change effect would be in the same direction as the one obtained after the very meagre "dissonant" justification (20 BF and relative deprivation) manipulated in Experiment Six and significantly greater than the attitude change of a control condition where the important "dissonant" reward would not be given.

We do not have to repeat that Festinger's hypothesis predicts that the attitude change would be inversely related to the importance of the justification for compliance. If the experimental design provides a condition with, and one without, important justification, the classical cognitive dissonance prediction would be that students will manifest less attitude change in the advocated direction in the condition with important justification. It should be noted that cognitive dissonance theory might predict a change in the attitude towards the compliance proper when the reward at stake is disproportionately high for the service rendered to the experimenter. The student might for example, enhance the perceived difficulty of the task ("if they pay me so much, it must be a very difficult thing to find arguments against exam reform") or he could try to work harder so as to achieve more consonance between the reward and the work performed. One could even predict, on the basis of cognitive dissonance theory, that the subject might change his attitude towards the exam reform in the direction opposite to the advocated position: if he considers the task of defending the traditional exam system as especially difficult for a fervent pro-reform student, he might try to deserve the reward better by manifesting a strongly anti-traditional exam position. The latter interpretation implies of course a shift of the central locus of the posited cognitive dissonance from the discrepancy between attitude and counterattitudinal behaviour to the discrepancy between costs and effort invested in the advocacy and reward or gain received for engaging in the advocacy.

The important point however, is that each of the above cognitive dissonance predictions can adequately be contrasted with our own position which predicts a greater change *in the advocated direction* for the condition where the important but "dissonant" reward is given than for the condition where the same important justification or disproportionate reward is absent.

The question could now be raised about the value of a prediction which coincides with the one made by various defenders of the *positive* relationship between importance of reward or incentive and subsequent attitude change. For the time being, our answer to this objection would be that the expected effect of a sizable attitude change in the advocated direction after important "dissonant" incentive or reinforcement does not differ from the prediction made for the relative deprivation and very low "dissonant" rewards of our 1969 research. It is difficult to see how any of the classical "direct relationship" explanations could account for a similar positive attitude change effect in *both* high and low reinforcement or incentive conditions.

Since we wanted to make some progress in pinning down the necessary and sufficient conditions for the production of a "dissonant" reward effect, the experiment was organized so as to provide more information with regard to the temporal contiguity between reward and advocacy. Therefore, in one condition, the highly appreciated non-monetary reward was given before the subject engaged in the preparation of his counterattitudinal plea, whereas in another condition, the experimenter did not allude to any reward until the subject had finished his advocacy. Although this comparison could also allow for an analysis in terms of "incentive" versus "reinforcement" (when given after the advocacy, the reward could not function as an incentive for biased scanning of arguments) it seemed especially useful as a control for a hitherto unmentioned aspect of the important "dissonant" reward for which cognitive dissonance theory might wish to give an alternative explanation. As will become clear, together with the description of the procedure, the highly appreciated non-monetary reward was not only very important to the student in the sense of being instrumental for basic need satisfaction, but was at the same time unusual, novel, unexpected or "dissonant" because illegitimate and against widely accepted ethical and academic standards. This means that the reward, when given to the subject *before* engaging in the counterattitudinal advocacy, could be defined as a *bribe* used by the experimenter to force the subject into the counterattitudinal compliance. If however, the subject, as is the case in our post-advocacy reward condition, makes his counterattitudinal speech under conditions which are strictly identical to a no-reward treatment, and only receives the reward immediately before emitting his post-advocacy attitude response, then it becomes difficult to consider the reward as a bribe given for compliance, since the compliance precedes the reward. Clearly, such a reward treatment cannot affect the quality of the advocacy, but more important, it becomes very unlikely that the post-compliance reward is seen as being related to the *counter*attitudinal nature of the advocacy. The argument that a bribe might be dissonance enhancing because of not fitting with cultural mores (Festinger, 1957, p. 14) does not seem then, to offer a basis for predicting a significant attitude change in the advocated direction, since the administration of the reward in the latter condition is by no means conditioned by the direction of the advocacy. It would indeed be a farfetched position to hold that the post-compliance reward becomes less unethical or more legitimate if one shifts, as a means for cognitive dissonance reduction, the attitude in the advocated direction.

Thus, on the basis of our reasoning about the role of "dissonant" rewards we predict that the attitude change will be similar for rewards offered prior to or after compliance provided that the reward is unusual, novel, strange or "dissonant". Moreover, the interpretation which eventually should account for the predicted effect ought to be different from the cognitive equilibrium process posited by Festinger, and from the incentive and/or reinforcement processes claimed by his opponents, since these theories do not account for our 1969 data. Obviously all this will not be achieved by the present experiment, which is only a first step in the untangling of our 1969 "dissonant" reward effect.

DESIGN AND PROCEDURE

In all conditions of the present experiment, the advocacy task was strictly identical to the one of the private counteratttudinal advocacy conditions of the previous experiment which had been run one year earlier, i.e., holding a private plea against exam reform in order to help the experimenter with her Ph.D. dissertation. Before presenting the full experimental design we shall describe the procedure for the administration of our highly valued "dissonant" non-monetary reward.

Differences between 1969 and 1970 macro-situation Let us first point to a few differences in the macro-situation of the experiment, some of which were necessary for the successful manipulation of the "dissonant" reward.

Again, the subjects were taken from the male (1970) Sciences pool. Volunteer bis-students were not sampled, since they might already have been selected for our 1969 research. Students expressed their willingness to volunteer on the usual invitation letter signed by the author and distributed at the occasion of a collective psychology exam. In view of the present experiment, the author had manifested his favourable attitude towards exam reform by complying with the urgent student request to organize an exam on an important part (approximately 2/3) of the psychology course, three months before the start of the official (and short) exam session. Besides making the student body happy with this diminution of their final exam load, this early exam prepared the stage for a real life manipulation of a highly appreciated "dissonant" reward. By participating, at their own request, in this collective exam in the midst of the second semester (the course had been taught during the first semester) the students also took some risk of ruining their July session three months before the official exam period started. The score obtained for this advanced exam was indeed irrevocable, since one could not take another exam on the same part of the course before the second (September) exam session. This means that a student who failed very badly on this early exam had almost no chance to succeed in the full exam series of the July session. Of course, during the official exam session there was still an oral exam—as imposed by government regulations—on a small part of the psychology course, but it was agreed, at the request of the students, that this would only be scored on one fourth of the points (5/20), so that it became rather difficult to compensate for a very weak result on the collective written exam. It will be remembered that, due to the prevailing exam system, any unsatisfactorily passed exam (even a score of

9 points out of 20) can become—when combined with other weak exam scores—a serious threat for overall success, and that approximately 60% of the students from our subject pool fail in the July exam session.

The following points are important for the realization of our "dissonant" reward manipulation: (1) The students are never supposed to be informed about the results obtained in any official exam until after the deliberation and proclamation of the outcome of the full exam series*. It was agreed with the students that this also would apply to the advanced exam, taken three months before the proclamation; (2) The student can of course have a rough (and often distorted) idea of the quality of his performance. Special precautions were however taken, so as to make it almost impossible for the student to make a precise estimation of the score obtained in the collective psychology exam, which took about two hours work and consisted of six open and six complex multiple choice questions of varying degrees of difficulty; (3) The collective psychology exam was carefully supervised by three male graduate students under the direction of Annie Beckers, the experimenter, clearly replacing the author who had been teaching the course; (4) Each student has a special identity card for the psychology course, which bears on the front his photograph and curriculum information signed by him, whereas the reverse side contains the detailed psychology exam record. Students, who have no access to this individual psychology record, all know that it is on this card that the final exam evaluation will be written to be used by the author when the exam jury will decide about his case; (5) The students are aware of the fact that, although the oral exams on the last part of the psychology course will be given by the author, his graduate students and assistants help him with the evaluation of the more than four hundred written exam copies.

Sub-sampling of subjects The reader will remember that our 1969 baseline condition in which the pre-advocacy attitude response was elicited, had almost no variability; all students being concentrated on the extreme anti-traditional exam side of the continuum. As one could expect, there was, for the total group of 1969 subjects, no significant correlation between attitude response and psychology exam score ($r = 0.007$ $N = 139$).

* It is worthwhile noting that the detailed communication of the exact exam scores is never done. One of the most recent victories of the exam reform movement consisted in the fact that the students who fail in July receive a letter indicating, within rather broad categories, how good or poorly they had performed in each of the exams taken. In 1970, this policy was not even followed in all departments of the Faculty of Sciences.

In view of the intended real life manipulation of our "dissonant" reward (see below) we could safely decide to sample our subjects from two different pools; a "rather bad" and a "good" student pool, without selecting at the same time on the basis of the crucial attitude. The "good" were all students who had a satisfactory (but not excellent) score on the collective psychology exam, whereas "rather bad" students had a score which was not extremely weak, but always under the required minimum for passing in that particular exam. Along with the description of procedure, it will be indicated from which pool—"rather bad" or "good"—the subjects were sampled. The rationale for this sub-sampling will be better understood when the operationalization of the reward is given.

Decision freedom It will be remembered that our 1969 "subjects" participated in a pseudo experiment before they freely decided to comply with the request for cooperation in the TV or radio programme. Clearly the perceived role of the experimenter in our 1969 private advocacy conditions was different from that of the interviewer in the various public conditions. In the private conditions, the experimenter was nothing but a Ph.D. student who asked for some help with her thesis. It was difficult to imagine that any student would refuse such help, when asked by a friendly graduate student after having been through an unexpectedly short "control condition". Undoubtedly there was much more conflict before taking the decision of complying with the request in the public than in the private condition.

The post-experimental ratings on question 7 ("How much did you hesitate before complying with the request?") are very clear in this respect, and so too are the non-verbal symptoms of hesitation witnessed by the experimenter. Despite these differences in conflict between public and private conditions, the attitude change after the relative deprivation treatment was equally dramatic in the public as in the private conditions. Thus it seemed no longer necessary to have the students go through the pseudo experiment, whose main function was precisely the creation of a true free-decision situation.

It should also be noted that the position of the 1970 experimenter was different in that she was for the first time perceived as having academic responsibilities (directing exam supervision, scoring written exams and keeping of examination records). This shift in perceived role of the experimenter obviously restricts the decision freedom of the student who is invited to hold a counterattitudinal plea. Since the consequences for self and/or audience of our private counterattitudinal plea were almost non-existent, we decided not to bother any longer about decision freedom, except by merely telling the subject at the beginning of the experiment and once more just before starting the preparation of the plea (after he had been informed of the crucial aspects of the treatment) that he should feel free to comply or not comply with the request to hold a unilateral private plea against exam reform. The decision freedom from now on can thus be considered as comparable to the classical dissonance experiments, where subjects were simply told that "the decision to hold the advocacy was entirely their own choice" (see, for example, Cohen's experiment in Brehm and Cohen, 1962, p. 72).

When initially volunteering for participation in the experiment, our subjects had been told, as usual, that various types of research were planned by different Ph.D. students, and that they would be randomly assigned to each of the projects. Upon arrival then in the experimenter's office, she explained briefly that she did not do any real instrumentation laboratory research, but was working on a thesis concerning exam reform, and that all she wanted was to have some anonymous and private help in her survey of arguments for and against exam reform. A comparison between two otherwise identical conditions of our 1969 and 1970 programme will allow us to examine if these and other modifications in the macro-situation of the experiment do have any effect upon the attitude responses emitted.

Temporal sequence of conditions The 1970 experimentation period started one month after the collective psychology exam and lasted for about two weeks. To check on the stability of the attitude issue and procedural features, we first ran a replication of one condition of our 1969 programme (zero BF). All other conditions were run simultaneously and in random sequence.

Control condition 1: private counterattitudinal advocacy, no reward Notwithstanding the absence of any correlation between the sub-sampling criterion and our dependent variable, six of the subjects of this condition were sampled from the "rather bad" and five from the "good" student pool. The instructions for the advocacy were identical to the ones used in the zero BF private counterattitudinal advocacy condition of Experiment Eight, run one year earlier. The subject is guaranteed that his anonymous advocacy only serves the purpose of privately helping the experimenter in her Ph.D. work. As said before, the experimenter is now clearly perceived as the author's assistant, who directed the advanced collective psychology exam. Moreover, upon subject's arrival in her office, she loosely "checks for identification" the photograph of the student's psychology record, which is filed before the experiment starts. Thus the subject is aware that the experimenter has his psychology exam record. Unlike all other conditions of the present experiment, the subject in this control condition receives no information whatsoever about his exam performance.

The reader will remember that the subject, after having explained to him what is expected, has a full fifteen minutes for preparing his plea and presents the plea before the experimenter, who afterwards plays the full text back "in order to have the subject check that he said all he wanted to". Immediately after this thirty minutes exposure to self-generated counterattitudinal arguments, the attitude response is elicited in the usual way.

Highly appreciated "dissonant" reward before advocacy All subjects for this condition are sampled from the "rather bad" student pool. The advocacy treatment is an exact replication of the above described control condition, except for the fact that the subject is given a very unusual but highly appreciated non-monetary reward before he engages in the compliance. As said before, in contrast to our 1969 research the student who is informed about the reward treatment before starting the preparation of his plea psychologically is not really in a position to freely decide about his compliance. As will become clear from the instructions, he is however made to feel free in his decision to accept or refuse the "dissonant" reward.

The experimenter administers the very delicate reward treatment in the following way. In contrast with the control condition, she does not file the psychology exam record but "inadvertently" plays with the card, while inviting the subject to prepare his counterattitudinal plea. When the usual instructions are finished, and just before the student is asked if he agrees with the proposed collaboration, the experimenter in a very spontaneous and mild way takes the role of the protecting older sister, who sympathizes with the student's bad exam situation. While making a move for filing the card, her attention happens to be caught by the 6/15 score which is written on the reverse side of the card (this was the case for all subjects from the "rather bad" pool) and in an uncontrolled burst of sympathy she says "Boy, that psychology exam of yours was rather bad! What a pity. Yet, I'm sure you must be motivated for the psychology course, since you are volunteering for psychology research. I am just wondering if, instead of paying you out of my research funds, I might not better give you some additional points so that you can be safe for your July session. Or would you prefer money?" Not a single subject did ask for money—"exam points are priceless"—(see also p. 185). Upon the clearly expressed preference for illegitimate rescue points, the experimenter changes under the eyes of the subject the 6 into 8 and while filing the card, continues in a confidential manner "I do not have to tell you that nobody ever should hear about this. If my boss knew that I am so compassionate, he would certainly fire me." A few students kindly asked if the experimenter would not run into trouble whenever the card was compared with the exam copy. Such altruistic questions were swept away by saying: "All I would have to do is change a few of your encircled multiple choice answers. The exam copies are in my file anyway. But be sure nobody ever cares anymore about the original exam copy." Then the student is asked if he agrees to cooperate in the experimenter's research and is left alone for the preparation of his plea.

Highly appreciated "dissonant" reward after advocacy The subjects for this condition were also sampled from the "rather bad" pool. The treatment was identical to the one in the no reward condition (control 1), except for the fact that (1) the exam record was not filed but put aside on the desk out of the subject's reach; (2) after the joint rehearing of the recorded plea, the experimenter inadvertently took the card, and while making a move for filing it, happened to see the 6/15 score and replicated the procedure for administration of the highly appreciated "dissonant" reward. The attitude response was tapped immediately hereafter.

Control condition 2: mere information "bad exam" The subjects of this control condition, sampled from the "rather bad" pool, were treated in the same way as their fellows of control condition 1, except for the fact that while filing the card, and at the very moment at which the reward treatment occurred in the experimental conditions, the experimenter simply said in a casual way "Boy, that psychology exam of yours was rather bad! That's a pity."

Control condition 3: mere information "good exam" These subjects all were sampled from the "good student pool". The treatment was identical to

E

that of control condition 2, except that the experimenter's casual comment was "You seem to have done a good job for your psychology exam! How nice." The rationale for both control conditions 2 and 3 will be commented upon in the discussion of results section.

Debriefing For all conditions in which information concerning actual exam scores was given, the students were told that they should completely forget about this information "since the exam copies were not yet scored". However reluctantly this false information was brought into the debriefing, we were convinced that this was the best and quite acceptable solution for the student. The confirmation of a bad exam score certainly could hurt the self-confidence of the weaker student and the confirmation of a good exam would discriminate between the students who were not sampled for the experiment. Not a single subject did show any resentment in this respect. They admitted having freely volunteered for psychological research and apparently understood that powerful non-monetary reward manipulation with human subjects is not easy to apply in a more or less standardized way.

Careful probing concerning arousal of suspicion failed to uncover even the slightest symptom of distrust in the experimenter. It should be conceded that the reward manipulation was imbedded in a most plausible macro-situation and that the experimenter is not only highly skilled but also quite exceptional in playing over and over again such demanding and very subtle "real life" like roles.

We would like to stress that the subjects of the "dissonant" reward conditions, who had been exposed to this delicate reward treatment, received an extraordinarily detailed and careful debriefing. Not only did the experimenter engage in a long and open talk with the subject, but in order to stress the point that we did care very much about the individual assimilation and integration of the highly unusual experimental treatment, each subject was brought by the experimenter into the author's office immediately after the experimenter's debriefing. The author then had an open "quasi therapeutic" conversation, taking on average thirty minutes per subject, explaining to the student why we decided to do such borderline unethical research. The main rationale given was that our focus concentrated on the problem of the gap between "intentions" and "real behaviour", or the conative dimension of attitudes and overt situational responses.

With each student we felt successful in turning this experience into a constructive event, in which the point was stressed that most human beings cannot resist temptations if the precipitating situation is so congruent with important need satisfaction. The main imperative for society thus being to create an environment in which man freely chooses to protect himself and his fellow men against his own fragile existence. Brief reference was made to the topics of aggressive behaviour and the Skinnerian view on the role of punishment discussed in the psychology course. The individual students always left in a manifest relaxed way and were guaranteed that, whenever they might want to discuss the ethics of this type of research, they were truly welcome to do so. The very fact that so much time was devoted to a relaxed "catharsis" presumably helped in convincing the students that they were not being treated as laboratory organisms but as deeply respected individuals.

RESULTS AND DISCUSSION

The main results of Experiment Nine are presented in Table 15. For comparison purposes the data of our 1969 baseline condition and 1969 zero reward private counterattitudinal advocacy are here repeated.

TABLE 15

Mean attitude response towards the traditional exam system as a function of highly appreciated but "dissonant" non-monetary reward

Baseline (pre-advocacy)	No Reward (zero BF)	Private Counterattitudinal Advocacy			
		Mere Information		"Dissonant" rescue points	
1969	1969	1970	Good exam	Bad exam	Before plea	After plea
2.3	4.5	4.3	5.1	4.7	9.5	7.4

With even a superficial glance at Table 15 one is shocked by the magnitude of the effect obtained. One should indeed realize what an average score of 9.5 means in terms of the psychological reality assessed; 9.5 being in the neutral zone and even leaning over to the pro-traditional exam pole of the attitude continuum (9 = the neutral point; 11 = the "rather pro" category of the 17 point rating scale). Remember that our subjects are students who, within a few weeks are going to suffer from a very heavy exam load, which for more than half of them, will end in failure. These students, all very strongly opposed to the traditional exam system before entering the laboratory, after half an hour exposure to self-generated counterattitudinal arguments under conditions of a highly appreciated but "dissonant" reward, endorse an attitude position which is at the right of the neutral point of the attitude scale. Not a single student of this condition says that he is very strongly or strongly opposed to the traditional exam system; *only four* score to the left of the neutral point (2 between "strongly anti" and "anti", and 2 "rather anti"). There is no doubt that the subjects of the sampled population would have participated in a most violent protest if the academic authorities had ever dared to take seriously arguments such as the ones preferred in the counterattitudinal advocacy. What if these registered attitude responses were used as a basis for new policy decisions? The idea that the researcher after half an hour's treatment can trigger a process which leads to such a drastic change in an important category of attitude responses is staggering, and calls not only for insight and understanding but also for a deep sense of responsibility from the social scientist. Indeed, it is very disconcerting when confronted with an adult student, who upon arrival in the laboratory is known to be ready to emit a strong negative attitude response towards an issue which concerns him above many others; but of whom it can also be predicted with almost certainty, *not* to emit such a negative response less than half an hour later, provided that he engages in a simple advocacy task and accepts a highly appreciated but "dissonant" reward. At this point, our main focus is the scientific understanding of the phenomenon. Let us start with a closer look at the results of Experiment Nine; discussing the implications of each of the conditions.

Control condition 1: comparability between 1969 and 1970 experiments Since there was a gap of approximately 14 months between our 1969 and 1970 experimentation periods, and in view of the above mentioned modifications in the macro- and micro-situations of the experiment, it was appropriate to start Experiment Nine with a replication of our 1969 zero reward private advocacy condition which at the same time could serve as a rigorous control condition for the other 1970 manipulations. As far as the comparability and stability of the studied phenomena is concerned, the data turn out to be most reassuring. Both distributions of the 1969 and 1970 zero reward conditions are very similar, the average attitude responses being 4.5 and 4.3 respectively. As far as the post-experimental ratings are concerned, the only noteworthy differences are the answers on rating 8 (I had the impression that I could have refused my cooperation very easily (1) . . . very difficulty (26)). As expected, the 1970 subjects felt it somewhat less easy to refuse their cooperation (15.3 versus 18.5 on a 26 point scale). We have already explained why perceived decision freedom could be lowered in 1970. It is interesting however to see that in both conditions the subjects express with equal strength the opinion that they were not forced by the experimenter to cooperate (post-experimental rating 13: Do you feel that the interviewer has forced you to cooperate? Strongly so (26) . . . not at all (1)). The 1969 average being 5.1, v. 5.5 for 1970. The average number of arguments developed (as assessed by blind content analysis) was also almost identical: 5.8 (1969) v. 6.3 (1970).

This quite satisfactory reliability of the studied phenomenon allows us to feel safe when continuing our progressive analysis of the "dissonant" reward effect.

Control conditions 2 and 3: mere information about "bad" versus "good" exam It will be remembered that the administration of the "dissonant" reward was preceded by the experimenter telling the student that his psychology exam was rather bad. Since this was the first official information he got about his exam, it might very well be that the confirmation or disconfirmation of his (unassessed) exam expectancies by itself would have an effect upon the attitude responses. Such a change could for example, be related to a difference in the mood of the subject; to an increased effort with preparation of the advocacy in order to compensate by making a good impression upon the experimenter (incentive effect), or to negative feelings toward the experimenter for telling him bad tidings. In terms of cognitive dissonance theory one could even hold that the knowledge that the early exam was a failure reduces considerably the dissonance generated by the attitude and the counterattitudinal behaviour. As a matter of fact, the early psychology exam was a typical instance of university reform in which wider spread of exams over the academic year was claimed. This first negative experience with exams during the year can be seen as consonant with at least some of the arguments generated in favour of the traditional system, thus reducing the total magnitude of dissonance and leading to an attitude change, which would be different from the one obtained in the "good" exam condition. It could also be that the mere negative experience with an early exam, by and of itself, would produce attitude change in the direction of the traditional system in which exams during the academic year are excluded. Simple avoidance conditioning could indeed decrease subject's liking for this aspect of exam reform. For all these reasons it seemed important to control for the possible effect of this part of the "dissonant" reward manipulation, which was conceptually independent from the administration of a highly appreciated but "dissonant" reward.

The results of comparison between the control condition 2 and 3 allows us not to attach much weight to this part of the treatment. As a matter of fact, the average attitude responses for "bad" (4.7) and "good" (5.1) hardly differ ($t = 0.43$; $0.60 < p < 0.70$) from each other. Moreover, the combined "information about exam" conditions do not differ significantly ($t = 0.82$; $0.40 < p < 0.50$) from the combined 1969 and 1970 control conditions (4.5 and 4.3).

For the time being however, we will concentrate upon the unusual "dissonant" reward effect. In this respect, there is one important conclusion we feel entitled to draw, namely, that the mere occurrence of an unexpected—satisfying or dissatisfying—event is not a sufficient condition for the production of a sizable effect, similar to that of our "dissonant" reward conditions. It should indeed be noted that the subject obviously did not expect to learn anything about his performance in the psychology exam. Clearly then, the agreeable or disagreeable "surprise" characteristic of the reward treatment should not be relevant for the ultimate explanation of the phenomenon under study. However unexpected the very message and its content could have been for the subjects of both conditions, the crucial feature might very well lie in the fact that there is nothing strange, embarrassing or "dissonant" in the experimenter having the exam information at hand and inadvertently and casually slipping out a general comment on the score obtained. Maybe the students simply processed the information as a confirmation of what they, at one or another moment, had hoped or feared. This was just another fact of life, as was also the quite unexpected but by no means strange or "dissonant" opportunity to collaborate in a TV or radio programme, offered to our 1969 subjects.

Highly appreciated but "dissonant" reward before advocacy What indeed is strange, embarrassing or "dissonant", is to receive undeserved and priceless rescue points from the hands of the very person who was in charge of the rigorous supervision of the collective psychology exam. As presented at the beginning of this section, the effect of this manipulation was dramatic indeed, taking into account the manifest resistance to change of the attitude at issue. The magnitude of the effect obtained in the condition where the "dissonant" reward was offered before the advocacy (9.5) can be specified furthermore as being significantly different in the predicted direction at the 0.01 level (t test) from each of the three control conditions taken separately (when combined, $t = 5.08$; $p < 0.001$), and at the 0.001 level from the baseline or pre-advocacy attitude response ($t = 6.09$).

In the formulation of the problem section we have already explained why Festinger's cognitive dissonance theory does not offer a valid basis for predicting and explaining the observed effect. Let us simply stress the following points. (1) Since all students clearly preferred our "dissonant" reward above any monetary gratification, Festinger's conceptual framework should lead to defining the non-monetary reward as an important cognitive element which is *consonant* with the counterattitudinal advocacy, thus reducing the total magnitude of cognitive dissonance and leading to an attitude change—if any—which is smaller than the one predicted for the control conditions in which this important justification was not made available. Our data hardly need any comment in this respect. (2) As said before, it is possible that some advocates of Festinger's theory would defend the position that the present experiment is not a classical instance of "forced compliance"—although it would be difficult to point to the crucial difference with, for example, the classical Cohen study—because of the manifest disproportion between reward and effort invested in the compliance. To this argument, it can be said that the very notion of minimal justification, and certainly as operationalized by cognitive dissonance psychologists (5 cents in the study of Lependorf, 1964), also implies a disproportion between reward and compliance. If however, the point is made that the focus of dissonance is being displaced in our study from the classical cognitive clusters concerning "attitude" and "attitude discrepant behaviour" towards the clusters concerning "the disproportionate reward" and "the task performed", then, if anything, cognitive dissonance should predict either a change in the effort invested in the advocacy (and to this we will come back in a moment) or a change in the attitude in the direction opposite to the advocacy. By showing how intense one's negative attitude is towards the traditional exam system, the disproportionately high reward could indeed become more deserved, since the negative attitude can be perceived as enhancing the costs invested in the counterattitudinal advocacy. Clearly such cannot have been the case with the observed effect in the present experiment. (3)

Finally, some might argue that cognitive dissonance theory, in its well-known flexibility, could also go the other way around by holding that the subject, when changing his attitude in the advocated direction, did reduce the dissonance generated by the acceptance of an immoral bribe. "I am an honest boy" versus "I did (choose and) accept an immoral bribe for holding a counterattitudinal plea". By changing the attitude into a neutral position, there is no firm basis left for the bribe characteristic of the reward offered, with the result that the magnitude of this particular kind of cognitive dissonance would be considerably reduced. As said before, this would be a farfetched derivation of a theory, which in the relevant literature is not used to make such versatile predictions. As a matter of fact, if taken seriously, the flexibility of the theory would only be matched by its uselessness. Still, our design does allow for a test of the latter contention, since the *post*-advocacy reward condition avoids the production of the cognitive element of having received a bribe for holding a *counter*attitudinal plea. It will be noticed that the "dissonant" reward effect also has been reproduced in the latter post-advocacy reward condition.

Highly appreciated but "dissonant" reward after advocacy Besides further pinning down the necessary and sufficient conditions for the production of a "dissonant" reward effect—with the hope of paralleled progress in the understanding of the underlying processes—a comparison between the *pre-* and *post*-advocacy "dissonant" reward condition provides evidence which might be considered as relevant for an incentive view upon post-advocacy attitude change.

Always taking into account the fact that our subjects obviously did *prefer* the dissonant non-monetary reward above a monetary reward, the attitude change in the advocated direction, according to the incentive view, would be greater when the reward is given before the subject starts the preparation of his plea than when given after advocacy (without any prior reward information). As shown in Table 15, this seems indeed to be the case, the pre-advocacy reward change (9.5) being greater than the post-advocacy reward change (7.4); the difference is almost significant by one tailed test ($t = 1.32$; $0.05 < p < 0.10$). In the pre-advocacy reward condition, seven of the eleven subjects are scoring on or to the right of the neutral point, whereas this is the case for only four subjects in the post-advocacy reward treatment.

The defenders of the direct relation between reward and post-advocacy attitude change could even go further by holding that both the incentive and the reinforcement view are sharing victory. As a matter of fact, the important—be it "dissonant"—reward could function as both an incentive and a reinforcing contingency in the pre-advocacy condition, whereas only reinforcement could be operating in the post-advocacy treatment. This relatively weaker mere reinforcement effect would then show up in the fact that the post-advocacy reward induces in its turn an attitude change which is significantly greater (and in the advocated direction) than the one observed, for example, in the most appropriate control condition where the students also were informed that their exam was bad, but did not receive any rescue points after their collaboration with the experimenter. The difference between 7.4 and 4.7 is significant indeed at the 0.05 level ($t = 2.09$).

Do these data then call for both an incentive and a reinforcement interpretation?

Let us first stress once more the point that the very use of the "reinforcement" notion is rather unclear in the attitude change area. The widely accepted meaning of "reinforcement" as a reward offered in temporal contiguity with, for example, the performance of a counterattitudinal advocacy task would simply allow for the prediction that the probability and/or intensity of the task relevant responses will be modified. This might imply that subjects would, in the future, become more willing to engage in counterattitudinal pleas, or work harder, at them after previously rewarded advocacy. Obviously the "reinforcement view" of the defenders of a positive relationship between rewarded advocacy and subsequent change in the attitude towards the isuse of the argumentation refers to a basically different process. As Rosenberg formulates it (1965, p. 39) the reward operates as a reinforcement "which fosters the internalization of the counterattitudinal cognitions". The incentive function of the reward (the expectation or promise of a reward or the administration of a reward before engaging in the task) is seen as affecting the amount and/or quality of arguments generated in the biased scanning of the attitude issue, whereas the reinforcement function of the reward given, contingent upon the production of (new) arguments, would lead to better acceptance, internalization and stabilization of these new cognitions, which—at least in Rosenberg's view—would then enhance the inconsistency with the affective components of the attitude, thus leading to an equilibrium restoring attitude change positively related to the magnitude of the reward. As said before, the latter inconsistency assumption is not essential for a "reinforcement" view which can be restricted to the hypothesis that reinforced arguments will have a stronger impact upon subsequent attitude responses, which are conceived as being partly determined by previous cognitive elaboration of the attitude issue.

Although the present design does not allow for an unambiguous test of such a reinforcement interpretation, we would, for the time being, like to defend the position that there is quite convincing evidence against this view if we also take into account some data obtained in the previous and perfectly comparable experiment. It will be remembered that an almost identical attitude change effect (7.1) was obtained in a private counter-attitudinal advocacy condition where the experimenter told the subject that there was unfortunately no more money left, to give him the reward normally received by other subjects (who did a less demanding job).

The important question then, for which the reinforcement view under consideration does not seem to have a ready answer, is the following: how could both these impressive attitude change effects (7.4 and 7.1) be explained by reinforcement if in the one condition a very important—and preferred—reward is given, whereas in the other condition the subjects are made to feel deprived from a normal reward? Getting an important reward for doing some task, and being deprived from a reward while performing an identical task should not have the same effect if the changes in the attitude response were mainly under the control of the manipulated reward contingencies. The fact that the temporal features of the reward contingencies are not exactly comparable, in our opinion, could hardly be used as a counter-argument.

We thus would argue that the obtained evidence is, to say the least, not consistent with a reinforcement view, and would prefer to defend the plausibility of our initial conception in which the effects are seen as related to what we have called the "dissonant" characteristic of the reward treatment. In the next experiment we will examine if manipulation of reward is *überhaupt* a necessary condition for the attitude change effect to be replicated.

What about the difference between the pre- and post-advocacy reward treatment and an *incentive* view on attitude change after rewarded advocacy?

It will be remembered that the results of our 1969 research were in manifest disagreement with incentive predictions. The attitude change effect obtained after a 20 BF reward, given before engaging in the advocacy, was greater (6.6 v. 4.8) than the attitude change assessed in a condition where everything was kept constant, except for the decupled size of the monetary incentive (200 BF). In the present experiment however, where the same important non-monetary reward is given either before (9.5) or after (7.4) the advocacy, the difference in the attitude change is almost significant ($t = 1.32$; $0.05 < p < 0.10$; one tailed test) in the direction predicted by the defenders of an incentive view. Does this mean that incentive theory is only working when the rewards at stake are very important (the non-monetary reward being preferred to a not specified amount of monetary gratification)?

To this, we would like to make the following comments: (1) Most incentive predictions have been tested with various magnitudes of monetary reward. Since our money manipulations do not confirm the incentive view, the theory should explain why only a non-monetary reward does work; (2) If the observed attitude change were mainly a question of incentive, how then do we explain the similar effect in the relative deprivation condition of both the public and private advocacy conditions? (3) The incentive interpretation implies that the students under high incentive will work harder, do a better job, or generate more convincing arguments. An analysis of our subsidiary data fails to reveal any supporting evidence in this respect. As a matter of fact, the average number of words used in the advocacy is 565 for the pre-advocacy incentive condition versus 627 for the post-advocacy subject who did not have the important non-monetary incentive for engaging in the task. Blind analysis of the number of arguments developed in the pleas revealed no difference between the two conditions (the average number of arguments being 5.9 for the pre- and 6.0 for the post-advocacy reward). Also the persuasiveness of the pleas, as rated by blind judges, did not produce a significant difference; the observed means even lying in the opposite direction (post-advocacy being slightly more persuasive than pre-advocacy). It should be noted that these data at the same time invalidate the above mentioned cognitive dissonance prediction concerning differential effort invested in the disproportionally rewarded compliance.

With regard to our post-experimental data, there is only one set which calls for attention, viz., the answers given to question 13 "Do you feel that the interviewer has forced you to cooperate?" (strongly so (26) . . . not at all (1)). The ratings for *both* the "dissonant" reward conditions are quite exceptional: as well in the pre- as in the post-advocacy reward condition, nine of the eleven subjects score at the very extreme "not at all (1)" pool of the continuum, in contrast to the "mere information about bad exam", where only three subjects do manifest such an extreme degree of experienced freedom. The difference between the combined "dissonant" reward (2.5 and 1.9) and the "bad exam" (8.3) conditions is significant at the 0.001 level ($t = 4.09$). The difference with the control condition, in which no information about exams was given (5.5), is significant at the 0.05 level ($t = 2.34$).

Although these data are impressive in their own right, our present focus is of course on their possible relation with the attitude response

TABLE 16
Average change in attitude towards the traditional exam
system and expressed degree of coercion

Experimental Conditions	Coercion Rating	Attitude Change
Counteratt. private "*bad exam*"	8.3	4.7
Counteratt. radio 20 BF	8.3	6.6*
Counteratt. TV 20 BF	7.7	6.1*
Counteratt. private 20 BF	6.6	5.1
Pro-att. radio rel. depr.	5.5	4.4
Counteratt. private rel. depr.	5.5	7.1*
Counteratt. private zero BF (1970)	5.5	4.3
Counteratt. radio zero BF	5.4	4.9
Counteratt. private zero BF (1969)	5.1	4.5
Counteratt. radio rel. depr.	4.6	7.1*
Pro-att. radio zero BF	4.5	4.2
Counteratt. radio 200 BF	4.5	4.8
Counteratt. private "*good exam*"	4.4	5.1
Pro-att. radio 20 BF	3.1	4.0
Counteratt. private *exam points pre-adv.*	2.5	9.5*
Counteratt. private *exam points post-adv.*	1.9	7.4*

Note. The higher the coercion rating, the more the subject felt "forced" by the experimenter. Not a single subject did score higher than 16 on the 26-point scale.
The experimental conditions are listed in decreasing order of expressed coercion.
* "Dissonant" reward effects.

under study. Could it then be that the attitude change effect is systematically related to perceived decision freedom or to experienced or expressed "coercion by the experimenter"? Would it make sense to think of a double reactance effect (Brehm, 1966), by which the subject, whose free cooperation was threatened by the acceptance of an unusually important reward, wanted to recover that freedom both by overemphasizing the absence of any coercive influence exerted by the experimenter and by shifting his attitude in such a way that the freedom to hold a "pro"-attitudinal plea seemed to be restored?

However appealing such a line of reasoning might sound, an inspection of the available data shows that both categories of responses are quite independent. In Table 16, the average attitude change for all thusfar reported conditions is compared with the average response to post-experimental question 13. Although at first glance, it looks as if there might be some promising clusters of conditions (e.g., the 20 BF reward) along the perceived coercion variable, it is obvious that the impressive attitude change effects are spread over the full continuum ($r = 0.09$).

Even when disregarding all public advocacy conditions, for which the post-experimental data might be of a rather dubious nature (the "subjects" becoming aware of their subject role), it suffices to compare the two conditions with mere information about "bad" versus "good" exam of the present experiment: notwithstanding the fact that both conditions are situated at opposite ends of the expressed coercion continuum (8.3 v. 4.4), the average attitude responses towards the traditional exam system hardly differ at all (4.7 and 5.1).

CONCLUSION

The hitherto discussed data leave us with negative conclusions concerning a plausible interpretation of the attitude change effects obtained, at least if reward is considered as related to perceived coercion, justification, incentive or reinforcement.

What if the reward treatment is considered as the administration of a strange, embarrassing, novel or *"dissonant" stimulus* which simply *disturbs and/or arouses* the subject?

Since relative deprivation, priceless rescue exam points and a trivial sum given by the BRT, all had a similar and dramatic effect upon the attitude responses, it seems warranted to forget completely about the "reward" aspects of the treatment and simply consider this feature of subject's environment as a "dissonant" stimulus which embarrassed and/ or emotionally aroused the subject. Let us try to have a fresh look at the behaviour of our subjects, who engaged in counterattitudinal behaviour under strange or "dissonant" stimulus conditions. Typically, a more or less complex and subtle environmental pressure induces the subject to concentrate upon a task which basically consists of the emission of one particular type of evaluative verbal response all of which have in common a depiction of the good qualities of the traditional exam system. For more than twenty minutes (solitary preparation and advocacy proper) the subject—probably for the first time in his life—does nothing other than generate, paraphrase and repeat the same arguments. Immediately after this active production of arguments, the subject is once more confronted with the same arguments when invited to carefully check his recorded speech. For half an hour he is thus exposed to one particular chain of messages which are essentially an instance of persuasive communication.

What happens now, when the reception or processing of persuasive communication is being disturbed by the occurrence of a strange, novel or embarrassing event? There is evidence in the literature that, in a social communication setting, the impact of a persuasive communication is enhanced when an unusual and embarrassing event occurs just before the message is transmitted. Miller and Levy (1967), for example, "inadvertently" insulted their slightly overweight women subjects for being obese just before they had to read a persuasive communication. It turned out that those subjects who had received the message immediately after being insulted, agreed very significantly more with the thesis of the communicator, than control subjects who had not been exposed to the strange, unusual and embarrassing "dissonant" treatment, whose meaning—it should be stressed—was totally irrelevant to the content of the persuasive communication and which could not readily be blamed on the communicator.

Whatever the underlying processes might be that account for this effect, we felt tempted to see an analogy between these provocative Miller and Levy results and our own data. As a matter of fact, taking into account that our "dissonant" reward treatment can be considered as a strange, unusual and embarrassing event, the main adaptation which was needed for making the two research paradigms comparable, consists in the fact that sender and receiver of the persuasive communication are one and the same individual in our experiments, whereas they are different persons in the social communication study at issue.

Since it is evident that our advocates not only actively produce, but also are passively exposed to the arguments proffered, it could make sense to consider the typical counterattitudinal advocacy situation as an instance of persuasive self-communication. The very fact that the role playing is counterattitudinal might be considered as supporting the view that the self-communication can be seen as persuasive. If disturbing or embarrassing events increase the impact of a persuasive communication, one could predict a similar effect for persuasive self-communication. This fits nicely with our data: under "dissonant" reward treatment, the impact of the counterattitudinal advocacy upon the advocate seems to be significantly greater than under normal conditions, the shift of the attitude responses in the advocated direction being seen as a consequence of enhanced self-persuasion.

As far as the differences are concerned between our two experimental conditions, one could argue that the magnitude of the self-persuasive effect is a function of the length of the time during which the "dissonant" stimuli could interfere with or affect the self-persuasion. Thus its influence would be greater when the disturbing event occurs just before the communication starts, than when given immediately after the reception of the messages. It does indeed seem plausible to hold that the elaboration of persuasive communication goes on for some time after the reception of the messages, and that the occurrence of a disturbing event at that time also could interfere with self-persuasion, for example, by inhibiting active counter-argumentation against the counterattitudinal arguments just proferred. However promising this parallel with the Miller and Levy study might be, it obviously does not uncover yet the process mediating the "dissonant" reward treatment and its attitude change effect. The various tentative interpretations offered by Miller and Levy do not seem to be useful for our purpose.

Another promising link with the relevant persuasive communication literature could be found in various experiments reviewed by Janis (1967). In his quite extensive and inspiring treatise on the effects of fear arousal on attitude change, Janis discusses several instances in which it might be useful to relate an increase in emotional arousal to an enhanced acceptance of a persuasive communication. Although our research setting is not typical for the study of effects of fear appeals, again one could make a parallel when considering emotional arousal, produced by our "dissonant" treatments, as affecting the acceptance in a self-persuasive communication setting. We will refrain from referring at this point to other possibly relevant research. The main point is that the above confrontation with social communication studies guided the development of our own research strategy as will become clear in Experiment Ten.

2. Experiment Ten: The effect of a "dissonant" aversive stimulus upon post-advocacy attitude change (1971 research)

PROBLEM AND DESIGN

After so much experimentation with various monetary and non-monetary rewards and under the growing conviction that the specific reward features of the treatments were irrelevant for the understanding of the attitude effects obtained, we decided to run an experiment in which the hypothesis would be put to test that the administration of a "dissonant" *aversive* stimulus would have a similar effect upon the attitude responses as the administration of a "dissonant" *reward*. If confirmed, the interpretation of the attitude change phenomena under study could dispose of the reward concept and the theoretical views which are centred around this notion. Provided that the common link between the various manipulations can be seen as being related to their unusual, novel, strange or "dissonant" character, the search for an interpretation could then be narrowed down towards the study of the effect of any disturbing and/or emotionally arousing stimulation (aversive or rewarding) upon the impact of a self-generated persuasive communication.

It should be stressed that the main guideline for our research consisted in the imperative that the aversive treatment should be "dissonant" in a similar way as the highly appreciated reward of the previous experiment. As a matter of fact, we know already that the perfectly plausible administration of an aversive stimulus, as realized in the "mere information about the bad exam" condition, does not lead to an attitude change effect which differs from that obtained in various not-"dissonant" advocacy conditions. We therefore made an effort to arrange the experimental situation in such a way that the occurrence of the aversive event would be truly strange, embarrassing and not fitting with the experimental situation in which the advocacy was induced.

Since we were tempted by the above discussed parallel with the Miller and Levy data, we finally decided to run a condition in which the subjects would be unjustly and severely blamed for something unrelated to the advocacy or the attitude at issue. The "dissonant" nature of the blame administered, will best be illustrated by the description of procedure. The results of this blame condition will be compared with the data of the "mere information about bad exam condition" and a comparable "no blame" condition of Experiment Nine. It must be conceded that, taking into account the fact that we wanted our experimental manipulation to be imbedded in a macro-situation which would ensure its validity, we did not see the feasibility of running a not-"dissonant" blame condition. Priority was indeed given to the question if the "dissonant" *reward* effect would be replicated under *aversive* stimulus conditions, which could be considered to be "dissonant" in the same vein as the important reward of the previous experiment. Since the present research was executed in 1971, another baseline condition was run in order to assess the stability of the attitude response studied.

PROCEDURE

Our continuous concern for an experimental procedure which could quite inconspicuously be embedded in the macro-situational changes of the student's university environment, induced us to exploit a circumstance which was standardized for both the present and the following experiment, run during the month of May 1971 (i.e., the four lecturing weeks between Easter vacation and the period of preparation for the July exam session).

Since the 1971 psychology course for the Science students had been scheduled during the second semester (February–May) and since the author—who until then had been the only teacher for this course—had accepted a visiting-professorship for the 1971 spring term at Dartmouth College, it was arranged that the experimenter (who in the meantime had received her Ph.D. degree) would replace the author for the two hours a week psychology lectures to be given during these last four weeks of the academic year. The reader belonging to cultures where the Women's Liberation movement has reaped already some important progress in the traditionally all-male academic world should note that the very fact that a young woman teaches an *ex cathedra* course to a four hundred, primarily male Science student audience is by itself a quite unusual event. In 1971, the University of Leuven had one woman among its 225 full professors and four in the total group of 540 tenured academic staff. The exam deliberations for the Science departments (and even for the Psychology and Educational Sciences Departments) still continue to be a one hundred per cent male enterprise. The importance of this feature will become even more salient for the "dissonant" treatment used in the next experiment.

Since the students knew that all remaining psychology lectures would be taught by Dr. Beckers and were not informed about the precise duration of the author's absence, it was a reasonable guess for them to expect that she would give the oral psychology exams of the imminent July session (which happened in fact to be true). At the end of Dr. Beckers' first psychology lecture, which was attended with perfect discipline, she invited the students to volunteer for an unspecified variety of experiments, which, especially taking into consideration the increasing time constraints of the students, would never exceed 45 minutes. It should be noted that the students were not made to expect that Dr. Beckers herself would be the experimenter: the students were essentially motivated to help in Ph.D. research of various graduate students who would be grateful for having data to work on during the summer period (when students are no longer available). All subjects for the present and following experiment were sampled from the pool of male non-bis-students volunteering at the end of this first lecture. In contrast to our 1970 research there was no sub-sampling criterion in terms of performance on an advanced collective psychology exam, for the simple reason that such an exam was not given in 1971.

Baseline condition 1971 The procedure for the 1971 baseline condition was essentially similar to that used for the 1969 baseline. The pseudo experimental 1969 treatment was of course omitted. As explained, the status of the identical experimenter was changed, also her fashionably equipped office in which the experiments took place, was twice the size of the one used in 1969.

Upon his arrival in Dr. Beckers' office* she thanks the student for lending his cooperation to a study which she herself is conducting, and continues: "Please sit down, I will explain to you what you can do for me in a moment, but first I would like to ask you one question". As was the case for the 1969 baseline condition (see p. 78) she then elicits the attitude response after having briefly explained the meaning of the attitude issue, so as to ascertain direct comparability with the advocacy-instructions, where a detailed description of the issue was given during the "eliciting of compliance phase". The subsequent treatment of the subjects in this 1971 baseline condition will be reported later on.

---

* It might be worth mentioning that the procedure for arranging precise appointments for experiments implies the use of an *ad hoc* invitation card which says that the student is expected to be at a fixed hour in the hall of the third floor of the Psychology Building for participation in experiment number X. This number is different for students of the same experimental treatment and appropriate signs in the hall lead the individual subjects to the experimenter's office.

"Dissonant" *blame* *condition* The procedure for this crucial condition of Experiment Ten is an exact replication of the "mere information of bad exam" condition of the previous experiment except for the fact that the unpleasant casual information about the poor exam performance was replaced by the administration of a truly "dissonant" aversive stimulus in the following way.

While making a move for filing the subject's individual psychology record, the experimenter's attention happens to be caught by a notice put on the reverse of the card (while clearly showing the front side with subject's photograph in the direction of the student). At this point the thusfar friendly experimenter completely changes her key when saying "How strange that you are volunteering for psychology research. You had much better stayed away from my lecture, since your disruptive conduct was a continuous source of distraction for me. Or do you think it is not disturbing that one and the same student continuously is giggling while one is teaching a course. You perfectly know that attendance at psychology lectures is by no means compulsory. If you cannot behave, I truly prefer you not to come any more to my lectures!" Upon the fumbling reaction of the appalled and obviously innocent subjects who invariably advance the argument that they cannot possibly see any grounds for the accusation made, the experimenter replied in a firm way "Your attitude was so salient and conspicuous that after my lecture I checked the photographs of the psychology records and had no doubt that you were the one who really did upset me. Well, let us not go now any further into this. For the moment just forget about it". While filing the psychology record she continues in the usual way by asking the subject if he agrees to make the plea and leaves him alone for a quarter of an hour.

RESULTS AND DISCUSSION

The data to be discussed in the present experiment are given in Table 17.

The stability of the strongly negative attitude towards the traditional exam system (no temporal spread nor exam exemptions for the September session) is shown by a comparison of the 1969 (2.3) and 1971 (2.5) attitude responses emitted before any experimental treatment. The variability in the 1971 sample remains very small: 4 students score "very strongly anti"; 6 "strongly anti" and 1 "anti".

The effect of the "dissonant" blame (7.5)—quite significant by a simple "interocular trauma test"—differs in the expected direction, from the "mere information about bad exam condition" (4.7) at the 0.01 level

TABLE 17
Mean attitude response towards the traditional exam system as a function
of highly unappreciated, "dissonant" aversive treatment

			Private Counterattitudinal Advocacy	
Baseline (pre-advocacy)		no aversive treatment	aversive information (bad exam)	"dissonant" aversive treatment (blame)
(1969)	(1971)	(1970)	(1970)	(1971)
2.3	2.5	4.3	4.7	7.5

$(t = 3.29)$ and the 0.02 level $(t = 2.76)$ from the condition in which neither rewarding nor aversive treatment was administered—zero BF private counterattitudinal plea, 1970—(4.3).

Going back to the Miller and Levy study concerning the enhanced impact of a persuasive communication sent to a blamed receiver, our data corroborate the plausibility of the proposed transformation of the latter paradigm: the embarrassing "dissonant" blame treatment had a similar effect in the social communication and in the self-persuasion setting.

The data obviously do not need much comment with regard to a positive reinforcement view on attitude change in the advocated direction. More important, they do offer evidence for the thesis that the administration of an appreciated but "dissonant" reward or the "dissonant" relative deprivation of a non-specified monetary reward cannot any longer be considered as a necessary condition for the impressive "dissonant" *reward* effect to be obtained. As a matter of fact, a perfectly similar change in the attitude response is being produced upon the administration of a "dissonant" aversive stimulus; a change which again is significantly different from the one assessed after administration of a not-"dissonant" aversive stimulus (information about bad exam). Taking into account the analogous differential effect obtained in the previous experiment for the administration of a not-"dissonant" reward (information about good exam) and of a "dissonant" but highly appreciated reward (rescue exam points), we would like to conclude that the specific reward (reinforcement, incentive or compliance justifying) features of the treatment are no longer useful in our search for an explanation of the phenomenon under study, and do feel more confident when stating, that it is the unusual, strange, novel or "dissonant" nature of an environmental feature, preceding the emission of the attitude response proper, which is responsible for the assessed effect. Since this environmental feature can be either rewarding or aversive, it seems justified to use the more general term *"dissonant"* *stimulus* by which we refer to an unusual, novel, strange or embarrassing aspect of the behavioural situation to which the subject is exposed immediately before his attitude will be assessed and which presumably controls the evaluative characteristics of the subsequent attitude response.

CONCLUSION

It might be useful to recall at this point the transformation of the conceptual meaning given to the experimental factor which is assumed to produce the crucial attitude change effect under study. Suffice it to recapitulate the various terms used to designate this factor in our progressive analysis of the classical cognitive dissonance effect.

(1) Minimal justification or barely sufficient *consonant reward:* the low reward in the classical Festinger and Carlsmith and Cohen experiments was conceived as a cognitive element consonant with the compliance but of so meagre importance that the total magnitude of cognitive dissonance generated by the simultaneous presence of the cognitive elements concerning the pre-experimental attitude and the attitude discrepant advocacy did result—as a means of dissonance reduction—in an attitude change (in the advocated direction) which was greater than the one observed in a high reward situation.

(2) *Dissonant reward:* as a first step it did seem plausible to consider the disproportionately low reward as enhancing the total magnitude of cognitive dissonance, in a similar manner as the relative deprivation of reward which in Festinger's terms also leads to the production of a cognitive element which is dissonant with the compliance. It should be conceded that at this point it might already be appropriate to use the term "dissonant" aversive stimulus. We refrained from doing so since we wanted to stay as close as possible within the conceptual framework of Festinger.

(3) *"Dissonant" reward:* this use of the term was made to indicate a reward which "does not fit" with one or another aspect of the situation preceding the emission of the crucial attitude response, but which has no implications whatsoever for Festinger's postulated cognitive equilibrium and thus merely designates an unusual, novel, strange, embarrassing "acognitive" reward.

(4) *"Dissonant" stimulus:* this last and most general term removes the

reward aspect of the former notion by widening its scope to any "dissonant" environmental feature which supposedly embarrasses and/or emotionally arouses the subject in a quite peculiar way. We are of course aware of the fact that blame and monetary or non-monetary reward can be conceived both as (negative or positive) reinforcers. We hope however to have amply documented the position that it would be meaningless to use in the present context the notion "dissonant" reinforcers.

The vagueness, neutrality and generality of the term "dissonant" stimulus accentuates however the importance of the question about the *interpretation* of the observed attitude change phenomenon which is still left open and unanswered.

Without pretending to be exhaustive we propose four—not necessarily completely distinct—lines of reasoning which might be relevant for an overall interpretation of the data and for which links could be made with the existing literature. It will be noticed that only the first two hypotheses do make explicit reference to the above discussed possible link between "persuasive communication" and "self-persuasion". The fourth hypothesis, whose relevance for the attitude change area might seem to be the least obvious, will be illustrated in the next paragraph.

(1) *Impaired counterargumentation hypothesis:* "dissonant" stimuli enhance self-persuasion because they are disturbing and impair active counter-argument or defence against the attitude discrepant argumentation in which the subject is engaged.

(2) *Emotional facilitation of self-persuasion hypothesis:* "dissonant" stimuli emotionally arouse the subject; enhanced emotional arousal facilitates the acceptance of persuasive communications generated and processed by the same person, as it does in social communication settings.

(3) *Social desirability hypothesis:* "dissonant" stimuli emotionally arouse the subject and make him more susceptible to the influence of social desirability cues. The experimenter concerned with the exam reform problem, even when not necessarily being perceived as part of the traditional establishment, can be supposed to have a much less extreme attitude towards the issue than the student.

(4) *Evaluative response contagion hypothesis:* "dissonant" stimuli emotionally arouse the subject who has been induced to emit for half an hour one particular kind of evaluative verbal responses concerning the attitude issue. An increase in arousal enhances the relative dominance and the impact of the most recent ongoing responses upon the immediately

subsequent attitude response, resulting in a greater similarity between the prevailing evaluative characteristics of the former and the latter responses.

This vast, and most likely not exhaustive repertoire of interpretational possibilities, might sound discouraging to the reader who is familiar with the complexity of the attitude change literature. Nevertheless, an effort will be made in the following experiment to test the relative plausibility and theoretical implications of the thusfar merely enumerated interpretational avenues.

3. Experiment Eleven: "Dissonant" stimuli and attitude change after pro- and counterattitudinal, persuasive and non-persuasive evaluative verbal responses

PROBLEM AND DESIGN

The thread running through the presented research supports the plausibility of our thesis that the impressive attitude change effects under study are a function of the strange, novel or "dissonant" stimuli impinging upon the subject in the experimental situation immediately preceding the emission of the attitude response proper. As explained, these "dissonant" stimuli are not any longer considered as affecting Festinger's cognitive equilibrium between clusters of cognitions concerning attitude and attitude discrepant behaviour, nor as having a positive or negative incentive or reinforcement function in the usual sense of the terms. An increased understanding of this phenomenon implies however, that its crucial determinants are further pinned down and the above suggested interpretational hunches weighed one against another.

It seemed to us that this difficult enterprise could profit from an experiment in which essentially three changes would be introduced, one concerning the attitude neutrality of the "dissonant" stimulus, one concerning the persuasive and one concerning the attitudinal nature of the advocacy.

Attitude neutrality of the "dissonant" stimulus

The reader might have felt uncomfortable with the apparent ease displayed in the discussion sections of the two preceding experiments where no attention was paid to a possible research contaminant of which behavioural scientists are becoming increasingly aware and which could be advanced as an artifactual interpretation for at least a part of the findings. After having read through our first chapter (and Appendix) we hopefully will not be accused of being blind to the important problem of uncontrolled aspects of the experimenter-subject interactions. Still, it must be conceded that the powerful "dissonant" treatments of the present chapter are not totally waterproof in this respect. As a matter of fact, both the exam rescue points ("dissonant" high reward) and the undeserved blame ("dissonant" aversive stimulus) could in some way or another trigger off a reaction of pleasing or ingratiating the experimenter, who had been giving undeserved exam points or who had severely blamed the student a few weeks before he was to take an exam with the same person. Thus one could argue that both exam relevant treatments did accentuate the experimenter's connection with the exam system establishment and that the student, especially in the "dissonant" conditions, would become sensitive to social desirability cues and try to tune in on the perceived attitude position of the experimenter by giving evidence of a much less extreme anti-traditional exam attitude. A similar social desirability reaction could be considered as a means for restoring the inequity generated by the administration of undeserved exam points, or undeserved disciplinary blame. In both "dissonant" conditions the treatment had to do with an aspect of the specific teacher-student hierarchic relationship. A rather mild attitude towards the traditional exam system could then be considered as instrumental to expressing one's gratitude or for winning a positive evaluation.

The very fact that the subjects of the 1971 baseline condition who, as part of an interview, were asked to estimate the attitude position of the experimenter, did concentrate their guesses around 3.9 (five "strongly anti" and four "anti" the traditional exam system) does not necessarily invalidate the above reasoning, since the specific "dissonant" treatment itself, particularly in the blame condition, might affect the subject's estimation of the experimenter's own attitude position on the issue.

It will soon become clear that the other modifications introduced in the present experiment will also contribute to an adequate test of the various explanations which refer to the perceived attitude position of the experimenter, and which we subsume under the "social desirability" hypothesis.

Our concern for an attitude irrelevant "dissonant" treatment equally was motivated by the fear that one or another imaginative adept of Festinger's cognitive dissonance theory might still point to the eventuality that the manipulated "dissonant" exam points and/or "dissonant" disciplinary blame, could lead to the (uncontrolled) creation of various new cognitions which, since they stemmed from a possibly attitude relevant manipulation, would affect the total magnitude of cognitive dissonance of one or another part of the cognitive cluster concerning the exam system. Under the given experimental circumstances, the only means for reducing the thus enhanced cognitive dissonance might then be a change away from the original attitude position.

For all these reasons, we made an effort to look for a "dissonant" treatment whose cognitive elaboration could be considered as truly irrelevant, or unrelated to the exam reform attitude issue. Probably influenced by the cultural shock which the author experienced upon his arrival in the Dartmouth College campus, where quite a few students, enrolled at this most expensive and high status "Ivy League" University, attended lectures and made appointments with their professors while going barefoot and in tatters which one would not even imagine in European slums, it occurred that having the experimenter wearing a *"dissonant" dress* might very well satisfy the requirements for an experimental treatment which in itself would be truly neutral with regard to the crucial attitude. It would indeed be difficult to maintain that the predicted attitude change towards the traditional exam system could be seen as restoring a cognitive imbalance affected by the experimenter's strange or "dissonant" dress.

It will become clear from the description of procedure, that our "dissonant" dress manipulation is comparable to the previous "dissonant" treatments in as far as the dress can safely be considered to be unusual, novel, embarrassing or strange and can be expected to be emotionally arousing and/or disturbing.

Persuasive nature of advocacy

We thought that our search for a better understanding of the phenomenon might be more successful if we could also more clearly isolate the persuasive advocacy character of the behaviour which the subjects were induced to emit during the experimental treatment. Although we had already covered a very large part of this variable by shifting from a nation-wide television speech to private and anonymous help in the exam reform research of the experimenter, the fact remained that in all experiments thusfar reported, the students were explicitly invited to hold a strong, persuasive and most convincing plea against, or in favour of the aspects of exam reform mentioned. It was precisely this persuasive aspect of the task which had guided us in the previous experiment, to examine the possible analogy with the social communication literature concerning the enhanced impact of persuasive messages. It remained however, an empirical question to see if the "persuasive communication" aspect of the advocacy was really crucial for the understanding of the observed effect. It will not have been left unnoticed that the last interpretational possibility enumerated at the end of the previous paragraph does not refer to the "persuasive communication" notion.

At the same time, it should be noted that any "persuasive communication" task could have implications in terms of "self-esteem", "commitment" and "social consequences" to which various theorists attach much importance (Aronson, 1966; Kiesler *et al.*, 1968; Kelley, 1967; Verhaeghe, 1970). It might be argued that one cannot feel yet completely safe with regard to the contention that commitment, threatened self-esteem and/or perceived aversive social consequences, are practically non-existant in our private advocacy conditions. Although it would be difficult to negate the immense differences in this respect between our public and private, identified and anonymous conditions, one might defend the position that some degree of commitment, threatened self-esteem and/or social consequences is persisting to serve as a necessary condition for the "dissonant" stimulus effect to be obtained. As a matter of fact, even in the private conditions the student is helping somebody whose research is focussing on the exam reform problem and he might believe that his advocacy in one or another way ultimately will affect the official exam policy.

We thus had enough reasons to test the plausibility of those interpretations centring around the notion of self-persuasion by manipulating the persuasive nature of the advocacy. This was hopefully achieved by applying the "dissonant" treatment to subjects who were merely invited to cooperate in a *verbal creativity* exercise, in which not the slightest allusion was made to a study of exam reform, nor was the subject invited to hold a strong convincing plea. As the description of procedure will clarify, the only thing the student was supposed to do was to generate arguments related to the exam reform issue *for the simple sake of showing off the creativity and productivity of his verbal repertoire.* The instructions did not refer to any such terms as advocacy, plea, convince, persuade.

Since the student in these conditions is really focusing on emitting evaluative verbal responses of a particular kind rather than on trying to hold a strong and convincing plea, we can expect that the persuasive communication setting, if not totally absent, is at least much weaker in these verbal creativity than in the true advocacy conditions. If then the notion of enhanced acceptance of a persuasive communication, either via the disturbing effect of the "dissonant" treatment—impairing active counterargumentation—or via an increase in emotional arousal, were to be the most plausible keys to a better understanding of the studied phenomenon, one would expect the "dissonant" treatment to be less efficient in the mere creativity than in the persuasive advocacy conditions.

If on the other hand an effect is found in the verbal productivity conditions, we would feel confident in rejecting the "impaired counter-argumentation" and "emotional facilitation of self-persuasion" hypo-theses and advance a probably more economical interpretation, which could dispose of various implications of a cognitive information proces-sing self-persuasion paradigm. Defying the fear of being covered with ridicule for oversimplifying and trivializing our impressive attitude change data, we would indeed propose to think somewhat along the following lines: we take for granted that the "dissonant" treatment does affect the emotional arousal of the subjects; one of the consequences being an enhancement of the relative dominance of the ongoing or most recent attitude related verbal responses emitted during the half an hour period preceding the emission of the attitude behaviour proper. This latter crucial response then is being significantly affected by the prevailing evaluative characteristics of the immediately preceding ongoing verbal behaviour; this "evaluative response contagion" effect manifests itself in an increased similarity between the prevailing evaluative characteristics of the attitude related verbal behaviour and the attitude response proper.

Obviously, a model for explaining the resultant of an underlying response conflict is in order, since the subjects are not predicted to evidence the attitude position of the extreme counterattitudinal verbal responses generated. But it might very well be that the mechanism of such a response conflict, in the circumstances under study, is of a very basic nature. It might be helpful at this point to digress briefly in an effort to illustrate our view by reporting a probably even more trivial real life experience which might help the reader understand the direction which we are hinting at.

One evening at the end of a family dinner, shared with a few playmates of the children, the level of excitement was quite high—partly as a function of wine for the adults, partly of the great fun the whole company was enjoying from a contest in pieces of wit. Clearly as a result of an arrangement among the children, my eleven year old daughter Katrien, as a spokesman of the youngsters, calls for my willingness to answer from now on all questions she would direct to me. Before the acquiescing and closely attending audience she invites me to repeat uninterruptedly ten times the Dutch nonsense word *work* while rolling the "r" and accentuating the "k". "All you have to do", she specifies "is to say 'work, work...' "—and she pronounces herself ten times the nonsense word while having me start immediately hereafter. As soon as my forced compliance was enjoyed by the audience, she asks me "with what do you normally eat your soup?" Since I had promised to answer all her questions I immediately said "with a *vork*". While I was expecting the next question, the conspiring children started laughing at me. Not understanding their reaction, I asked for the following question, and it was only when a triumphant Katrien insisted upon asking me if I am sure that I usually do eat soup with a fork (which in Dutch is *vork*), that I realized that the proper answer should have been spoon (or *lepel* in Dutch). The very fact that the children enjoyed having taken in a presumably learned adult, proved that I was not the first subject which had been successfully treated in this child-game experiment.

I was so impressed by the retrospective awareness of the earnestness and conviction with which I had given a foolish answer to such a simple question that I puzzled about the necessary and sufficient conditions for this response change effect to be obtained. My own effort in producing the effect in more formal settings with friends in the lab mostly ran into failure. However, a senior psychology colleague, who had never been "tested" by somebody like me—in full earnest did emit the wrong response, and when asked a second time, after having repeated in a normal fashion the ten "work" responses, with what he usually did eat his soup, his reaction was "*vo . . . eh, lepel*".

Although the issue is apparently very simple to study, I did not explore the point any further. I think that basically there could be an intriguing analogy between the processes leading to the emission of a wrong response in the children's game and our observed and/or predicted attitude change under "dissonant" response contingencies. There is no doubt that the answer "spoon" is the one hundred per cent dominant response to questions such as "with what do you normally eat your soup". And yet, the stimulus evokes a quite different response, belonging to the same category of utensils (the answer given was not a stimulus unrelated existing word, such as *werk* or *lork*—in English, "work" or "larch") on condition that the immediately preceding ongoing responses—under arousing and/or distracting contingencies?—do share some prevailing common elements with the response predicted by the game.

The main point here might well be that the problem of the underlying response conflict, and the precise laws for its solution (*vo . . . eh lepel*, or pointing at the attitude position somewhere in between the recently made responses and the pre-experimental attitude position) is not so much a problem for social psychologists, but rather has to do with a very basic and elementary phenomenon of response contagion, chaining and/ or generalization to be studied by behavioural scientists with more modest and fundamental research orientations.

It is unnecessary to stress the point that we do not pretend that the above example could be used as a fully adequate analogy for the complex phenomenon of "subtle and enduring attitude change"—be it for the simple reason that from now on Katrien can be sure that I will not any longer be taken in this particular game. *But what exactly does "enduring attitude change" and "be taken in" mean*, at least as operationalized in an important part of the relevant literature, and *even in "real life"*? We are going to deal with these problems in Chapter Four. The reader will however have understood that we do contend that the risks are that social psychologists will accentuate the differences between the phenomenon under study and the, (trivial?), example just described.

The attitudinal nature of the advocacy or verbal responses emitted

Let us now briefly point to the possibilities offered by a third comparison which will be made in the present experiment, and which has to do with the discrepancy between the attitude and the advocacy or verbal responses which the subjects are induced to generate. In the previous chapters we have already documented the rationale for controlling counterattitudinal advocacy with otherwise identical pro-attitudinal advocacy conditions. In the present study the manipulation of the attitudinal nature of the "compliance" serves usefully some further purposes. With respect to the self-persuasion notion, taking into account the extreme pre-experimental attitude position of the subjects, the self-persuasive function of a pro-attitudinal plea would be less than in the counterattitudinal conditions. This is not to say that producing and elaborating arguments in favour of one's own attitude position could not result in increased intensity of the position held before this activity. (It will however, be remembered that in all comparable pro-attitudinal advocacy conditions thusfar reported, the effect is clearly one of tempering the extremity of the pre-experimental attitude response.) However, since the discrepancy between the persuasive communication and the attitude position held by the receiver of the communication is by far, smaller in the pro-attitudinal conditions, it makes sense to expect that the "dissonant" stimuli would be more operative in the persuasive counterattitudinal than in the less (self-) persuasive pro-attitudinal conditions if the underlying processes essentially were to be linked to enhanced self-persuasion. If on the other hand, persuasion related processes are not crucial for the predicted "dissonant" stimuli effect, one would expect the latter to be independent of the persuasion-related features of the experimental treatments under comparison. The effect then should go in the direction of an increased similarity between the evaluative characteristics of the ongoing (pro- or counterattitudinal) responses and the subsequent attitude response, or in other words, an attitude response which is more extreme in either direction than in otherwise similar conditions where no "dissonant" treatment is given.

At the same time, the manipulation of the attitudinal nature of the "compliance", especially in the verbal productivity conditions, allows for another test of the hypothesis that increased arousal—induced by the "dissonant" treatment—would alert the subject to social desirability cues in the situation in which the attitude response proper is elicited. Since the experimenter herself clearly would be the main, if not the only source for such cues, and since this factor is kept constant across conditions, one would expect a similar attitude change in the social desirability direction in both pro- and counterattitudinal "dissonant" conditions if this were the crucial process at issue. As said before, the notion of social desirability could also include such experimenter-subject interaction phenomena as evaluation apprehension, desire to please the experimenter, to display maturity, etc.

Needless to add that the hypotheses sketched are not necessarily "all or nothing" alternatives and that observed interactions would simply complicate the issue.

As far as the concrete experimental *design* is concerned, taking into account the imperative time constraints of the experimentation period, we finally performed the following sequence of comparisons which was expected to offer us the most economical test of the various hypotheses described. We first ran two counterattitudinal "dissonant" dress conditions: one advocacy and one verbal creativity; immediately after came a pro-attitudinal "dissonant" and a normal dress condition, both verbal creativity; finally, a pro-attitudinal "dissonant" blame advocacy condition was run together with a partial replication on four subjects of the counterattitudinal blame condition run three weeks earlier (Experiment Ten)*. The rationale for having a *pro*-attitudinal "dissonant" blame, if not yet obvious, will be made clear during the discussion of results.

Together with the penultimate set of conditions, one more "dissonant" dress verbal creativity condition was run, for which no attitude responses were elicited immediately after the treatment, but for which, by intention, the attitude responses were tapped five weeks later together with the other persistency data. The strategic value and the results of this *delayed first attitude response condition* will be commented upon in Chapter Four.

As explained before, the progressive development of this design was inspired by research-economy considerations. For the sake of clarity, the data of Experiment Eleven will be presented as gathered in a truly simultaneous design, which essentially is a 2 × 2 design with two control and one baseline condition (see Table 18, p. 150).

PROCEDURE

The procedure section can be short. The reader is already familiar with the changes in the experimental macro-situation described for Experiment Ten, which had been terminated one day before the start of the present experiment. Especially, the unusual circumstance that the experimenter was formally teaching the *ex cathedra* psychology course is considered to be relevant. The only new experimental procedures are related to the "verbal creativity" and the "dissonant" dress manipulations.

"Verbal creativity conditions" This manipulation is in all respects identical to the private and anonymous conditions in which the subjects were invited to help the experimenter with her research on the exam reform problem, except for the following changes in part of the instructions.

---

* The reason for partially replicating the counterattitudinal "dissonant" blame condition was that there had been a gap of three weeks between the running of the pro- and counterattitudinal blame conditions. Especially in view of the fact that the exam period became so much more imminent, we wanted some extra guarantee that this time factor would not artifactually facilitate the predicted effect. Since the data obtained with the four subjects were 6, 7, 7 and 6, and thus perfectly in line with the results gathered three weeks earlier (cf. Experiment Ten) there seemed to be no problem in this respect.

The experimenter explained that she was studying various factors related to *verbal output problems* and especially cognitive or mental creativity and productivity.

It was important for me, although not easy, to find a topic which would be equally familiar and relevant for all subjects. I finally decided to try the exam system topic. One can indeed presume that each student is able to produce some verbal output on this issue. You will however understand that, in order for me to make a sensible analysis of the productivity and creativity aspects, we have to agree upon certain constraints within which your creativity and productivity efforts should stay. Somebody could indeed be very creative and talk a lot on the comparison between the present exam system and that of his grandfather who studied at a Chinese university in the past century. For comparison purposes I would like to ask you to limit your thinking to the exam system of our university, and more precisely the two issues of exam spread and exam exemptions for the September session (which were described as usual).

Then the instructions differed as a function of the pro- or counter-attitudinal nature of the treatment: "I would like to put one final constraint upon your thinking and talking: you only consider the pro (or contra) side of the two issues mentioned. The main point is that, within those limits *you try to be as productive and creative as possible*". As said before, there was no reference at all to a study of the exam reform problem, nor to any such terms as persuade, plea or advocacy.

"Dissonant" dress conditions During the Easter vacation immediately preceding the experimentation period (spring 1971), after the manifest failure of the maxi-dress—at least in this country—the commercial world tried to launch the hot-pants fashion. A few days before the experiment started, a leading newspaper read by many students and academics, dedicated a long article to the question if secretaries and other female personnel should be allowed to wear hot-pants during office hours. The hesitation of the public at large was manifest, and months later this proved to have been just another eccentric fashion campaign which failed completely. In the Louvain University milieu, it was simply not conceivable, even on a sunny spring day, that a female student would come to lectures or take exams in hot-pants, nor that any female personnel would wear them during office hours.

Taking into account the fact that our experimenter was teaching the psychology *ex cathedra* course—in normal dress—it will be understood that the subject was exposed to a quite strange, novel, embarrassing or "dissonant" treatment when he was welcomed by an experimenter who was dressed in very short hot-pants and an exceptionally low-necked T-shirt. The only other differences with the thusfar reported conditions were: (1) the experimenter and subject were not sitting at a desk, but around a small low smoking stand, the experimenter in a rather standard armchair, the subject in a deep pink sponge armchair of a most avant-garde tub-design (part of the furniture for all 1971 conditions); (2) the experimenter did not leave the subject alone during the usual fifteen minutes solitary preparation phase, for the simple reason that she did not want to meet anybody in the lab while wearing her experimental attire. These two alterations were also introduced—for control purposes—in the normal dress, pro-attitudinal mere creativity condition.

We would like to emphasize the fact that we would refuse to label the above described "dissonant" dress manipulation as a mere sexual arousal condition. This would not only be a theoretically irrelevant but also an unwarranted interpretational definition. Since Schachter's pioneering work (1959, 1971) on the social determinants of emotional states, we should be aware of the fact that the subject who finds himself under the complex circumstances described, confronted with our "dissonant" treatment, must have problems in labelling the emotional arousal experienced. "Embarrassment" is the label the experimenter advances if asked to use one term to describe the subject's emotional expressions. For us, the problem is not crucial since we have reasons to consider the manipulation as "dissonant" and unrelated to the exam-attitude at issue.

Debriefing The fact that we discontinued detailed information on the debriefing should not lead the reader to believe that this very important scientific and ethical part of the experiment was neglected. In view of our planned study of the persistency of the attitude change over time (for both the 1969 and 1971 programmes), the main imperatives of our provisional debriefing were still that the student left the experimenter's office (1) understanding the reasons for and reconciled with the rationale of the treatment; (2) unaware of our central scientific focus on the problem of attitude change; (3) guaranteed of the anonimity of his cooperation which served only a fundamental research purpose (with *ad hoc* plausible presentation of one of the possible problems which could in fact be studied with his data), and (4) formally committed to secrecy for reasons made once more very explicit. We cannot refrain from stressing again the fact that the Science student subjects were truly remarkable for their understanding of our research imperatives. It also can be taken for

F

granted that the final phase of the experimenter-subject interaction was an instance of (mutual) positive reinforcement. We will come back to this later.

RESULTS AND DISCUSSION

The data for Experiment Eleven are displayed in Table 18.

Although the design used does not meet all requirements for a classical 2 × 3 design, our interpretational goals can usefully be served by an analysis of variance which takes into account the variance of the two not-"dissonant" control conditions (baseline excepted).

The overall data of Experiment Eleven offer a remarkable and powerful basis for narrowing down the interpretational frame in which the phenomenon under study should provide better understanding.

TABLE 18

Mean attitude response towards the traditional exam system as a function of persuasive and attitudinal nature of the task performed under "dissonant" stimuli (hot-pants or blame)

Peformance	"Dissonant" stimuli (dress or blame)		Not "dissonant" stimuli (normal dress)	
	Advocacy	Verbal Creativity	Advocacy	Verbal Creativity
Counterattitudinal	7.0 (dress) (blame)	7.2 (dress) (dress)	4.3	
Pro-attitudinal	1.9	1.8		4.5

Note. Baseline mean is 2.5.

TABLE 19

Analysis of variance for data of Table 18 (without baseline)

Source	SS	df	MS	F
Between treatments	301.17	5	60.23	16.20†
Attitudinal (A)	300.76	2	150.38	40.45*
Persuasion (P)	0.14	1	0.14	
A × P	0.27	2	0.14	
Within treatments	223.09	60		
Total	524.26	65		

* $p < 0.005$
† $p < 0.01$

The analysis shows there is no difference at all between the effects obtained under persuasive advocacy and mere verbal creativity or productivity conditions. Moreover, the "dissonant" treatment for *both* the pro- and counterattitudinal performances has a highly significant effect upon the attitude response in the direction of the advocacy or verbal performance. The differences between the combined "dissonant" counterattitudinal and the combined not-"dissonant" control conditions (7.0 and 7.2 v. 4.3 and 4.5) is significant at the 0.001 level ($t = 4.16$). The same two control conditions equally differ at the 0.001 level ($t = 4.58$) from the two pro-attitudinal performance "dissonant" treatment conditions (1.9 and 1.8), the effect being so strong that the latter means are almost significantly more extreme than the already very extreme attitude responses of the combined 1969 and 1971 baseline conditions (for 1.9 and 1.8 v. 2.3 and 2.5, $t = 1.44$; $0.05 < p < 0.10$; one-tailed).

Let us now briefly confront these data with the various theoretical considerations which guided us in the progressive realization of the above design. As said before, this was not an heuristic simultaneous design, but a sequence of various steps for each of which predictions were formulated by the author while at Dartmouth and confirmed by research executed in Leuven by our experimenter Annie Beckers who, by intention, had accepted not to be informed about these predictions and the precise hypothetical infrastructure of the various strategic moves.

It will be remembered that we started Experiment Eleven with the simultaneous running of two counterattitudinal "dissonant" dress conditions, one advocacy and one mere creativity. The fact that the advocacy under "dissonant" dress treatment (7.0—different at the 0.05 level ($t = 2.49$) from the 4.3 control condition which was used in Experiment Ten) produced an almost identical effect as the advocacy "dissonant" blame condition of the previous experiment (7.5)—run a few days earlier (together with the 1971 baseline)—increased our confidence that the "dissonant" blame and rescue exam points effects were not due to the possibility that these treatments in one or another way could be seen as interacting with the issue of the attitude used for the study. One could have argued that the student evidenced a much less extreme attitude, because this might be instrumental in restoring the inequity produced by the experimenter giving him extra exam points or severely blaming him a few weeks before an important exam situation, but it is now very unlikely that the "dissonant" dress treatment would produce a similar effect via dynamics of that kind.

The effects obtained under advocacy and mere creativity conditions (7.0 and 7.2) offer an important confirmation of our increasing convictions concerning the basic nature of the underlying processes. To begin with, it does not seem anymore rewarding to search for interpretations which refer to concepts such as "commitment", "threatened self-esteem" and/or "perceived aversive social consequences". Further, a probably even more important conclusion was that the previously discussed analogy with persuasive communication research—which suggested the cognitive self-persuasion conceptual framework—no longer appeared useful.

As a matter of fact, if for example, impaired counterargumentation were the key notion to explain "enhanced self-persuasion" one would not expect an equally strong effect in the mere verbal productivity condition where the subject had no incentive whatsoever to counterargue since he was not invited to defend a strong position but merely had to show off the productivity of his verbal repertoire.

It is not that the results obtained under mere creativity conditions induce us to abandon the comparison with social communication studies, but rather that the results recommend the intriguing possibility that some persuasive communication research might economize its interpretational efforts by simply "de-socializing" the research-paradigms used.

The interpretation of the impressive effect obtained under counterattitudinal mere creativity "dissonant" treatment (7.2) is further narrowed down by the chronologically next set of creativity conditions run, viz., the pro-attitudinal "dissonant" (1.8) and normal (4.5) dress. The differences are clearly very large ($t = 4.86$; $< p\ 0.001$) and the reader should fully realize how powerful these data are. In each of the three conditions under comparison, the experimenter and subject are sitting around the small smoking stand, and the subject is showing off his verbal creativity and productivity for his teacher who is studying verbal output problems. While the experimenter is sitting in front of him during the full performance—fifteen minutes of silent paper and pencil preparation, followed by dictating the product of his thinking in the microphone and then carefully listening once again to the recording—there are only two factors which systematically differ: dress of the experimenter and pro- or counterattitudinal restraints put upon the verbal creativity exercise.

When the experimenter wears a normal dress and the student produces anti-traditional exam statements, the subsequent attitude change response is 4.5 which is by no means different from the various pro-attitudinal public advocacy conditions of our 1969 programme. If how-ever, the experimenter is wearing a "dissonant" attire, while the subject produces the same kind of anti-traditional exam statements (the quality of the products analyzed by blind analysis, fails to reveal any consistent differences) his attitude response (1.8) becomes even more extreme anti-traditional exam system than in the baseline condition (2.5); if the restraint is to only talk pro-traditional exam, the "dissonant" dress results in a significant attitude change in the pro-traditional exam direction (7.2). The three conditions under consideration do not leave any doubt about the clarity of the effect: for 7.2 v. 4.5, $t = 3.51$, $p < 0.01$; for 1.8 v. 4.5, $t = 4.86$, $p < 0.001$ (see also Table 20).

TABLE 20

Distribution of attitude responses towards the traditional exam system for the three verbal creativity conditions of Experiment Eleven

Verbal Creativity Conditions	Attitude Responses						
	very strongly anti	strongly anti	rather anti	anti	neutral	rather pro	pro
Normal dress pro-att.	—	5	6	—	—	—	—
"Dissonant" dress pro-att.	8	3	—	—	—	—	—
"Dissonant" dress counteratt.	—	1	3	3	3	1	—

Obviously then, these effects produced by the "dissonant" dress treat-ment in a mere verbal productivity situation, seem to corroborate the evaluative response contagion hypothesis, and invalidate the "social desirability" hypothesis, the experimenter not being committed to exam reform research but to the study of verbal productivity problems. Since it is difficult to consider the mere verbal productivity as instances of per-suasive advocacy, the effect amounts basically then to an increased similarity between the evaluative characteristics of the attitude response and the immediately preceding verbal responses produced under the "dissonant" dress treatments.

The phenomenon seems to be pretty well under control. It suffices to have the subject emit during some time a certain kind (pro or contra) of attitude related evaluative verbal behaviour, to expose him to the "dissonant" stimuli and to tap the attitude response. The observed effect is that the latter becomes more similar to the prevailing evaluative characteristics of the former ongoing responses.

As a last check on the reliability of this evaluative response contagion effect, John Lanzetta, who shared our excitement about the increasing predictability of the phenomenon, urged us to cable instructions for a *pro-attitudinal* replication of the crucial "dissonant" blame condition of Experiment Ten. A few days later the 1.9 mean attitude response not only did confirm our predictions, but also corroborated our confidence in the fundamental nature of the effect: notwithstanding the fact that the student was being severely blamed by the person who would take his psychology exam only a very few weeks later, the attitude responses emitted were frankly and extremely in the anti-traditional exam direction (for 1.9 v. 4.3, $t = 2.42$, $p < 0.05$; for 7 v. 4.3, $t = 2.49$, $p < 0.05$). "Dissonant" blame and "dissonant" dress clearly had a similar effect, whose direction was only determined by the evaluative nature of the immediately preceding ongoing verbal behaviour.

We would like to point to another implication which the data of the present experiment seem to have, viz., with regard to the relative unimportance of the precise moment in the experimental sequence at which the "dissonant" treatment is administered. It will indeed be noted that, for example, in contrast with the blame condition, the subject of the "dissonant" dress manipulation is exposed to this crucial environmental feature from the very first moment of his interaction with the experimenter, i.e., before he had any information concerning the nature of the task. It will be remembered that in all experiments of our 1969 programme the "subject" only was informed about the monetary reward just before he could take a decision to comply and that the reward was administered before he started the preparation of his advocacy. All other non-monetary "dissonant" treatments were also applied only after the student was informed about the nature of his experimental task, except for the one condition in which the "dissonant" exam rescue points were given immediately after the advocacy. Although the difference between the latter, before—and—after advocacy treatment, could suggest that the intensity of the effect is a function of some characteristics of the temporal contiguity between the attitude related verbal behaviour and the "dissonant" stimuli, there does not seem to be any decisive temporal constraint, as long of course as the "dissonant" treatment precedes the tapping of the attitude response. Clearly this temporal aspect is one of many instances which is in need of further research.

Finally, it should be noted that our evaluative response contagion hypothesis implies not only that the "dissonant" treatment effect precedes the attitude response but also that the latter is emitted in rather close temporal contiguity with the preceding attitude related verbal behaviour. A rough but valid test of this aspect of our interpretation will be made in Chapter Four, where the results will be analyzed for the "dissonant" dress, counterattitudinal creativity exercise condition for which the attitude response was only elicited five weeks after the dissonant treatment.

Conclusion of Chapter Three

The experiments presented in this chapter (1970 and 1971 research) not only provide a powerful substantiation of the "dissonant" reward effects discussed in the previous chapter but also lead to considerable progress in the elimination of various interpretational alternatives. Let us briefly recapitulate the impressive chain of attitude change effects in the advocated direction which were obtained when our subjects, exposed to various "dissonant" treatments, had produced their *counter*attitudinal argumentation: low reward for TV and radio advocacy 6.1 and 6.6; relative deprivation for public and private advocacy 7.1 and 7.1; highly appreciated illegitimate reward before 9.5 and after 7.4 advocacy; strong aversive stimulus before advocacy 7.5; embarrassing dress during advocacy 7.0 and during mere verbal creativity exercise 7.2; when exposed to an identical a-cognitive "dissonant" treatment while producing *pro*-attitudinal evaluative statements, the attitude change was equally strong but in the pro-attitudinal direction: advocacy under "dissonant" aversive stimuli 1.9 and mere verbal productivity under "dissonant" dress 1.8.

Our progressive conceptual analysis of the above listed effects, reproduced under the most diverse "dissonant" circumstances while using appropriate control devices, does not seem to support an interpretation based on such concepts as cognitive dissonance or consistency, reward, incentive, commitment, aversive social consequences, threatened self-esteem, perceived decision freedom, evaluation apprehension, social desirability, impaired counterargumentation or emotional facilitation or self-persuasion.

The "dissonant" dress effects obtained under both pro- and counter-attitudinal mere verbal productivity conditions, corroborate an evaluative response contagion hypothesis which is offered as an explanation for the observed enhanced similarity between the prevailing evaluative characteristics of the most recent ongoing verbal responses and the subsequently emitted attitude response. This response contagion effect is conceived as being determined by the peculiarly arousing nature of the strange, novel, embarrassing or "dissonant" stimuli which precede the attitude response and which enhance the relative dominance and the impact of the most recent ongoing responses upon the immediately subsequent attitude response.

4

The Illusion of Post-advocacy Attitude Change: an Evaluative Response Contagion View of Persuasion*

As said before, the underlying response contagion process and the peculiarly arousing role played by "dissonant" stimuli are in need of theoretical and empirical consolidation by experimental psychologists studying fundamental response chaining and/or response generalization phenomena. It seems to us that our primary concern as social psychologists should be to substantiate the theoretically and practically very consequential position which is being taken when we propose to deal with complex attitude change phenomena by using a *mere evaluative verbal response paradigm.* In this last chapter an effort will be made to demonstrate the plausibility of this paradigm and of an evaluative response contagion interpretation of the observed "attitude change" effects. In a first section we will study the long term persistency of these effects. It will soon become clear that we are not taking irrelevant bypaths: the analysis of the persistency data obtained for our 1969 and 1971 research not only will corroborate our theoretical position with regard to our own experimental data, but hopefully will lead to a fundamental new approach for the understanding—and shaping—of what traditionally are called "social attitudes".

* First presented as an invited lecture at the Annual Convention of the American Psychological Association, Honolulu, September 1972.

157

1. Enduring attitude change versus stability of a changed attitude response

Experiment Twelve: Enduring attitude change five weeks later? (1969)

PROBLEM

Our 1969 research, in which various monetary rewards were given for public and private, counter- or pro-attitudinal advocacy, was conducted in such a way that the provisional debriefing did not jeopardize an assessment of the persistency of the attitude change effects obtained. Before leaving the laboratory, the students answered some fifteen post-experimental ratings and also received a plausible explanation for the full pseudo- and experimental treatments which made them believe that the choice of the exam-attitude issue was made on a rather arbitrary basis and that the research was not focusing on the problem of attitude change. The rationale given for tapping the attitude response was simply that it might be worthwhile to know what the position of the individual student was, since this might correlate with the experienced difficulty of the experimental tasks.

At that time, our main incentive for gathering persistency data was the striking scarcity of such evidence in the cognitive dissonance literature. We knew of no studies in the area of post-advocacy research and only the Aronson and Carlsmith (1963) and Freedman (1965) research on the effects of sufficient and insufficient threat of punishment upon dissonance reduction, which we in vain tried to replicate (Mertens, 1967; Cré, 1970), have examined long term persistency of attitude change effects.

Besides the heuristic value of the study of persistency of attitude change effects, there was also a theoretical reason which is generally overlooked. Although never explicitly stated, the cognitive dissonance view implies that attitude change, resulting from dissonance reduction after "forced compliance", ought to be a quite temporary and unstable restoration of a cognitive equilibrium. Not only is the attitude change usually too small by far to achieve consonance between attitude and counterattitudinal behaviour, but more important, the change in the least resistant cognitive element—the one concerning the attitude—is bound to lead to new or increasingly dissonant cognitive relations (e.g. with the various cognitive elements which were consonant with the initial attitude position). Since the experimental verification of the cognitive dissonance hypothesis implies that the cognitive element concerning the attitude is among the least, if not the least, resistant to change, one has to expect then that the consonance restoring attitude change would be a quite vulnerable and transitory phenomenon with questionable utility for a theory of "enduring attitude change". These were the main reasons we had in 1969 for studying persistency data after a relatively large time interval.

PROCEDURE

Despite various efforts to obtain attitude responses from the same subjects in a situation which would have a minimum of common elements with the laboratory situation in which the first attitude response was emitted, we finally had to have recourse to a rather unsophisticated procedure which might, in the eyes of some critics, be insufficiently protected against contamination. It should however be stressed that we were not interested in the long term effect of our experimental manipulation upon attitude *related* behaviour emitted in more complex situations. Our endeavour was indeed very modest and restricted to the following question: will there be a significant relation between the crucial attitude ratings obtained immediately after the various advocacy treatments and the attitude responses emitted by the same individuals after an average interval of five weeks?

To achieve this, each subject of our 1969 conditions, while with his family during the Easter vacation, received at his home address a letter, mailed on April 3rd 1969, signed by the experimenter (referring to herself as an assistant of the author) in which essentially the following was said:

> Dear Sir, A few weeks ago we were fortunate to have your cooperation in the Research Centre of Professor J. M. Nuttin. I want to thank you once more for your highly appreciated help. As promised, Professor Nuttin will send you around May 15th a brief report on all studies run. While analyzing our data, it occurred to us that it might be very useful to obtain a few more items of information from you. Since I should finish the analysis of the research done so far before the end of Easter vacation, I dare bother you now with the very short enclosed questionnaire. It would be appreciated if you were willing to give a spontaneous and sincere answer to the questions asked, without attempting to remember whatever answers you might have given a few weeks ago. We are only interested in the opinion you have right now when you answer the questionnaire. We urge you to do this on a strict individual basis, without discussing the issue with others*. Enclosed you will

---

* Since the students were not on campus, the chances were very small that they would feel tempted to search out the opinions of other students. Also it will be remembered that the subjects were committed not to discuss the experiments before May 15th, until the reception of a clearance letter from the author.

find a prepared envelope. It really does not take more than a couple of minutes to pay us a highly appreciated service. Please do so right now. With most sincere thanks.

On a separate sheet (with code number for identification purposes), the crucial exam-attitude rating was presented and defined as during the experiments proper, besides three filler questions. Once more, the formulation stressed that we were not interested in how the student felt a few weeks ago, but in his opinion right now. It will be remembered that the exam reform attitude rating used in the laboratory was not mimeographed but hastily written down by the experimenter on the scratch paper the student had used for the preparation of his plea.

RESULTS AND DISCUSSION

Out of the 143 subjects who participated in the thirteen conditions of our 1969 programme, only 4 did not return the questionnaire, one from each of the following conditions: pro-attitudinal radio, zero BF and 20 BF, counterattitudinal private and TV both 20 BF*. For the time being, we will restrict ourselves to the persistency data for eleven of the twelve thus-far discussed conditions. The persistency data for our 1969 baseline condition, which are not strictly comparable for reasons to be explained later on, will be discussed at the end of the present section. The persistency data of a thirteenth 1969 condition, to which until now no reference was made, are included with the other 1969 conditions: this "unrestricted or free advocacy" condition was identical to the private pro- or counterattitudinal advocacy treatments (no reward) except for the fact that no pro- or contra exam reform restraints were put on the advocacy: the student was completely free in his choice of pro and/or contra arguments.

In Fig. 2 (p. 160) the average attitude responses are compared for the 1969 (except baseline) conditions, obtained with an average interval of five weeks. Although one can see in all conditions a change in the direction of the pre-experimental attitude position, the difference between the

* We will not speculate about the fact that three of the four "refusals (?) or missing answers" belonged to 20 BF conditions, nor about the circumstance that it was precisely one of the only two students whose attitude response did not seem to be affected by the "dissonant" TV treatment who did not reply (scoring very strongly anti, four categories below the next negative answer). Exactly the same happened with the only "very strongly anti" student of the counterattitudinal private 20 BF advocacy condition. No doubt there is room for a personality and differential psychology approach to the problems under study. It will hopefully be accepted that this is beyond the scope of the present monograph.

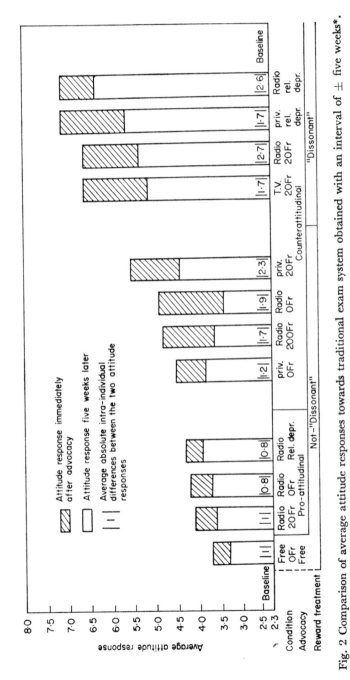

Fig. 2 Comparison of average attitude responses towards traditional exam system obtained with an interval of ± five weeks*.

*The minor differences in the average score of the first attitude responses are due to the loss of four subjects for whom no second attitude response was available.

baseline attitude responses (2.3) and the ones emitted in the second rating
continues to be large. The fact that for the TV and the counterattitudinal
radio conditions the interval was close to *ten weeks*, indicates the remarkable stability of the attitude change obtained after the "dissonant" treatments. The sequential designs used do not allow for a more detailed
analysis in terms of length of the interval between the two ratings. It
might however be worthwhile noticing that the variability of the intra-
individual differences within conditions was quite small. The absolute
differences between the attitude responses emitted by the same individuals can be summarized as follows: an average of 0.9 for the four pro-
attitudinal conditions; 1.8 for the four not-"dissonant" and 2.2 for the
four "dissonant" counterattitudinal conditions. The average attitude
change scores (taking into account the direction of the change) are −0.5
for the four pro-attitudinal conditions, −1.1 for the four not-dissonant
and −1.3 for the four "dissonant" counterattitudinal conditions. The
overall correlation between the first and second attitude response emitted
by each of the subjects is 0.60 which is significant at the 0.01 level
($N = 128$). For our present purposes it does not seem worthwhile to
analyze these data in any further detail.

CONCLUSION

The long term (average of five weeks) persistency of the attitude change
effects is quite impressive, especially taking into account that all these
changes are in the direction away from the pre-experimental baseline
position, and that the Easter vacation is for most students a period of
hard preparatory work for the imminent exam session. We would however like to stress one very important restraint which, because of the
design, is put upon any interpretation of the above data, and which most
social psychologists and social engineers seem to have neglected alto-
gether. It would be tempting indeed to conclude that counterattitudinal
advocacy under "dissonant" treatment has *by itself* a rather large and
enduring effect upon well entrenched and important social attitudes.
However, the absence of a control condition whose necessity is easily
overlooked, makes such an inference unwarranted. The design does not
permit one to distinguish between two conceptually quite different
phenomena, "enduring attitude change" and "stability over time of a
changed attitude response". The sole conclusion which can be drawn
from these results is that there is a relationship between the evaluative
characteristics of the attitude responses emitted immediately after the

experimental treatment and those emitted several weeks later. However, the design employed in our later research does permit an indirect test of whether the response changes obtained reflect "enduring attitude change" or "long lasting stability (or resistance to change) of a *changed* attitude *response*" and we turn now to consideration of these data.

Experiment Thirteen: Stability of a changed attitude response five weeks later? (1971)

PROBLEM

Our 1971 persistency research* was designed in such a way that it should allow us to draw some conclusions with regard to the above formulated alternative of "enduring attitude change" versus "stability of a changed attitude response". It will be remembered that during the 1971 spring period two "dissonant" dress (hot-pants) counterattitudinal, verbal creativity conditions were run which only differed by the fact that in one of them the usual attitude response was not tapped immediately after the advocacy, but some five weeks later (the *"delayed first attitude response condition"*) whereas for the other condition the attitude response was immediately after the advocacy as well as some five weeks later.

The value of the "delayed" condition as an indirect test of the validity of our evaluative response contagion hypothesis is obvious: on the basis of our 1969 persistency data we can expect that the (second) attitude response obtained in the "dissonant" dress condition will remain significantly different from the baseline after a five weeks period. If then the otherwise identical but *delayed* attitude response condition also results in a significant long term effect, it would become almost impossible to maintain our evaluative response contagion interpretation of attitude change. How could an increase in arousal enhance the relative dominance and the impact of the most recent ongoing responses upon an attitude response emitted for the first time five weeks later? Such persistency of an arousal effect would be extremely unlikely and changes in the attitude responses obtained in the "delayed" condition could thus not reasonably be attributed to response contagion.

It should be noted that we are not saying that the absence of an effect in the delayed response condition would prove in any definitive way the validity of our interpretation but it certainly would, together with other

* No persistency data were gathered for the experiments run in 1970.

evidence, corroborate it whereas the opposite result would invalidate our interpretation and support the position that the treatment affected in one or another way the cognitive, affective and/or conative dimensions of the underlying attitude system (e.g., via some form of self-persuasion) so that the symptoms of this enduring attitude change still can be made manifest five weeks later.

PROCEDURE

Our first point of concern was to obtain persistency data which would be minimally biased by contaminating factors. The contamination problem is not solved by assessing in a disguised manner, various "real life" attitude related forms of behaviour. This commonly held belief is simply an obstinate misconception—leading to quite a few theoretical and practical wrong decisions—by people who are obviously not aware of the important conceptual difference between attitude responses (whose evaluative characteristics ideally should not be affected at all by the situation in which the response is being emitted, see below p. 187: "a situation-free evaluative response") and attitude *related* "overt" behaviours which are a function of more complex antecedents than the attitude *per se*. We believe we were successful by adopting the procedural changes described below.

"Laboratory" versus "Field" setting Once again use was made of a macro-situational feature which might be so unique to the Louvain situation that some background information is in order. At the City of Louvain (Leuven) there are two universities that recently became fully inde-pendent: the "Université Catholique de Louvain" (UCL, French speak--ing) and the "Katholieke Universiteit Leuven" (KUL, Dutch speaking). In the late sixties, long lasting conflicts led to the political decision that the UCL would be transferred to a new campus (Louvain-la-Neuve), some 20 miles distance from Leuven in the Walloon (French speaking and culturally autonomous) part of the country, whereas the KUL would stay in Leuven which is in the Flemish, and also culturally autonomous, northern part of Belgium. The fact that the transfer is planned over a ten year period, means that at the time of our 1971 research the two univer-sities were still sharing the same buildings and facilities. It should be noted that ever since the political decision was taken by the government (in 1968), not a single Walloon-Flemish student riot has taken place and that students of both universities were and still are, joining forces in public

(bilingual) manifestations or riots related to the almost universal repertoire of student-revolt topics. This is relevant because, as will become clear in a moment, it is important that we can take for granted that the subjects used in our 1971 research are not likely to manifest a negative attitude towards a research programme undertaken by the UCL, and especially not if they are accosted by an African Negro student who, after trying out a couple of sentences in Dutch, apologizes for not being able to speak the language of the subject. The important point is indeed that African Negro students who come to Belgium are typically French speaking so that no Negro students are enrolled at the undergraduate level in the Flemish university, and only very exceptionally at the doctoral level, but this safely can be considered to be unnoticed by the student pool of our research.

We were fortunate in gaining the cooperation of Dr. Celestin Kabundi, a Negro post-doctoral student from Zaire (the former République du Congo) enrolled at the UCL, which enabled us to confront what we call a "Field" approach with the usual (1969) "Laboratory" approach of the persistency problem*. It will be remembered that our 1971 experimentation period finished a few days before the exam preparation period ($\pm$ 3 weeks) started. In the midst of the exam period (an average of four weeks after the experiments), Dr. Kabundi visited "his" subjects individually in their rooms. The subgrouping between "Field" and "Laboratory" approach was done within each 1971 experimental condition, matching for "first" attitude response (except of course for the "delayed response condition"). Dr. Kabundi was given those students whose study rooms were located as far as possible from one another, so that the subjects would not notice that "another fellow Science student" also received a visit from a Negro sociologist†.

After having excused himself, both for not speaking the subject's native language (which he did while making an effort to speak Dutch) and especially for interrupting the student who was in his most busy exam time, he asked for a ten minute interview on the quite salient topic of the use of drugs (stimulants and/or tranquillizers) during the exam session. He explained (in French) that he was preparing a Ph.D. in medical sociology at the UCL, and that he also had planned to include a random

---

* Dr. Celestin Kabundi is herewith thanked for the dedication and competence which he manifested in his highly valued cooperation with the research-project.
† Various post-experimental probings from Dr. Beckers with Dr. Kabundi's subjects offered ample guarantee for the success of the disguise used.

sample of Flemish students for comparison purposes. As a rule the subjects were quite interested in the opportunity to talk to somebody who presumably was an expert in the effects of such widespread exam drugs, so that our interviewer, who had prepared himself in order to be able to give valid information to the students, often had to excuse himself for not being able to spend more time with his friendly and quite cooperative host. The standardized interview was centred around three (Dutch) ratings, none of which were identical to the crucial question asked during the experimental treatment proper, for reasons which will become clear later on: (1) What is according to you the percentage of Flemish students from your Faculty who take drugs during the exam period? (2) What about your own behaviour in this respect? (anonymity was guaranteed); (3) Survey data have shown that the use of exam drugs was very much lower ten years ago. To what factors do you attribute this increase?

The latter question invariably led the student to talk about the sizable aggravation of the study-material and the stressing features of the exam system. Dr. Kabundi, following his interview schedule on *ad hoc* protocols (mimeographed on green paper, a colour "never" used in the social psychology lab) thus quite naturally came to an exam attitude *related* question which read: "*How desirable would be, according to you, a return to the exam regulation of ten years ago, when among other things, all exams were taken in a one week period?*". The subject could then express his opinion on an eleven point (Dutch) rating going from "very desirable" to "not desirable at all". We will call this the "*Field interview, attitude related rating*".

After having enquired about the end of the exam period for the student and where he could be reached if more information was needed, the student was thanked for his cooperation and left with his busy work.

Since the exam period ends at approximately identical dates for all subjects involved in the study, it was not difficult to send to their home address, either a "laboratory" or a "field" paper and pencil persistency questionnaire. For the "Field approach", this was a letter, mimeographed on green paper, with the appropriate stationary reference of Dr. Kabundi (in French) and with a Dutch translation of essentially the following: "Dear Friend, I am the Congolese student who dared to bother you during your exam period. I want to thank you once again for your highly appreciated collaboration in my study on the use of drugs during the exam period. Since you must have terminated your exams by now, and be informed about the results, I take the liberty of asking you a few short questions which are especially useful for my work". Then five questions follow, the student is reassured of the anonymity of his answers, invited to give any further comments he might have on the drug problem and thanked once more for the enjoyed hospitality which is appreciated "as an instance of a promising cooperation between a Flemish and a Congolese student".

It might be worthwhile to point to the disguising nature of the quite plausible questions asked: (1) "Did you succeed in your first exam session?" (2) "Do you have exam exemptions for September? How many?"* (3) "Did you use drugs (tranquillizers or stimulants) during the exam period proper?" (4) "In case you did use drugs, do you think or suspect that this might have influenced your exam results? Please check off with an x one of the points along the vertical line which expresses best your own opinion." (Follows a vertical—in contrast to the horizontal ratings used in the 1971 laboratory experiments—eleven point rating labelled from "very large influence" to "no influence at all". (5) The last question, which for our purpose is called the *"Field attitude response"* is a close approximation to the ratings used immediately after the experimental treatment and reads as follows:

"Are you happy with the current exam system or do you prefer a return to the former exam regulation, in which all exams were taken during a one week period and no exam exemptions were given for September". Another vertical 17 point rating is labelled "I am very strongly against the former exam system, against, rather against, indifferent, rather in favour, in favour, strongly in favour, very strongly in favour"†.

As said, the subject was invited to freely comment upon the answers given. An enclosed (green) envelope was prepared for mailing the questionnaire to the real private address of Dr. Kabundi, which happened to be situated in the street of the well-known University Medical Hospital.

The "laboratory" approach persistency letter was a close replication of the 1969 letter, with some obvious modifications as far as filler questions are concerned. Besides the crucial attitude response rating the student was asked how happy he felt about his concrete exam schedule of the past session, whereas the third and last question was a replication of the "field interview attitude *related* rating" which Dr. Kabundi had used in his

---

* This can for obvious reasons be perceived as an indication of the intensity of the failure.
† The standard laboratory rating was labelled: "very strongly *anti* the traditional exam system, *neutral*, and *pro* . . .".

preparatory interviews. Needless to say that no information was asked about the use of drugs nor about exam results. As said before, the crucial attitude rating was identical to the one used in the 1969 persistency research and, except for being mimeographed, a replication of the rating around which all the experiments reported in Chapter Two and Three were concentrated. Both the "Field" and "Laboratory" persistency questionnaires were mailed simultaneously.

Design

Because of the temporal constraints within which Dr. Kabundi had to visit his subjects, it was decided to restrict ourselves to the following six 1971 conditions:
(1) *Pro*-attitudinal: "*dissonant*" blame, advocacy and "dissonant" dress, mere verbal creativity; (2) *Counter*attitudinal: "*dissonant*" blame and dress, both advocacy and "dissonant" dress, mere verbal creativity; (3) Counterattitudinal "dissonant" dress, mere verbal creativity, *delayed attitude response*. In each condition the "Field" or "Laboratory" assessment of long term effects was randomly given to either five or six of the eleven subjects, taking into account the above described criteria.

In view of the obvious reduction of number of subjects due to the "Field" v. "Laboratory" comparison and the fact that the evaluative response contagion effect throughout our 1971 experiments only seemed to be a function of the pro- or counterattitudinal nature of the advocacy or verbal creativity exercise, the various "dissonant" treatments will be pooled within the pro- or counterattitudinal conditions.

We have then a 2 × 2 design, namely the "Field" versus "Laboratory" approach for both the pro- and counterattitudinal "dissonant" treatments. In addition there is the delayed attitude response condition which is crucial for the theoretical interpretation of the persistency phenomenon. For the latter condition, 5 data were gathered under "Field" and 6 under "Laboratory" approach.

RESULTS AND DISCUSSION

First we will present and discuss the data which are directly related to the rationale of our "Field" v. "Laboratory" comparison. The *delayed attitude response* data whose validity clearly is contingent upon the answer given to the former methodological issue, will be presented and discussed afterwards.

The data for our 1971 persistency research (except for delayed attitude response condition) are presented in Table 21.

TABLE 21

Persistency (over 4 to 8 weeks) of 1971 attitude responses towards the traditional exam system for pro- and counterattitudinal "dissonant" treatments as a function of "field" or "laboratory" approach

Pooled "dissonant" 1971 conditions	"Laboratory" approach average attitude response		change	intra-ind. absol. change	"Field" approach average attitude response		change	intra-ind. absol. change
	First	Second			First	Second		
Counterattitudinal (N = 33)	7.0	5.8	−1.2	1.5 (N = 18)	7.6	6.6	−1.0	2.0 (N = 15)
Pro-attitudinal (N = 22)	2.0	2.9	+0.9	1.1 (N = 10)	1.8	2.8	+1.0	1.3 (N = 12)

Note. The 1971 baseline mean is 2·5.

What can we learn from these data? When looking at the average first attitude responses (all emitted in the laboratory) we can feel rather comfortable that the subjects submitted to the "Laboratory" versus "Field" approach for the persistency data, as a result of our matching effort, do have quite comparable average initial attitude responses (7 v. 7.6 and 2 v. 1.8).

With regard to the methodological issue which induced us to realize a more contamination free "Field" approach for the assessment of the second attitude response, the data offered reassuring evidence for the validity or comparability of the second attitude responses given on an almost identical attitude rating scale under otherwise quite different "research settings", viz., the former experimenter and examiner towards whom response-consistency might be motivated by various kinds of social needs, versus the foreign exam-drug researcher to whom no commitment concerning the attitude issue was made in the form of the crucial attitude rating. Both the intra-individual relative and absolute change scores for "Laboratory" versus "Field" approach are very similar (−1.2 v. −1; +0.9 v. +1; 1.5 v. 2 and 1.1 v. 1.3). The only point worth mentioning is that the average absolute change is somewhat—although not significantly —larger in the "Field" approach, which could indeed be considered as a very weak indication of diminished stability of the attitude response in conditions where the attitude is tapped by two totally unrelated re-searchers. So far we have examined the methodological problem of the possibly artifactual nature of the correlation between the two attitude responses emitted withan interval of several weeks.

Given the above confidence in the validity of our persistency data, we can now return to the theoretically much more exciting problem—at least in the development of our own research—concerning the "enduring attitude change" versus "stability of a changed attitude response" issue. The important test which our research design enables us to make in this respect, is of course, the comparison between the two 1971 "dissonant" dress, counterattitudinal mere verbal creativity conditions, which only differ in so far that in one condition it was in fact the second time that the same attitude response was tapped, whereas in the other, *delayed first* attitude response condition, the subject's attitude was assessed for the first time five weeks after the treatment, since no rating had been given during the experimental session in the laboratory.

The data for this comparison are so remarkable that we cannot refrain from displaying in Table 22 the individual responses for both conditions.

Taking into account the apparent validity of the persistency responses tapped approximately five weeks after the "dissonant" treatment, the data

TABLE 22

Individual attitude responses towards the traditional exam system five weeks after the "dissonant" dress counterattitudinal mere verbal creativity treatment as a function of temporal contiguity of first attitude response with the immediately preceding attitude related verbal responses

Attitude responses 5 weeks after treatment	Attitude Rating Scale										
	1	2	3	4	5	6	7	8	9	10	11
Second response				×							×
				×	+		×				+
				+	+		+	×			+
Delayed first response	+	+	+	×							
	+	+	×								
	×	×									
	×	×									

+ = individual response assessed with "Laboratory" approach
× = individual response assessed with "Field" approach
Note. The 1971 baseline mean is 2.5; the average "dissonant" dress effect assessed in laboratory is 7.2.

of Table 22 strongly corroborate the plausibility of the evaluative response contagion interpretation of the "dissonant" stimuli effect and at the same time prevent us from misinterpreting our 1969 and 1971 persistency data.

There appears to be no trace of any attitude change effect in a situation where the attitude response was not emitted in close temporal contiguity with the ongoing counterattitudinal verbal responses (under "dissonant" treatment). The average attitude response five weeks later is 6.9 for the "second response condition" v. only 2.2 for the "delayed first response condition" (2.2 is not different from the 1969 (2.3) or 1971 (2.5) baseline conditions). The difference between 6.9 and 2.2 is highly significant ($t = 3.82; p < 0.01$). It is also clear from Table 22 that the "Laboratory" versus "Field" approach did not affect the evaluative characteristics of the delayed response data. It is apparent that the delayed first attitude response is *not* similar to the second attitude response emitted by the not-"dissonant" advocacy conditions, but almost identical to the *baseline* responses given by students who had not been previously invited to advocate in favour or against the traditional exam system.

Our "response contagion" interpretation for the "dissonant" treatment effects implies that the attitude response be elicited in close temporal contiguity with the evaluative verbal responses produced during the role playing (advocacy or mere creativity exercise). If the attitude response is not emitted within certain temporal constraints, there is indeed no possibility for evaluative contagion to spread to the latter response. *Only if emitted* (in the present example: elicited by the rating) is the response likely to be influenced by the evaluative characteristics of the preceding verbal productions. The above data are indeed completely in line with an evaluative response contagion view where contagion, which is conceived to be a direct function of the emotional arousal or disturbance produced by the "dissonant" treatment, is assumed to shape the evaluative characteristics of the response given on the attitude rating. It is then this *new* or *changed response* which, *once emitted*, becomes stabilized and relatively resistant to change.

CONCLUSION

Obviously we are faced with a phenomenon of *stability* (over time) *of a changed* evaluative verbal *response* instead of a process of enduring attitude change triggered off by the "dissonant" counter-, or pro-attitudinal advocacy. This is a very important conclusion with wide ranging theoretical and practical implications for the attitude change tactics used in much social psychological research. In essence, we are saying that it is *not* the "underlying organized and structured social attitude" towards the exam system which has been affected by the "dissonant" advocacy or verbal creativity treatment, but the evaluative loading of an *emitted* evaluative verbal *response* and that it is this particular changed response which has become stabilized. This conclusion not only corroborates the plausibility of our evaluative response contagion view, but also seems to seriously challenge the validity of quite a few theoretical and practical conclusions of the classical attitude change and persuasion literature, where the observed change in an attitude response is readily interpreted as *one among many testable symptoms of a change in an underlying system which itself was affected by the persuasive manipulation*, and where one seems not prepared to consider the possibility that the very assessment of the "attitude change"—by eliciting the "attitude" response(s)—might function as a crucial condition for "attitude" change to be produced. As a matter of fact, our "delayed first attitude response" treatment warrants the formulation of the following paradox: *attitude change tactics will only be effective provided that their effect has been assessed under appropriate conditions.* The very paradox however, implies such a drastic devaluation of the social attitude concept, that after its reduction to the mere evaluative verbal response level, it does not seem any longer to be a useful tool for the study of the phenomena which are traditionally called "social attitudes".

FURTHER DATA ILLUSTRATING THE RESISTANCE TO CHANGE OF A ONCE EMITTED ATTITUDE RESPONSE

The results reported above provide us with demonstration of the plausibility of our proposal to approach complex attitude change phenomena by using a *mere evaluative verbal response* paradigm. At the same time however, the long term persistency of a changed attitude *response* raises the problem of its remarkable stability or resistance to change. We frankly have to admit that we are not in a position to offer any compelling evidence for explaining this phenomenon. Some social psychologists reminded of the classical work of K. Lewin, might wish to refer to the notion of "commitment" to a publicly taken position (public here in the sense of "before an experimenter"). The striking similarity between the second attitude responses obtained in our Laboratory and Field approach, although not incompatible with a commitment explanation, would invite us to look for an interpretation which does not imply this rather complex process. Personally we prefer to point to the plausibility of a social reinforcement explanation. Although the behaviour of the experimenter was not contingent upon the particular evaluative characteristics of the attitude response emitted by the subject, the experimenter always remaining neutral when the latter response was emitted, one should not forget that the student was debriefed by the experimenter a very few minutes after having emitted his first attitude response. Taking into account the macro-situational features in which all experiments were imbedded, this might be seen as an instance of very strong social reinforcement: a quite friendly and attractive experimenter not only relieved the subject from the blame and other embarrassing "dissonant" features of the treatment, but also made a serious and presumably successful effort to establish a mutually rewarding social relationship with the individual student, who agreed to continue collaboration in her research project by pledging secrecy. As said before, we do not have control data for such a social reinforcement view as affecting the stability of the changed attitude response, but we believe the interpretation has high face validity.

We do however have some interesting data from our very first 1969 baseline condition which illustrate the remarkable resistance to change of a once emitted "attitude" response.

Let us first briefly supply the procedural information about the treatment of our 1969 baseline and free plea conditions to which we have already referred on various occasions. The subjects of the 1969 baseline condition, *after* having emitted their *first* attitude response towards the traditional exam system, were treated exactly in the same way as the subjects of the 1969 private anonymous advocacy condition (no reward), except for the fact that there were no pro- or contra restraints put on the attitudinal nature of the arguments. Their attitude response was tapped a *second* time, immediately after the advocacy, and a *third* time approximately one month later.

For our present purposes, it is especially useful to compare the stability or resistance to change of the attitude responses of the baseline condition with the data obtained in the "free advocacy" condition which was run simultaneously. The latter condition is identical to the former, except for the fact that no attitude response was elicited before the subject engaged in the free advocacy task. In order to increase the strength of the comparison, we will also display the data obtained for the next closest condition, viz. the 1969 private counterattitudinal advocacy no reward treatment.

To use well known learning theory concepts, we could say that the comparison allows us a very modest and rough enquiry of the resistance to change as a function of habit strength (other factors being kept constant), or as a function of previously emitted (and socially reinforced) verbal operants, or—in terms which sound familiar in the attitude change area—as a function of "commitment" to an already expressed attitude. Let us not bother about conceptual labels, but have a look at the data displayed in Table 23.

The long term stability of the attitude responses in the baseline condition is indeed remarkable. Only three subjects reveal a minor half a point change between their second rating in the laboratory and the one mailed several weeks later. In the other two conditions seven and eight

TABLE 23

Long term stability of attitude responses towards the traditional exam system as a function of number of previously emitted responses

Subjects	Baseline Conditions				1969 Private Anonymous Advocacy, No Reward					
					Free Advocacy			Counteratt. Advocacy		
	First	Second	Third	Change 2nd-3rd	First	Second	Change	First	Second	Change
A	1	1	1	0	1	1	0	1	4	+3
B	1	1	1	0	1	1	0	3	2	−1
C	1	1	1	0	2.5	3	+0.5	3	1	−2
D	1	1	1	0	3	2.5	−0.5	3	2	−1
E	2	4.5	4	−0.5	3.5	5	+1.5	4	4	0
F	2	2	2	0	4	5	+1	5	5	0
G	3	3	3	0	4	2.5	−1.5	5	3	−2
H	3	3	3	0	5	1	−4	5	5	0
I	3	5	5	0	5	3	−2	6	5	−1
J	4	3.5	3	−0.5	5	5	0	7	5	−2
K	4	4.5	4	−0.5	7	7	0	7	6	−1
Average	2.3	2.7	2.5	0.1	3.7	3.3	1	4.5	3.8	1.2
Number of Ss whose att. resp. remains unchanged 5 weeks later	8				4			3		

Note. The data are displayed with increasing order of first attitude response.

subjects do manifest a change. Not only more subjects change, but the changes are also more important as shown by the average change scores (0.1 v. 1 and 1.2).

It will also be noticed that the three baseline subjects who slightly changed their third attitude response (with respect to the second) had already given proof of instability with regard to their first attitude response (emitted immediately before the plea). Only one subject changed his second response and left it unchanged during the third assessment

(3, 5, 5). It seems as if again, inter-individual differences (fast versus slow "learners" ?) are at issue.

Although we do not have at our disposal an adequate control condition which is similar to the baseline condition except for the fact that no advocacy would be made in between the two responses, it does seem warranted to emphasize the important point that the free advocacy of the baseline condition did not affect the second attitude response in any marked way, although such was clearly the case in the "free advocacy" condition where no preliminary attitude response was elicited (the difference between 2.3 and 3.7 is significant at the 0.05 level ($t = 2.24$)). This indirectly confirms our view that a once emitted "attitude" response is very resistant to change, even under conditions of "unbiased" or "biased" scanning of arguments related to the attitude issue. Obviously this problem could be studied in a much more sophisticated way with more appropriate designs.

2. Social attitudes: a mere evaluative response view

In the previous sections we have been confronted with evidence of the impressive long term persistency of "dissonant" attitude change effects. The most important finding however, was the predicted absence of any "dissonant" treatment effect in the *delayed* first attitude response condition. Moreover, since these delayed attitude responses were not different from the usual baseline responses, they clearly were not influenced by the evaluative verbal statements proferred during the creativity exercise, which, even in the absence of "dissonant" treatment, still affect the immediately subsequent attitude response by making it less extreme in both pro- or counterattitudinal advocacy conditions. Although we do not have direct experimental evidence for the view that a delayed first attitude response of a not-"dissonant" condition also would fail to show any effect of the advocacy treatment, it seems plausible to accept the position that the long term persistency of the attitude change effect in both "dissonant" and not-"dissonant" advocacy, or creativity treatments, is conditioned by the critical circumstance that the attitude response be emitted in temporal contiguity with the previously produced evaluative verbal responses. At this point we will not comment upon the implications for an evaluative response contagion interpretation of the assessed attitude change in the not-"dissonant" conditions, since we want first to substantiate our mere evaluative response paradigm for the study of social attitudes. It is hoped that, indirectly, this also will eventually contribute to the plausibility of the evaluative response contagion interpretation of the reported attitude change effects.

CHANGE OF SOCIAL ATTITUDE OR CHANGE OF A PARTICULAR EVALUATIVE RESPONSE: COMPLEMENTARY EVIDENCE

The data presented so far, concerning the "stability of a changed attitude response", shed some light upon the very restricted meaning of a presumed change in the "social attitude" affected by counter- or pro-attitudinal advocacy. A different approach to the same basic issue consists in the study of the effect of the experimental treatment upon the responses given to *another* attitude rating, which because of its face validity, can be considered as just another symptom of the same, presumably, underlying social attitude. The procedure of our "Laboratory" versus "Field" setting persistency research (see Experiment Thirteen) provides data which are relevant for this purpose.

The subjects of Experiment Thirteen had been invited to answer the following attitude *related* question: "How desirable would be, according to you, a return to the exam regulation of ten years ago, when among other things, all exams were taken in a one week period?" The students of the "Field-approach" did so when Dr. Kabundi paid them an individual interview visit, whereas the students of the "Laboratory-approach" answered this question together with the other items of the persistency questionnaire mailed by the experimenter. It is obvious that the above rating is very closely related to the attitude response rating concerning the traditional exam system used throughout our research. Both ratings safely can be considered as attitude stimuli taken from a large universe of ratings concerning the complex attitude towards the university exam system, offering two opportunities for the subject to express or manifest his own "attitude".

The important point now is, that if the "dissonant" pro- and counter-attitudinal experimental treatment affects *attitude* in the classic sense, i.e., modifies the complex structure of *interdependent* cognitions, feelings and behavioural dispositions, one ought to expect that an "enduring attitude change" would manifest itself by a change in response to attitude scales which have not been used during the experimental treatment, but which can be considered as another verbal expression or symptom of the same underlying attitude. Concretely then, one would predict that the responses given to both the "Field interview attitude related rating" and the "Laboratory attitude related rating" would be affected by the "dissonant" pro- and counterattitudinal experimental treatments in a similar direction as the critical attitude responses which had been emitted immediately after the advocacy or verbal creativity task.

There is however, no theoretical imperative to predict an effect on an attitude *related* rating if we do not assume that an interdependent system of cognitions, affects and behavioural dispositions is being changed by the experimental treatment, but rather, that the treatments merely affect an evaluative verbal response which has been emitted under conditions favouring evaluative response contagion and relative stabilization of the new response. The absence of any effect upon an attitude related response would, under the present circumstances, corroborate the "mere evaluative response" conception of the attitude change phenomenon under study. We therefore expect that the subjects should respond similarly to the attitude related rating scale, whatever their previous experimental treatment.

In Table 24 we present the attitude responses given on the attitude related ratings during the "Field interview" and in the "Laboratory persistency questionnaire", and compare them with the long term effects upon the critical attitude response assessed in Experiment Thirteen.

These data hardly need any comment. It is clear that the experimental

TABLE 24

Average attitude responses on an attitude *related* rating as a function of "dissonant" pro- or counterattitudinal experimental treatment (five weeks earlier) and "laboratory" v. "field" approach

Pooled dissonant conditions (5 weeks earlier)	Attitude Related Rating		
	"Laboratory persistency questionnaire"	"Field interview rating"	
Counterattitudinal (N = 33)	(5.8)*	9.7 (N = 18)	9.4 (N = 15)	(6.6)
Pro-attitudinal (N = 22)	(2.9)	9.7 (N = 10)	10.3 (N = 12)	(2.8)

* The average *second* "Laboratory" or "Field" attitude responses given by the same subjects to the critical attitude rating which had been used immediately after the "dissonant" treatment (see also Table 21).

Note. The reader's attention is called to the fact that, in order to avoid an unwarranted direct comparison between the two ratings under discussion, the attitude related rating has been scored in such a way that a large number indicates an anti-traditional exam position (1 = return is very desirable; 11 = return is not desirable at all).

treatments have no effect on the evaluative responses to the "attitude related" question. This is in sharp contrast with the fact that, when the *same* attitude rating used in the experimental session is again administered, responses were significantly different between experimental treatments as they were for the measurement taken five weeks earlier, i.e., immediately after the experimental treatment.

CONCLUSION

These findings clearly corroborate our "mere evaluative response" view, and infirm the prevailing conception in the attitude change literature. Since the "forced compliance "research is imbedded in a theoretical background which conceives of social attitudes as enduring organized interdependent systems of cognitions, affects and behavioural dispositions, the implications of our thesis are far reaching. While recognizing this, we are also aware of the quite impressive amount of experimental attitude change literature which apparently contradicts our thesis. However, we do not contend that there are not myriads of instances available for which the consistency or interdependence between various "attitude related responses" is compelling and obvious. Equally compelling as the fact that most Chinese students talk, eat and evaluate various issues in a way which is consistently different from the way Flemish or Inca youth does or did behave.

The question to be asked however is if, for the attitude change literature under study, the paradigm of an enduring attitude change, induced by "forced compliance", is the most appropriate and parsimonious way of explaining the experimental data which form the empirical foundation of the challenged attitude change theories. The data discussed so far suggest not, and further support for this contention can be found in a quite unsuspected source, viz., the classic cognitive dissonance literature itself. In the pioneering Festinger and Carlsmith (1959) study, the minimal reward justification manipulation was considered to change the *attitude* of the subjects towards a boring task. If the attitude rating contained the verbal responses which the subject was induced to emit and/or expose himself to (we will come back to this aspect later), then a significant cognitive dissonance effect was obtained. When however other attitude *related* ratings were presented, the effect was not replicated. The same is true for the famous Carlsmith, Collins and Helmreich (1966) study. These authors, without any further comments, point to the following phenomenon which is highly relevant for our thesis: "As Festinger and Carlsmith found, *this effect seems to be quite specific to the particular words used in adopting the counterattitudinal position*. When subjects (the subjects of the Carlsmith, Collins and Helmreich study) were asked *how pleasant* the experiment had been, or how much they had learned from it, or whether they would recommend it to a friend, there were no effects in the role playing conditions, and only one significant effect in the essay-writing condition . . . Only the questions asking the subjects how interesting and *how much fun* the experiment had been, seem to show the effects of role playing which are predicted" (p. 10, italics added).

Are we dealing with attitude change or with change of a *particular evaluative response* emitted in close temporal contiguity with the "particular words used in adopting the counterattitudinal position"? Even the classical cognitive dissonance studies, it seems to us, contain evidence in support of our argument: how else could one explain that the effect only obtains for the rating "how much fun" and not for the rating "how pleasant" which obviously also taps the underlying *attitude* towards the boring experimental tasks.

Hopefully we will be excused for concluding this paragraph with a quotation from our own 1966 article, which contains a partial presentation of our replication of the Festinger and Carlsmith study, and in which the results section was preceded by the following remark:

It will be recalled that we used three different ratings for the assessment of the attitude towards the dull experimental tasks . . . which could be considered, on *a priori* grounds, as very similar phrasings for an evaluation of the tasks: rating A, not enjoyable—enjoyable; rating B, boring—interesting; rating C, monotonous—varied. The intercorrelations between the answers given by the whole sample ($N = 120$) on these quite similar looking ratings are however not high: $r = .66$ between A and B; $r = .54$ between A and C; $r = .44$ between B and C. It will be recalled that, in the original Festinger and Carlsmith experiment, the main dependent variable was measured by a single rating which was phrased: "Were the tasks interesting and enjoyable?" It is worth noting that, if we split this double question into two different ratings, the reactions correlate only .66. It is very unlikely that these low correlations are mainly due to a lack of reliability of each of the instruments used. We do not have accurate estimates of the reliability, but some indication is given in the correlations found between the answers collected by the interviewer in the attitude measurement phase (A. Beckers) and the answers given by the same subjects on the identical ratings to the interviewer of the post-experimental treatment phase (the author). Notwithstanding the difference in the interviewing situation, these correlations ($N = 120$) are rather high: for rating A, $r = .86$; for rating B, $r = .77$ and for rating C, $r = .80$. It seems unlikely that this constancy (*stability of changed responses*) would be due to the short time interval, since subjects had to fill out a whole series of similar ratings and there was a complete absence of any memory-set (p. 47, italics added).*

3. Dominant "situation-free" evaluative responses and "unpredicted" response change in a precipitating situation

So far we have documented the point that it would be hazardous and unwarranted to consider a change in the experimental attitude response, even when stabilized over time, as evidence for a change in attitude; i.e., in an organized and structured system of interdependent cognitions, feelings and behavioural dispositions. We have proposed instead to interpret the effects as a change in evaluative *responses* produced by response contagion and stabilized by social reinforcement. Our interpretation may not only antagonize an important group of social psychologists, but also incur the scepticism of experimental psychologists interested in response change processes. After all, in our "dissonant" counterattitudinal conditions, the attitude response emitted immediately after the experimental treatment was quite different from, if not incompatible with, the dominant evaluative response repertoire acquired during a relatively long history of pre-experimental experiences concerning the exam reform issue. Since the habit strength of the strongly negative baseline attitude response can be considered to be much greater than the habit strength of the most recent ongoing counterattitudinal verbal responses, it becomes difficult—especially under the hypothesis of a multiplicative drive or arousal function, to explain the changes obtained as reflecting response enhancement or contagion.

We have already argued that the fundamental substantiation of the proposed response contagion interpretation lies beyond the scope of social psychological research. In the present section we will however make an effort to illustrate the point that one should not too rapidly reject the response contagion view on the basis of the argument that a well learned and "deeply rooted" or dominant evaluative response cannot be made to change suddenly as a function of the evaluative characteristics of a sequence of *recent* responses (active or passive exposure to counterattitudinal verbal statements) which are incompatible with, or quite different from, the dominant evaluative response repertoire.

* The above paragraph and the (not quoted) comments on it, was left out by the editor who reprinted this 1966 article in his book of readings "Role Playing, Reward and Attitude Change" (Elms, 1969).

The problem obviously is very complex, and far from being able to propose any compelling solution, we can hardly formulate it. For the present purposes, it might however help to call attention to the well known fact that human behaviour is sometimes characterized by the "unpredicted" emission of responses whose prevailing characteristics, along one or another dimension, are very different from those of the dominant, well learned response. This is especially relevant for some social psychological studies where one is interested in the discrepancy between "social attitudes" and attitude related "overt" social behaviour. Since we are defending an evaluative response paradigm for the study of social attitudes, we will try to illustrate the parallel between attitude response change and sudden changes in "overt" behaviour, while assuming that all these response changes might obey the same fundamental response change mechanisms which—it must be conceded—are not yet fully understood. The principal idea guiding our modest endeavour, is that attitude responses are by no means different from other forms of behaviour, and that real progress in the understanding of so-called "social attitudes" will depend upon the progress made in the study of the fundamental laws of "behaviour".

"Unpredicted" response change as a function of specific features of the precipitating situation

The term "precipitating situation" is proposed as referring to a behavioural environment which induces the subject to react rapidly to its more or less unexpected fast changes. The changes in the environment might be primarily related to the "internal" antecedents of overt behaviour (for example, changes in emotional arousal, confrontation with a sequence of representations, ideas or images) or to external factors (for example, urging demands of another person, active and/or passive self-exposure to a sequence of verbal responses), or to a combination of both.

Let us briefly illustrate the wide range of phenomena which we have in mind by giving two rather extreme pieces of anecdotal evidence. The first example, which refers to precipitating situational antecedents of an "unpredicted" mere verbal non-evaluative response, is similar to the one already mentioned concerning the induced emission of the wrong answer "fork" to the question "with what do you normally eat your soup?" A local elementary school-teacher reports to be very successful in eliciting an "unpredicted" response at the end of a class-game experiment which she conducts every year when entertaining the children on her birthday.

G

One should know that the Dutch term "stoppen" means "to stop" and also serves as the plural for a "stopper of a bottle". The excited children are expected to call out collectively the completion of a sequence of ten sentences like "If we have one bottle of wine, we have?" "One stop!" "If we have two bottles of wine, we have?": "Two 'stoppen' ", etc., until ten. This series is terminated by the question "What do you do when the traffic light is green?" The enthusiastic answer invariably sounds, "stoppen!". There can be no doubt that the dominant or well learned response to the latter question is the opposite of the emitted answer. The response change can only be explained by taking into account some specific (phonetic) features of the immediately preceding ongoing responses which are part of the behavioural and situational antecedents of the crucial response at issue.

Another example we have in mind is taken from a tragic event which was in the headlines of last week's Belgian newspapers. One will easily find analogous, although hopefully less dramatic examples, in other real life situations. Mr X was notorious as a model husband and father. For years his primary sources of enjoyment seemed to be his charming family and his fine collection of old rifles which decorated the walls. One afternoon he shops with his daughters in order to buy birthday presents for his wife. The same evening the birthday is celebrated in the best of traditions. Towards the end of the celebration a trivial quarrel spoils the party. One argument entails another . . . feelings run high. The model husband takes the nearest rifle, shoots his beloved wife and two of his grown up daughters. The third one tries to escape with the help of a casual passer-by. Both however become the new target of the "mad" man who finishes the series of available targets by pointing the rifle to himself. Nobody could "understand" this sudden and totally "unpredicted" behavioural sequence.

Needless to say that we are far from pretending to have an adequate explanation for this drama, nor for the many other examples where love suddenly turns into hatred and firmly formulated intentions are closely followed by discrepant acts. However, saying that the man "lost his head" or self-control or that he had repressed his aggressive feelings for years and had them sublimated in a rifle collection does not offer much of an explanation either. He certainly could not have repressed aggression towards the unknown passer-by. And even if he basically hated society, including himself, why did the drama break out a few hours after he took the initiative to buy birthday presents for one of his victims. We would argue that the fact that the birthday party ended with murder instead of its opposite cannot be adequately explained if specific features of the precipitating situation (emotional arousal, evaluative nature of arguments proferred in the quarrel, rifle within reach, etc.) are not fully taken into account. It seems to us that the pre-existing complex attitude, in its cognitive, affective and conative components, and even "personality" as approached by classical clinical psychology or psychiatry would not offer a more valid basis for an explanation of the unpredicted outcome of this behavioural sequence.

At this point, the purpose of the two birthday celebration examples (the school-teacher and the model husband) is to illustrate the fact that, under the influence of some (eventually identifiable) features of the precipitating internal and/or external situation, an unexpected response ("stoppen" or shooting) can be emitted whose prevailing characteritics (phonetic or evaluative) are very different from those of the response, which can safely be supposed to have much greater habit strength. We are of course aware of the fact that there are, in many respects, important differences between the two examples given. One might for example, wish to point to the difference in the motivational dynamics of the two classes of responses. For the time being we would like to document the same point while making use of behavioural data which are closely related to the response repertoire with which we are dealing in our research programme.

"UNPREDICTED" WILLINGNESS TO HOLD A PLEA AGAINST EXAM REFORM BEFORE A NATION-WIDE AUDIENCE

There can be no doubt that, for the student population used in the reported experiments, the dominant evaluative response repertoire concerning the exam reform issue was characterized by a homogeneous and strongly negative evaluation of the two crucial aspects of the traditional exam system which were chosen as the topic of the experimental advocacy (all exams within a one week period and abolishment of exam exemptions for September). The data obtained in the two baseline conditions supplement the face validity of the commonly held belief that a massive and violent student revolt would be unavoidable if the local academic authorities ever dared to reintroduce the traditional exam system.

The "behavioural disposition" or dominant conative attitude responses of the students can be further illustrated by the following data obtained from the 1969 baseline and free advocacy conditions. After having collaborated with the experimenter in holding a private free attitudinal plea (without restrictions upon the pro- or contra exam reform nature of the arguments), these subjects were invited to estimate the willingness of their fellow-students to hold a public counterattitudinal plea on the issue and also to express their own willingness in case the interviewer would have asked them to do so. In an individual interview situation the students were given a full description of the "real life" situation to which our counterattitudinal public advocacy "subjects" had been exposed and were urged to try to enter into the position of the students when confronted with the decision to comply or not with the request of holding a false plea before the national TV (identified) or radio (anonymity guaranteed).

   In Table 25 we display the answers given to the question "what percentage of second year Science students would, according to you, accept to hold a plea (under the circumstances described) in favour of the traditional exam system on TV or in an (anonymous) radio broadcast?"

TABLE 25

Distribution of estimated willingness of fellow-students to hold a TV or radio plea in favour of the traditional exam system $(N=22)$

	Estimated percentage of complying fellow-students							
Circumstance	1–2%	3–5%	6–10%	11–15%	16–20%	21–25%	26–30%	More than 30%
identified TV	7	7	3	2	2	—	1	—
anon. radio	5	4	5	1	5	1	1	—

   The data clearly show that most students agree that only a very few of their fellow-mates would comply with a similar request. More than half of the subjects (14 out of 22) estimate the percentage for TV compliance not to exceed 5%. The median estimated percentage is approximately 4%. The circumstance that the (radio) advocacy is described as completely anonymous raises the median estimated percentage to approximately 8%.

   Even more important for our present concern are the answers given by the same subjects to the question: "Do you think that *you* would have complied with a similar request to hold a public speech in favour of the traditional exam?" Invariably, and with much confidence, *all subjects affirmed that they would never comply;* and when asked if they might do it for money the refusal remained equally strong. The typical comments were "one can never tell of course that one or another conservative student would lend himself to a public defence of the old exam system, but certainly never me!" When asked why not, the usual answer was that one does not betray one's deepest conviction in such an important matter. Several students also spontaneously pointed to the unavoidable ostracism which would follow from a TV plea against exam reform.

Let us now confront the above results with the actual number of refusals to hold a counterattitudinal public plea in the real life "precipitating situation" arranged for Experiments Five, Six and Seven. The relevant data are given in Table 26.

TABLE 26
Number of refusals to hold a plea in the various 1969 public
advocacy conditions

	TV 20 BF	0 BF	Counterattitudinal radio 20 BF	radio 200 BF	rel. depr.	0 BF	Pro-attitudinal radio 20 BF	rel. depr.
N of subjects	12	11	13	13	11	11	12	11
N of refusals	1	0	2	2	0	0	1	0

The most fascinating result is obviously the fact that only 1 out of 12 subjects refused to comply with the request to hold a clearly identified counterattitudinal plea on the nation-wide TV screen. It will be remembered that in a perfectly comparable random sample of 22 subjects, everyone affirmed with much confidence that they would never "be taken in" or lend themselves to such false public advocacy, and that the typical estimated percentage of complying fellow-students was around 4%.

A similar striking contrast is found for the willingness to hold an anonymous public plea. Not less than 44 out of 48 students or 92% accepted in fact to defend the traditional exam system before the radio whereas the median estimated percentage was approximately 8%. Although we are not interested in analyzing the justifications given for the refusals, it will be noted that there was also one subject of the *pro-*attitudinal radio condition (20 BF) who did not want to collaborate "since he was no good at making speeches". We should add that no refusals were incurred for the private advocacy conditions.

Overall then, 55 out of 60 students or 92% accepted in a real life situation and under conditions of high decision freedom, to deliver before a nation-wide audience, a counterattitudinal plea on the very important exam reform issue, whereas in a comparable sample each of 22 students proclaimed in an individual interview that he himself would never make such a plea and that only a very small percentage of fellow-students (4–8%) would comply with a similar proposal.

"UNPREDICTED" CORRUPTIBILITY OR LACK OF INTEGRITY

A second series of data which might also contribute to the substantiation of the point at issue, is taken from Experiment Nine in which a "dissonant" high reward was offered either before or after private counterattitudinal advocacy. It will be remembered that the students after being informed that they failed in an important exam, were given the choice between a monetary reward and illegitimate additional exam rescue points. The import of this real life test of the corruptibility or integrity of the students has been amply documented in the description of procedure (pp. 112–113). We should add here that the students of the "mere information about bad exam" condition, who were told that they had done poorly in their exam but who were not offered the "real life" opportunity to receive the illegitimate reward, had been asked at the end of the post-experimental interview to answer two evaluative and conative "attitude" items: (1) "Would you consider it unfair if additional exam points were given as a reward for the student's collaboration in research?" All students answered without hesitation that this would be an utterly unfair practice; (2) "Do you think that you yourself would resist the temptation if I offered you—in a safe manner—additional exam points which would change your failing into a passing score?" Out of eleven students only one said that he might agree to such a proposal. He justified his answer by referring to the bad luck which often affects exam scores in an unfair way and that succeeding in an exam is so important that it is legitimate to exploit any opportunity which might compensate for bad luck. All other students affirmed that they would not lend themselves to such practices.

The contrast between these "attitude" responses and the "overt" behaviour emitted in the precipitating situation to which the students of the "dissonant" high reward conditions were exposed does not need much comment: out of the 22 students (of the "before" and "after" advocacy" conditions) who as part of the experimental manipulation were actually confronted with the real life choice between a (legitimate) monetary reward and the illegitimate additional exam rescue points, not a single student did refuse the latter unfair reward.

It should be noted that the instrumental value for need satisfaction of the unfair reward is identical for the two groups of subjects under comparison, all of whom had been informed that they made a poor exam.

Apparently the crucial difference between the two classes of related behaviour can only be explained by reference to the circumstance that the students who proclaimed their ethical immunity had not been exposed to the specific precipitating situation which induced their fellow-students to accept the "counterattitudinal" unfair reward.

We would like to stress the point that the occurrence of "unpredicted" behaviour in a precipitating situation does not necessarily imply that the subject evidences a restriction of his behavioural freedom. As mentioned before (see pp. 127–129), the acceptance of the unfair reward clearly affected the expressed degree of experienced coercion. When asked "Do you feel that the interviewer has forced you to cooperate?" 18 out of 22 "unfair reward" subjects did score at the very extreme "not at all" pole of a 26 point rating scale in contrast to 6 out of 22 in the "mere information about good or bad exam" conditions (9 in each of the former and 3 in each of the latter conditions). If anything then, a situation which pushes the subject into "unpredicted" behaviour might entail an overaccentuation of experienced freedom. Reactance (Brehm, 1966)? Taking into account the striking discrepancy between the integrity proclaimed by 10 out of 11 students in a strictly comparable interview situation and the complete lack of resistance to a real temptation (all of 22 students accepted the unfair reward) one might indeed conjecture that people experience (or express) freedom especially in situations where decision freedom was almost non-existent since all subjects could be predicted with unusually high certainty to accept the unethical reward. It looks indeed as if subjects stress behavioural freedom especially when they are in fact least free.

ATTITUDE RESPONSE: A SITUATION-FREE EVALUATIVE RESPONSE?

It is obvious that the above presented data deserve attention in their own right. They throw a grim light upon the vulnerability of human intentions (the conative dimension of "attitudes") and convictions (the cognitive dimension of "attitudes") and add to the impressive body of scientific and pre-scientific evidence illustrating the strong situational determination of high level forms of human behaviour. The import of these and similar data for the understanding and social engineering of individual and society is manifest. For our present purposes however, they serve to illustrate our position with regard to the problem raised at the outset of this paragraph: does it make sense to explain a change in a "deeply rooted" evaluative response by referring to some features of *recent* ongoing evaluative responses, i.e., to characteristics of the precipitating situation which immediately precedes the emission of the critical attitude response? In essence we have made an effort to show that responses which reasonably may be considered dominant can quite suddenly change under the impact of subtle and not easily identifiable features of a precipitating situation. It should be noted that in contrast with much research on obedience, the emission of "unpredicted" responses is not being attributed to explicit coercive forces manipulated by the experimenter. The "real life" creation of a situation allowing for perceived decision freedom was a major source of concern and no subject ever used the excuse that he had been forced by the experimenter. On the contrary, as said before, the reported freedom from situational constraints was at a maximum precisely in those conditions where the discrepancy between the pre-experimental "behavioural disposition" and the "overt" behaviour was most striking.

What then can be the meaning of a "dominant pre-experimental behavioural disposition" or "dominant pre-experimental evaluative response repertoire"? It seems to us that one should fully realize not only that the underlying hypothetical attitude construct is inferred from con-sistency in the evaluative responses given to so-called "attitude ratings", but also that these attitude responses *are* samples of "overt" behavioural reactions to specific questions or stimuli, and that these responses are not necessarily more "situation-free" than other samples of so-called "overt" behaviour. Ideally and in theory a valid attitude response is conceived to be a "situation-free' evaluative (cognitive, affective and/or conative) response. By situation-free we mean that the evaluative characteristics of the response (how much pro- or anti, how good or bad, etc.) are not at all, or at a minimal level, determined by features of the specific situation in which the response is elicited. It is indeed only on condition that the situational determination of the evaluative characteristics of the attitude response is non-existent or minimal that the attitude response can be con-sidered as controlled by *pre*-situational determinants and thus as revealing a "disposition" or "attitude" towards an object resulting from previous experiences related to the attitude object. Attitude responses are typically conceived as samples of behaviour *in vitro*, i.e. emitted in an artificial environment which ideally is so designed that none of the environmental stimuli is likely to affect its evaluative nature.

Such a conception of an attitude response however, might be quite fallacious and misleading since any behavioural reaction is under control of more or less complex situational determinants and the important problem is that we simply do not know very well what the meaning is of "situation" with regard to a response. Theoretically, the notion *pre-situational* determinants of an attitude response would refer to the multitude of determinants which were operative in the lifelong chain of antecedent attitude related responses (antecedent with regard to the specific situation in which the attitude response proper was tapped). But what can be the use of a theoretical attitude construct which basically coincides with the behavioural history of the individual with regard to a specific class of objects?

As a matter of fact, when we are talking about attitudes, what else can we refer to except behaviour, sequences of behaviour and the impact of past behaviour on new behaviour (emitted in more or less complex situations). The fundamental issue we are dealing with amounts to the study of the impact of past behaviour—old or recent—upon new responses, and of new responses upon future responses. It seems to us that it is only due to certain historical circumstances in the development of social psychology, that so many scientists have become attracted to the study of that quite a-typical sample of social behaviour referred to as "attitude response". The main and probably most valid reason for this interest, might be that attitude responses are rather simple reactions to assess in a standardized manner and that the responses easily deal with value loaded objects which are "relevant" for social behaviour. But what can we learn about the impact of values upon man and the way man deals with values if we restrict our observations to evaluative reactions *in vitro*? And again, what exactly does *in vitro* mean?

Let us try to clarify this point by coming back to the assessment of the "attitude" towards accepting an unethical reward. It will be remembered that the students of the "mere information about bad exam conditions" were invited to give an answer to the following question: "Would you consider it unfair if additional exam points were given as a reward for the student's collaboration in research?" One will agree that such a question currently is considered as an "attitude rating", i.e., a question which taps the underlying attitude towards the issue of giving additional exam points as a means of rewarding experimental subjects. The responses to this question were quite unambiguous: all students strongly rejected the policy as being utterly unfair. From this, one can infer that the "behavioural disposition" or "attitude" towards the object is negative.

It will also be remembered that all subjects of the otherwise strictly identical "additional exam rescue points before and after advocacy" conditions reacted positively by accepting the unfair reward, to the following

H

question (see p. 117): "I am just wondering if, instead of paying you out of my research funds, I might not better give you some additional points so that you can be safe for your July session. Or would you prefer money?" This question is not supposed to tap an attitude but to elicit "overt" behaviour, which is conceived to be in part determined by the underlying "behavioural disposition".

To us, it is not clear what the crucial conceptual difference could be between the two questions and the two responses. Although the two responses are incompatible in their evaluative loading (saying that it is unfair practice or that one would never comply with such practice, versus accepting without much hesitation the offered unethical reward), it is difficult to argue that the first response would reveal a "behavioural disposition", whereas the second would not be largely determined by the same antecedent response repertoire. The ambiguity of the notion "situation" or "response eliciting question" can be exemplified further when we simply marry the two verbal stimuli (which did entail the "incompatible" responses) and imagine for a while that the experimenter had induced the compliance as follows, (without assessing a response to the first question): "Would you consider it unfair if additional exam points were given as a reward for the student's collaboration in research? I am just wondering if, instead of paying you out of my research funds, I might not better give you some additional points so that you can be safe etc. . . . ?" Our conjecture would be that the latter "situation", consisting of both the stimuli for the attitude response *and* the "overt" behaviour, would lead to the same reaction of accepting the unethical reward, provided that the subject is not invited to *react* to the first part of the question. However, if he would be allowed to react to the first part of the question, then the impact of this reaction upon the subsequent behaviour would not illustrate the impact of some "behavioural disposition", *but merely the impact of a previous behavioural response* which, as any antecedent response, can be supposed to affect a subsequent response according to universal response change mechanisms whose complexity are not yet ascertained or understood.

CONCLUSION

What we have been trying to convey is our scepticism with regard to the theoretical and practical usefulness of the "attitude" construct for students of social behaviour. Dominant "situation-free' evaluative responses, or "underlying attitude" are concepts which essentially refer to the residue of past behaviour. It has been shown once more, that the "underlying attitude" does not offer a valid basis for predicting behaviour which ought to belong to the same response repertoire. The "unpredicted" response change assessed at various occasions, can most plausibly be viewed as under the control of changes in the behavioural situation. Attitude responses as well as so-called "overt behaviour" are both instances of behavioural responses emitted under more or less complex situational control. The situational constraints upon any behaviour are however, very difficult to isolate from the impact of previous, old or more recent responses. There is apparently, no compelling reason to attach less importance to the impact of recent responses and/or specific features of the situation than to the so-called "dominant evaluative response repertoire" or "underlying attitude".

It thus seems plausible to consider "attitude responses" as mere evaluative responses whose determinants can be studied without reference to the underlying attitude construct. As said before, this is not solely a task for social psychologists. Still, in the next section we will take a chance to spell out some rudiments of a response contagion view which might suggest a plausible direction for interpreting the various evaluative response change phenomena assessed in the reported research.

4. Perturbation and evaluative response contagion: rudiments for a theory of persuasion

PERSUASION AND THE EVALUATIVE RESPONSE PARADIGM

The classical cognitive dissonance experiments which were the starting point of the present monograph, are linked historically to the vast communication and persuasion research programmes initiated by Carl Hovland and his associates who, during the Second World War became involved in the study of the effectiveness of military propaganda and indoctrination techniques. Their relevance for the study of persuasion is widely accepted and obvious,* although not all attitude change phenomena are related to persuasion; the "forced compliance" paradigm essentially induces the subjects to active and/or passive self-exposure to attitude

---

* The Festinger and Carlsmith (1959), Rosenberg (1965) and Carlsmith, Collins and Helmreich (1966) studies are, for example, reprinted in Rosnow and Robinson's "Experiments in Persuasion" (1967), a volume of the American Social Psychology Series (Academic Press, New York and London), which intends to provide an introduction to current experimental research and theory in the psychology of persuasion.

discrepant arguments or persuasive messages. Since our critical analysis of post-advocacy attitude change has questioned the plausibility of interpretations centred around such notions as "attitude discrepant" and "persuasive arguments", it seems appropriate to examine how the proposed evaluative response paradigm can be applied to the persuasion research.

The main operational criterion for the inference of persuasion in its most elementary form, consists in the assessment of a change of the recipient's attitude in the direction of the prevailing attitude position reflected in the persuasive message. When applying the proposed evaluative response paradigm, a persuasive message can be defined as an evaluative (verbal) statement or response emitted by a sender which, with a certain probability, will affect the "attitude", i.e. an evaluative response of the recipient, in the direction of the "attitude" position of the message.

If sender and recipient are two different persons, we are dealing with persuasive social communication or social persuasion; if they are one and the same individual, the phenomenon is called self-persuasion. While the distinction between social and self-persuasion can be useful for structuring the vast area of persuasion research, it is by no means fundamental if the focus lies on the persuasion phenomenon itself.

The following elements then, it seems to us, can be considered as constitutive for the persuasion phenomenon in its most elementary form:

(1) a *temporal* sequence of evaluative responses, the responses of the sender preceding the response to be emitted by the recipient; since sender and recipient are the same person in the case of self-persuasion, we propose to simply use the terms *prior* and *subsequent evaluative responses;*

(2) an increased similarity of the evaluative characteristics or *evaluative assimilation** of the subsequent to the prior responses.

We thus propose to consider persuasion as an instance of evaluative assimilation of subsequent to prior evaluative responses. The magnitude of persuasion can be defined as the extent to which subsequent evaluative responses became more similar to prior evaluative responses.

Let us briefly illustrate this by referring to a classical example of self-persuasion. Self-persuasion is said to have occurred if subjects, after holding a counterattitudinal plea, manifest an attitude change in the

* The first meaning of "assimilate", according to "Webster's New Collegiate Dictionary" (1961), is "to make similar or alike"; assimilation then is defined as "the act or process of assimilating".

advocated direction. Counterattitudinal advocacy can be considered as self-exposure to a series of prior evaluative statements, messages or responses; attitude change has been shown to amount to the emission of a new evaluative response; self-persuasion then is inferred if the evaluative characteristics of the "subsequent" (attitude) response prove to be affected by the evaluative characteristics of the "prior" (advocacy) responses, in the sense of an enhanced similarity of the subsequent to the prior responses. In the case of social persuasion, the message (prior response) which has its source in a sender is said to entail persuasion if the subsequent (attitude) response of the recipient has become more similar to the evaluative characteristics of the prior responses.

Although the rationale for the use of the notion "evaluative response assimilation" is based upon our progressive analysis of the post-advocacy attitude change effect, it should be conceded that the term as such is not much more than a descriptive reformulation of the experimental effects assessed in the reported research. At the same time however, it serves as a label which reveals a particular conception of the observed phenomenon. Hopefully it will be granted that the proposed reformulation is more economical, since it reduces the number and the complexity of the concepts involved in current research, (for example, counter- or pro-attitudinal advocacy or persuasive communication and attitude change). Also it looks as if it can be more easily applied to a wide range of phenomena including conformity and imitation which could be approached as special cases of *response assimilation*.

The main task however, is to uncover the underlying process which might account for the observed evaluative response assimilation. As said before, our modest contribution in this respect is doomed to be predominantly negative, in the sense of defending, as we have done several times, the plausibility of the rejection of alternative explanations. We will however make an effort to convey an outline of the process as conjectured in our evaluative response *contagion* hypothesis.

RESPONSE CONTAGION

The term "evaluative response assimilation" was used to denote—at a rather high level of abstraction—the observable endresult of persuasion. We use the term response *contagion* as a label for the hypothesized process leading to evaluative response assimilation. The choice of a label is of course to a certain extent arbitrary and unimportant. We did however opt for the term contagion* since it evokes rapid spread of an influence or emotional state and temporal contiguity or contact (between prior and subsequent responses) while not referring to persuasive information processing aspects. A disadvantage of the term contagion could be its "social" contact implication. It will be remembered that the concept of behavioural contagion was introduced by Le Bon (1896) to explain certain undesirable aspects of the spread of "animal-like" behaviour of people in crowds†. It should be stressed that we consider the term "contagion" equally neutral with regard to its possible social implications as, for example, the term persuasion. "Self"-contagion and "social" contagion are conceptually interchangable terms.

Response contagion then is conceived to be a function of three factors: (1) *the nature of the prior responses;* (2) *the degree of perturbation or arousal;* (3) *the temporal contiguity between prior and subsequent responses.*

In line with the Lumsdaine and Janis (1953) and McGuire (1964) analogical use of the term "inoculation" for the study of resistance to persuasion, we could compare these three factors with those of a simple biological analogy which would hold that contagion of disease is a function of (1) type of germs; (2) virulence of the germs; and (3) contact.

Let us illustrate the model by applying it to the anecdotical examples which have been advanced as instances of response contagion. It seems plausible to refer to the three posited factors for explaining the unpredicted emission of the subsequent response "fork" as an answer to the question "with what do you normally eat your soup?" or the response "stop" to the question "what do you do when the traffic light is green?": (1) the subsequent response obviously is a function of the (phonetic) characteristics of the "prior" responses, a series of ten times "work" or *stoppen;* (2) a certain degree of emotional arousal seems to be necessary before the skilled real life "experimenters" take the risk of starting the game; (3) it is self-evident that the phenomenon is a function of constraints put on the time interval between the emission of the prior and the subsequent responses.

The same factors seem to be relevant for the dramatic birthday

* "Contagious: spreading or communicable from one to another; exciting similar emotions or conduct in others. Contagion: the spread or communication or the tendency to be communicated of any influence, doctrine, emotion or emotional state; an influence, doctrine or emotion that spreads rapidly". ("Webster's Third New International Dictionary", 1961).

† For a more recent, also social psychological use of the term, see for example, Wheeler (1966).

celebration example: the extreme forms of unpredicted aggressive behaviour most plausibly are related to the fact that (1) at some moment, the
nature of the prior responses was very aggressive; (2) the emotional arousal
relatively high (end of a party) and (3) the time interval between subsequent and prior responses quite small. It should be noted that each of the
three factors involved are considered to be necessary conditions: it seems
very unlikely indeed that the subsequent murder response would have
been emitted if either, (1) the evaluative nature of the verbal interactions
would have been reflecting an "attitude position" of mutual love; or (2)
the emotional arousal was not enhanced by the specific features of the
party; or (3) the emission of any (overt or covert) response after the
"prior" responses had been delayed (for one or another reason) until some
later time.

So far this illustration of the hypothesized response contagion process
which implies that the above mentioned three conditions are met
simultaneously.

While the first and third factor (nature of evaluative responses and temporal contiguity) do not need much comment when applied to our post-
advocacy attitude change research, this might not be the case for the second
factor which is considered to affect the intensity of the prior responses.

PERTURBATION AND INTENSITY OF PRIOR RESPONSES

Our progressive analysis of the cognitive dissonance effect led to the
rather compelling conclusion that the impressive attitude change effects
in the advocated direction were to be linked to what we finally called the
occurrence of "dissonant" stimuli. The variety of "dissonant" stimuli
used was quite large: a trivial remuneration, relative deprivation, priceless illegitimate exam points, unexpected severe blame and hot-pants.
The common element between these "dissonant" treatments seemed to be
that they all could be depicted as embarrassing, strange, novel or unusual.
The face validity of this interpretation of the various manipulations has
been amply demonstrated in the description of procedure section of the
various experiments. Since we prefer not to use any longer the term
"dissonant" stimuli, which might be misunderstood by the reader because
of its resemblance to the terms used in a cognitive dissonance approach of
the phenomena, and at the same time want to have a short hand label for
denoting the presumed state of confusion created in the subject exposed to
the "dissonant" stimuli, we propose to use the term *perturbation* which
reflects pretty well the typical state of affairs caused by the experimental

treatments. According to Webster, the meaning of perturbation implies among other meanings: "to disturb considerably in mind; make quite *uneasy*; cause to be *upset* or worried or alarmed; to put in considerable disorder or confusion; to *modify the usual* or expected course . . ."

Again, perturbation is only a label and we are completely at a loss when asked for a precise operational definition. Even worse, but not unlike frequent practice in the field, we cannot offer any independent check for the occurrence of perturbation*. As said before we are very sceptical towards the use of retrospective paper and pencil "checks" of such manipulations. Also we have never used any physiological measures, partly because the usefulness of such measures often proves to be misleading, but mainly because the very tapping of physiological data would have ruined the real life character of the strong psychological manipulations. Our primary interest clearly was not the study of psychophysiological processes.

And yet, it might very well be that further consolidation of the response contagion hypothesis will depend on research done simultaneously at the behavioural and the physiological response levels. When discussing the motivational significance of collative variables and arousal, Berlyne (1968) mentions that high levels of arousal can be produced in situations characterized by *novelty, surprisingness, complexity* and *ambiguity*. While referring to Berlyne's discussion of relevant work, Berkowitz (1969) writes "Strange, new stimuli which stand out sharply against a background of familiar stimuli or previous experiences presumably lead to disturbingly sharp increases in arousal level. Unduly complex stimuli have a similar effect, as do conditions of sudden change and great uncertainty".

It thus seems plausible to consider arousal as a mediating variable. If arousal then fosters the intensity of the ongoing responses or energizes whatever responses are in progress, it becomes plausible to expect that these relatively new dominant "prior" responses will have a stronger

* The only scant piece of evidence which might indicate a relative enhancement of arousal comes from a short concentration task which was given just before the provisional debriefing to the subjects of the dissonant dress counterattitudinal advocacy and the normal dress pro-attitudinal verbal creativity condition of Experiment Eleven. During 90 seconds these students had to fill in the substitution subtest No. 7 of the Wechsler Adult Intelligence Scale (Dutch adaptation) and were instructed to work at a maximum speed with minimal errors. The result was that in the perturbing dress condition, five out of eleven subjects made at least one error (three with one and two with two errors) whereas no errors at all were made by the eleven subjects of the normal dress control condition. The amount of work done was slightly although not significantly larger in the hot pants condition (an average of 62 versus 61 substituted symbols).

impact upon the "subsequent" responses than in a comparable situation where the intensity of the prior responses was not enhanced by the sudden increase in arousal. It should be noted that we restrict our reasoning to the sample of ongoing prior responses and do not take into account the so-called dominant pre-experimental response repertoire whose weak relevance for the prediction of behaviour in a precipitating situation has been discussed previously.

One could also think along the lines that an increase in arousal, enhancing the dominance of a class of recent responses, causes behavioural *rigidity* and that the enhanced assimilation of the subsequent response is a symptom of rigidity. One is here reminded of a study of Cowen (1952) who studied problem-solving rigidity as a function of varying degrees of psychological stress. He found that under increasingly stressful conditions there was a greater tendency to adhere to an induced behaviour which had become inappropriate. It thus looks as if arousal, caused by stressful instructions, produces response contagion, i.e., enhanced similarity between subsequent and prior responses. Maybe the behavioural rigidity and response contagion of prior to subsequent responses basically refers to the same phenomenon. As already mentioned, the further substantiation of the response contagion view does not fall within the scope of social psychologists. Our principle contribution might indeed be to have documented the plausibility of a mere evaluative response view of post-advocacy attitude change phenomena. We do however defend the position that response contagion offers the thus far most economical way for explaining our own experimental results and for reinterpreting and reconciling an impressive amount of relevant research literature which led to competing views of similar phenomena. In the next section we will make an effort to further substantiate this position.

Note: *relative degrees of arousal and response contagion in not-"dissonant" conditions*

As already mentioned, the vagueness of the proposed relation between response contagion and perturbation is in need of more sophisticated research explicitly designed to test and specify the basic assumptions made. Of the many puzzling questions this raises, we would like to comment briefly on the assessed significant "attitude" change effects in the twelve not-"dissonant" advocacy or creativity conditions of our research programme.

At the outset it should be noted that none of the discussed attitude change theories attempt to explain the observed post-advocacy baseline data. As a consequence of the methodological strategy used, all predictions relate to differences in one or another direction between various monetary rewards and/or other variables manipulated. The quite often observed differences between any of the experimental advocacy conditions and a no-advocacy control or baseline attitude level, are however sometimes more impressive than the differential effect produced by the manipulated variable.

As an example we refer to the Mintz and Mills (1971) study in which students were exposed to a three page warning against annual X-ray examinations. As will be explained in more detail in the next section, the experiment focuses on the effect of arousal and information about its source upon attitude change. For half of the subjects the favourability towards chest X-rays was assessed before exposure to the persuasive communication: the data for the three pre-communication conditions were 10.2; 10.9 and 9.9 reflecting a fairly positive attitude. For the other half of the subjects the attitude responses were only tapped after exposure to the persuasive communication. The average favourability attitude-score went down to 3.1 for the control condition and as far as 1.3 and 1.8 for the two manipulated arousal conditions. The point now, is that the author's theoretical analysis is limited to explaining the difference between 1.3, 1.8 and 3.1, whereas the overwhelming exposure-to-communication effect, viz., the difference between 3.1 and 10 (10.2; 10.9 and 9.9) is left totally unexplained.

It seems to us that theories about post-advocacy attitude change ought also to try to integrate these quite important categories of data which are directly related to at least equally powerful aspects of the exposure to what we have called "prior responses". In our own research, the very significant differences between any non-"dissonant" advocacy or mere creativity condition, and the pre-advocacy baseline attitude response, provided a remarkably constant result. Does it make sense to integrate these data in a response contagion explanation? We venture the following considerations which might illustrate the plausibility of such an integration.

It is obvious that the mediating arousal notion has to be conceived as a variable which can represent various degrees of perturbation. The specific development of our research project, using a very central attitude issue and struggling with the strange a-cognitive "dissonant" stimuli effect, led us to a rather extreme manipulation of perturbation. Perturbation clearly is a label used to depict the endresult of some very powerful "unusual" treatments which triggered off response change in a deeply entrenched evaluative response repertoire. The fact that some manipulations led to stronger response contagion effects, than other manipulations, can easily be interpreted as due to differences in relatively very high degrees of perturbation. Although we lack any independent assessment of the mediating arousal variable, we are, retrospectively not surprised that the strongest effect of all was produced in Experiment Nine where the students held their plea after having accepted the undeserved exam rescue points. The very fact that this was the only experiment for which beforehand an exceptional debriefing procedure was organized (cf. p. 118), illustrates the highly unusual nature of the treatment.

At the other end of the relative arousal continuum, one could defend the position that even in the non-"dissonant" advocacy conditions an enhanced arousal level did produce a relatively weak amount of response contagion. As a matter of fact, the very novelty and uncertainty created in most experimental situations could be considered as leading to excitement and an increase in arousal. A response contagion approach then would predict that under relatively mild arousal, some evaluative assimilation would occur between subsequent and prior responses. Under conditions of relatively equal arousal (the conditions which were called non-"dissonant") the response contagion effect thus should be solely a function of the evaluative nature of the prior responses. The data obtained for our twelve non-"dissonant" advocacy or creativity conditions appear to be in line with this reasoning. The average "attitude" change obtained for the five non-"dissonant" *pro*-attitudinal conditions are 3.7; 4; 4.2; 4.4 and 4.5, whereas the average "attitude" change scores for the seven non-"dissonant" *counter*attitudinal conditions are 4.3; 4.5; 4.7; 4.8; 4.9; 5.1 and 5.1. When ranks are assigned to the above twelve averages, a Mann-Whitney test reveals a very significant difference between pro- and counterattitudinal conditions ($p = 0.009$, one-tailed; $U = 3$; $n_1 = 5$ and $n_2 = 7$). The average attitude score for the pro-attitudinal conditions is 4.1 ($N = 55$) against 4.8 ($N = 77$) for the counterattitudinal conditions (difference significant at the 0.05 level; $t = 1.89$; one-tailed test).

The above data thus can be considered as indicating evaluative assimilation between subsequent and prior responses, since the prevailing evaluative characteristics of the prior responses (pro- versus counterattitudinal) seem to be reflected in the subsequent "attitude" response.

The problem with testing any further the limits of evaluative response contagion might basically be related to the assessment of an empirical zero point for response contagion. This is an utterly difficult if not unsolvable question. One should realize that even in our well controlled laboratory situation it is simply impossible to have a full record of the ongoing prior evaluative responses. Especially during the first and third phase (the private preparation and the rehearing of the recorded speech), but also during the advocacy proper, one can safely assume that the students who were invited to produce one-sided arguments or evaluative responses could not avoid to (covertly) expose themselves to arguments in defence of the *opposite* side of the issue. The attitude responses obtained in our no-advocacy baseline conditions cannot be considered as providing such a zero point since the subjects are not being exposed at all to prior evaluative responses. Also such a zero point or minimal response contagion level is clearly dependent upon various—yet unspecified—parameters of the advocacy or prior responses. Mintz and Mills (1971) provide us with some interesting data which illustrate this aspect of the problem. In their first experiment, all subjects were exposed, under varying degrees of arousal, to an identical persuasive communication (A), containing approximately 600 words, against annual X-ray examination. For reasons which are irrelevant to our present purpose, they decided to run a second experiment in which the persuasive communication (B) was shortened to approximately 550 words by deleting a number of emotional terms and authoritative references. Since all other factors were presumably kept constant, we can consider the two experiments, taken together, as a manipulation of the length, and the prevailing evaluative characteristics of the communication or prior responses. There are in fact three prior response conditions: communication A, 600 words; communication B, 550 words and communication C, zero words. The interesting point now is that the evaluative characteristics of the assessed subsequent response (attitude towards X-rays) are clearly affected by the evaluative characteristics of the prior responses. For each of the two experimental conditions, arousal being kept constant, the favourability of the attitude towards X-rays varies as follows: A (600 words) = 1.3 and 1.8; B (550 words) = 3.2 and 4.7; C (zero words) = 10.9 and 9.9. It looks as if response contagion could be plotted as a direct function of the length and/ or the number of emotional terms and authoritative references.

One should realize that in our experiments, the subjects were not exposed to prior responses which were controlled by the experimenter. Since our subjects had themselves to produce, within the pro- and counter-attitudinal restraints, all prior responses, one can speculate that, under the concrete experimental situations, the minimal response contagion level of half an hour exposure to self-generated prior responses is situated somewhere between 4.1 and 4.8, depending upon the evaluative nature of these prior responses (pro- or counterattitudinal). Obviously, there is room for parametric studies of both arousal and evaluative assimilation. The benefit for enhanced understanding of the basic phenomena might however be problematic.

5. A response contagion reinterpretation of some representative persuasion experiments

No one who is familiar with the vast attitude change literature will expect to find here a detailed reinterpretation of even a small sample of this rich and controversial repertoire. We merely wish to examine briefly a few typical research paradigms in order to see if data obtained by other investigators, working within quite different theoretical frameworks, could fit the basic response contagion assumptions and predictions outlined before. We first turn to an experiment which in a more direct way might illustrate the appropriateness of the mediating physiological arousal concept.

MINTZ and MILLS (1971)

Mintz and Mills' recent studies on the "Effects of Arousal and Information about its Source upon Attitude Change" grew out of the very influential research programme conducted by Stanley Schachter (1964) on the interaction of cognitive and physiological determinants of emotional state. We also feel tempted to defend a response contagion interpretation of the important Schachter and Wheeler (1962) and Schachter and Singer (1962) experiments, where our "prior responses" could be substituted for the euphoric or angry evaluative verbal and non-verbal responses emitted by the stooges; our "subsequent responses" for the observed behaviour and the verbal self-reports used to label and assess subjects' emotional state. Although we are convinced that a mere response contagion approach to the study of emotional labels (*verbal self-evaluative responses*) and even of overt or covert motor reactions (see, for example, Berger, 1973) could create promising links between thus far almost totally unrelated areas of social and general psychology, we finally decided not to postpone for another year the publication of this research report and to restrict ourselves for the time being to the Mintz and Mills study which directly deals with persuasion, i.e., attitude change after exposure to a series of arguments.

Basically, Mintz and Mills manipulated physiological arousal by administering 300 mg of caffeine to college students who were then invited to read carefully a three page plea against annual X-ray examinations. An appropriate assessment of subjects' own attitude towards chest X-rays showed that the persuasive communication was more successful when the students had been reading the communication under caffeine produced arousal than in a placebo control condition. Moreover, the effect was stronger when the subjects had no appropriate information about the source of their physiological arousal, viz. when the caffeine was described as an analgesic.

It is obvious that the paradigm of this study, reduced to its most elementary form, is similar to that of the "forced compliance" or "role playing" experiments discussed throughout this monograph. In essence, the subjects are exposed to a series of arguments (generated by the experimenter) before their attitude towards the object of the plea is measured. The independent variable is not reward or justification but physiological arousal. Inspired by Schachter's theorizing, the authors propose a highly cognitive interpretation for their findings, which amounts to the assumption that "if a communication produces a positive or negative attitude toward an object, the degree of emotion that is associated with the object will be used to infer the strength of the attitude. If the degree of emotion experienced is increased by an increase in physiological arousal, then a stronger attitude will be inferred" (p. 562). It should be noted that the authors attach much importance to the effect of the cognitive labelling of the arousal, and had predicted that "when the source of the increase in arousal is not known, the increase in the degree of emotion should be greater and thus the attitude change produced should be greater" (p. 569). However, it seems to us that it is not proven that the cognitive labelling was manipulated independently from arousal. The authors hold that the amount of physiological arousal was the same for the caffeine-stimulant and the caffeine-analgesic subjects, the only difference being the label (p. 570). We agree that the amount of caffeine produced arousal was the same, but there is no guarantee that the total amount of arousal was not affected by the presentation (labelling) of the drug. A subject who has to take an analgesic drug after being told that this will raise his threshold of pain, and who has to wait 20 minutes before the experiment proper starts, might rightly become so worried about the unrevealed purposes of the Health Clinic research team, and thus become more aroused than his colleagues who were given a stimulant drug. A comparison between a placebo-stimulant condition and the placebo-analgesic condition might have shown that the labelling itself is confounded with the physiological (caffeine) arousal variable.

For our purposes then, Mintz and Mills have three conditions with increasing degrees of arousal: placebo-analgesic; caffeine-stimulant; and caffeine-analgesic. A response contagion approach would predict that the evaluative assimilation between the prior responses (plea against X-rays) and the subsequent responses (attitude towards X-rays) is a direct function of the degree of arousal, provided temporal contiguity between prior and subsequent responses (which was the case in the after-communication conditions of the experiment).

The data are completely in line with this prediction: the favourability towards chest X-rays decreases with increasing arousal. In the conditions where the "attitude" response was tapped before the communication was given, there was of course no possibility for response contagion to occur, and as expected the differential arousal had no effect upon the "attitude" response.

This confirmation of our results obtained in for example, the blame and hot-pants experiments is striking, notwithstanding the important differences in the conceptual and procedural approach. The more economical response contagion interpretation deals with the data without having recourse to such complex notions as "interpretation of emotion, inference of strength of attitude, attitude change produced by a convincing communication". Also the study offers more direct evidence in support of the arousal notion which was proposed as mediating perturbation and response contagion.

FESTINGER and CARLSMITH (1959)

Let us now turn back to the very first experiment which started the minimal reward controversy, and see how a response contagion approach could explain the famous one versus the twenty dollar reward data. The experimental procedure is so well known that we will merely point to a few details which might help us in restructuring the experiment and set the stage for a simple test of response contagion. On the basis of our own 1964 replication (Nuttin, 1966), where we found that the cognitive dissonance predicted minimal reward effect was at least equally strong in the *pro*-attitudinal as in the original counterattitudinal role playing condition, we have defended the position that the attitudinal nature of the role playing was not crucial for the minimal reward effect obtained. How then could the assessed attitude change fit a response contagion analysis? Basically such an analysis implies that under a condition of relatively high perturbation, evaluative assimilation occurs between subsequent and prior evaluative responses (which are not separated by a long time interval).

The following quotations should illustrate how perturbation was produced in the one dollar condition:

> I'll tell you what we had in mind: the thing is, if you could do it for us now, then of course you would know how to do it, and if something like this should ever come up again, that is, the regular fellow couldn't make it, and we had a subject scheduled, it would be very reassuring to us to know that we had somebody else we could call on who knew how to do it. So, if you would be willing to do this for us, we'd like to hire you to do it now and then be on call in the future, if something like this should ever happen again. We can pay you a dollar for doing this for us, that is, *for doing it now and then being on call* . . . The experimenter then paid one dollar, made out a hand-written receipt form and asked the subject to sign it . . . After two minutes the E returned . . . thanked the subject for talking to the girl, *wrote his phone number to continue the fiction that we might call on him again in the future* . . . (p. 205, italics added).

The embarrassment of the subjects who were thus taken in by the experimenter to stay on call for a trivial "dissonant" one dollar reward, hardly needs any comment. The fact that seven of the eleven discarded subjects did belong to the one dollar condition might further document the perturbing nature of this manipulation.

The important point now, it seems to us, is that at the very peak of perturbation, immediately after the experimenter wrote down the telephone number of the embarrassed subject, a precipitating series of "prior and subsequent responses" starts. We continue our quotation from the original article:

> As the experimenter and the subject started to walk to the office where the interviewer was, the experimenter said: "Thanks very much for working on those tasks for us. I hope you did *enjoy* it. Most of our subjects tell us afterwards that they found it quite *interesting*. You get a chance to see how you react to the tasks and so forth." This short *persuasive communication* (for the present author these are the *prior responses*) was made in all conditions in exactly the same way. The reason for doing it, theoretically, was to make it easier for anyone who wanted to persuade himself that the tasks had been, indeed, enjoyable. When they arrived at the interviewer's office . . . the interview consisted of four questions (p. 206, italics added).

REINTERPRETATION   205

By now, it is well known that the very first question was "Were the tasks *interesting* and *enjoyable*?" and that this was the only question for which a significant experimental effect was obtained. It is also clear that the labels used in this question are identical to the short persuasive communication which the subject received immediately before contacting the interviewer.

A response contagion approach would then predict that evaluative assimilation between subsequent (attitude) and prior (persuasive communication) responses would be a direct function of degree of perturbation, provided temporal contiguity between the latter and the former responses (which was indeed the case). It seems plausible to state that perturbation or arousal was highest in the one dollar condition, lowest in the control condition (no role playing, no reward, no telephone number for long term commitment) and intermediate in the twenty dollar condition. The data + 1.35 (one dollar); —0.05 (twenty dollar) and —0.45 (control) are in line with the expected relative degrees of evaluative assimilation. Basically the interpretation is identical to the one offered for our pro- *and* counterattitudinal mere verbal productivity exercise under blame or hot-pants perturbation. Moreover, the response contagion analysis holds that the assessed verbal evaluative response change is highly specific (as confirmed in the 1966 Carlsmith, Collins and Helmreich study; cf. supra, p. 177) and would not show up in a delayed first response condition which would prevent the occurrence of evaluative contagion.

JANIS and KING (1954)

Another well known classic, and one of the very first experiments studying the effect of more elaborate advocacy upon attitude change, was done by Janis and King who compared the effect of active versus passive advocacy using three topics: cinemas, meat supply and effective cure for the common cold. Suffice it to point to a few details of the procedure: ". . . The active participant was not told what the topic of his talk would be until his turn came to present it. He was given about three minutes to look over the prepared outline, during which the others (passive controls) also were requested to study duplicate copies of the same outline so as to be prepared for judging the adequacy of the speaker's performance . . . In all three communications, the conclusion specified an opinion estimate which was numerically lower than that given by any of the students on the "before" test (four weeks earlier) . . . The influence of each communication could readily be observed by noting the degree to which the

I

students in each group lowered their opinion estimates on the "after" test" (p. 212).

Janis and King thus provide us with an experiment in which the "prior responses" (the persuasive communication) are identical for all subjects as far as the outline is concerned, and identical within each performing group also for the improvised parts. The main independent variable was active versus passive exposure to these prior responses. It seems quite plausible to postulate that arousal was relatively higher while the active participants were exposed to their "prior responses" than when the same subjects passively listened to the same communication.

In line with the response contagion assumptions, one would thus expect evaluative assimilation between prior responses (the various communications) and subsequent responses (the "after" test opinion) to be greater for the active than for the passive conditions. This is exactly what the data show. It should also be noted that our interpretation can also deal more easily with a puzzling part of the Janis and King findings, viz., the fact that for communication C (common cold cure) the effect was equally strong for the passive communication C participants as for the active improvisers of the three communications. The authors indeed specify that communication C contained "a greater amount of unfamiliar technical material . . . The "cold cure" outline referred to a great many technical details concerning the cold virus, antibiotics, allergic reactions and histamines. Many of these details were probably unfamiliar to the subjects and consequently it may have been difficult for them to spell out the implications of the arguments" (p. 216). These comments might in fact mean that both active and passive participants were equally confused, embarrassed or aroused when exposed to this highly technical form of argument. Since the active participants who presented communication C "appeared to adhere much more closely to the prepared outline, making little attempt to reformulate the main points, to insert illustrative examples, or to invent additional arguments" (p. 215) it is not surprising that the improvisation had no differential effect with the equally embarrassed passive listeners who were facing the difficult task of judging the adequacy of a performance they were unable to evaluate. Since perturbation or arousal might have been relatively high for both conditions, response contagion should lead to a similar effect on the subsequent evaluative response.

We would like to stress the point that we are fully aware of the fact that the absolute degree of perturbation or arousal most probably is much lower in the Janis and King study than, for example, in our own blame and hot-pants experiments. It is obvious that all predictions have to be made within the restraints of "all other factors being kept constant" and that, for example, the underlying response conflict in the exam reform issue could be quite different in several respects from the one triggered off by the Janis and King communications. The comparisons made in the discussed experiments deal with relative differences along one or another hypothetical variable, thus we always refer to relative degrees of perturbation and clearly, it is beyond our interest to establish "absolute base levels" for perturbation or response contagion to occur.

ZIMBARDO (1965) and ZIMBARDO and EBBESEN (1970)

In Experiment Eleven we have compared a mere verbal creativity condition with a true advocacy condition in both a pro- and counter-attitudinal direction. One of the major objectives for this design was to eliminate alternative explanations which would centre around the idea that self-persuasion is enhanced by exposure to stimuli which are distracting and thus prevent the subject from actively counterarguing the defended position. The results obtained for the mere verbal creativity condition clearly did not support a disrupted argumentation interpretation. Zimbardo proposes however a quite different approach to the distraction of persuasion experiments, and tries to integrate them in Festinger's cognitive dissonance theory via the notion of differential *effort* invested in the advocacy. His research is presented as "a test of the general derivation from dissonance theory that the amount of attitude change toward an object or goal is a function of the magnitude of the barriers or aversive stimuli to be overcome in attaining the goal. The major hypothesis to be tested is that the greater the physical effort required in publicly reading and understanding a communication discrepant from one's own attitude, the greater will be the resulting dissonance and consequent attitude change in the direction advocated by the role performance" (1965, p. 106).

In his 1965 experiments then, effort is manipulated by having the subjects deliver a counterattitudinal plea (from a prepared outline) with a 0.3 second versus a 0.01 second delay of the auditory feedback of their own voice. Immediately after two successive public readings of the plea (exposure to prior responses) the attitude (subsequent response) was tapped and the assessed change in the direction of the advocacy proved to be a direct function of length of the feedback delay and thus presumably of amount of effort exerted to hold the plea.

In 1970, Zimbardo and Ebbesen further substantiate the cognitive dissonance-due-to-effort interpretation by using a more adequate control condition, in which a 75 decibel white noise is superimposed upon subject's normal feedback speech. The rationale given is that "the act of giving a speech under delayed auditory feedback is a novel experience which might conceivably increase acceptance of the content associated with this novelty. It is also a distracting experience . . . which might in itself be the variable responsible for greater attitude change . . . loud white noise superimposed upon one's speech is *also* a novel and distracting experience, but is significantly less effortful than the delayed auditory feedback experience." (p. 208, italics added). The results show that both on the affective-cognitive and conative dimensions of the experimental attitudes, the more effortful role playing was more effective.

The validity of this conclusion is of course contingent upon the independent manipulation of effort, for which, it seems to us, no clear evidence is given. Zimbardo and Ebbesen are probably right when arguing that white noise is *also* a novel and distracting experience. The crucial question might however be if white noise is an *equally* novel and distracting circumstance for delivering a speech. We would defend the position that delayed auditory feedback is distinctly more novel and distracting to the subjects than white noise. Since unusual, novel and disturbing stimuli have been identified throughout the monograph as the critical necessary condition for the impressive series of experimental effects obtained, we would argue that in all Zimbardo's effort studies, the auditory delayed feedback manipulation basically affects degree of perturbation or arousal, which safely can be considered (1) to be higher in the long than in the short delayed auditory feedback; (2) to be higher in the delayed auditory feedback than in the white noise condition; and (3) to be lowest in the normal feedback conditions.

Response contagion then predicts that evaluative assimilation between subsequent (attitude) and prior (advocacy) responses will be a direct function of relative degree of perturbation, which is exactly what was found in the discussed experiments. The complex cognitive dissonance interpretation, holding that the subject changes his attitude as a means to restore the imbalance produced by the amount of effort invested in the defence of an attitude discrepant position thus is substituted by a more economical interpretation which easily integrate ssimilar effects which cannot possibly be related to effort expended in publicly defending a counterattitudinal position (see the mere creativity hot-pants conditions of Experiment Eleven). It should be noted that the proposed response contagion reinterpretation not only makes no use of the cognitive imbalance restoring dissonance assumption but also completely disposes of the attitude notion as a helpful analytic concept. Moreover, evaluative response contagion theory would predict that Zimbardo's attitude change effects will not be produced unless the subsequent response change be assessed within certain (yet to be specified) constraints of temporal contiguity between the subsequent and prior responses.

Finally we would like to briefly point to another plausible application of response contagion theory, suggested by a footnote in Zimbardo (1965) which reads as follows: "It is surprising to note that Hess (1962) reports as one of the most reliable findings in ethology the positive effect of effort on imprinting. The strength of imprinting during the critical period is a function of the logarithm of effort expended by the duckling in following the imprinting object. In another study, ducklings who had to overcome aversive stimulation (painful shocks) for following a model imprinted more strongly than those not presented such a barrier. Both results are in clear agreement with the cognitive dissonance theory formulation" (p. 119).

Personally we are very sceptical with regard to the proposed applicability of cognitive dissonance theory to these imprinting data. We would however, defend the plausibility of a response contagion approach to the Hess data. Following the imprinting object in fact implies an enhanced (motoric) assimilation between subsequent and prior responses, whereas aversive stimulation or painful shocks can be considered as perturbing or arousal enhancing (see our blame treatment). As said before, we are convinced that the *evaluative* assimilation between subsequent and prior response is only one of several dimensions along which a temporal series of responses can become more similar as a result of response contagion. The prevailing characteristics of the prior responses which affect the subsequent response in principle can relate to any category of discriminative stimuli.

COLLINS and HOYT (1972)

With his sixteen "Studies in Forced Compliance", Barry Collins undoubtedly beats the record for a sustained and systematic analysis of the

effects of counterattitudinal advocacy upon attitude change. In an extensive treatise, reprinted as a 1973 Warner Modular Publication, Collins
and Hoyt give a comprehensive review and reinterpretation of the forced
compliance literature culminating in the presentation of a $2 \times 2 \times 2$
factorial experiment on the effects of high versus low financial reward
given for counterattitudinal advocacy under conditions of high or low
personal responsibility for high or low perceived social consequences of
the plea. The results are interpreted as supporting the crucial role of the
personal responsibility-for-important-consequences notion. Also, for the
first time in the relevant American literature, Collins and Hoyt obtain,
for approximately 50% of the subjects, an independent mail survey-post-
test two weeks after the experimental treatment and conclude to the
successful production of enduring attitude change.

Let us see if it would be justified to apply a mere evaluative response
contagion analysis to the Collins and Hoyt data. First it should be noted
that both the overall results for the immediate post-treatment and for the
delayed post-test effects (two weeks later) are very weak: no single cell
mean is found to be significantly different from the non-advocacy
baseline or control mean (see footnotes for Table 2 and 3, p. 576 and 577).
This is especially puzzling since the crucial effect, on which the proposed
reinterpretation of the whole relevant literature is based, is to be found in
the low reward, high responsibility for important consequences condition,
whose numerical value is indeed by far the most impressive of all cells but
which still does not differ significantly from a not-treated control sample.
A straightforward conclusion would of course be that the observed attitude
change does not provide reliable evidence for the theoretical position
defended. However, since the authoritative *Journal of Experimental Social
Psychology* assigned 35 pages to the presentation of these data, we are
perfectly willing to join the authors and the Journal in giving credit to the
reliability of the findings. As a matter of fact, our liberal position with
regard to statistical confidence limits could even profit from the consideration that the authors took a pre-test three weeks before the same
subjects were exposed to the experimental treatment. As we have shown
in Table 23, such a pre-test might very well have enhanced the resistance
to change of the already emitted attitude response.

Our principal question then will be if the low reward—high responsibility—high consequences data could be understood in terms of the relative high perturbation experienced by the subjects while exposed to the
arguments of their counterattitudinal essay. We invite the reader to role

play the treatment of the subjects of this experimental condition while reading the following extensive quotations.

The present experiment was conducted in *the week after* institution of the popular co-educational open visitation policy . . . Such a policy change had been sought by dormitory residents for several years, and residents' evaluation of the new policy was overwhelmingly positive . . . Each subject . . . had indicated (on the pre-test) a pro-visitation attitude. Additionally, all subjects had also made a behavioural commitment toward open visitation, in that they *had explicitly chosen to live on an open floor*, a choice that entailed completing applications and acquiring *signed parental consent* . . . The experimenter proceeded door to door on open floors . . . each subject (of the condition under discussion) heard the following: "Hi, I'm . . . from the (fictitious) Administration Research Committee, and we are working on a report about the open visitation issue. Can I have a couple of minutes of your time ? . . . It's been found that one of the best ways to get all the arguments on both sides of an issue is to have people write an essay on only one side. So this week we've been going around to all the dorms and paying residents, like yourself, 50 cents to spend a few minutes writing a couple of paragraphs about open visitation. We now have enough essays in favour of open visitation, and *we still need some more essays against it. The essay we'd like you to write is going to be used by administrators in deciding whether or not to make open visitation a permanent dorm policy;* we want to let you know that because *you are, of course, responsible for the effects your essay may have.* I have the paper right here, and the essay won't take more than 5 minutes to write. Like I said, I'll pay you 50 cents to write the anti-visitation essay. Will you do it ?" Upon receiving an affirmative response to this request, the experimenter then produced the following receipt: "*I have chosen to write an Open Visitation essay for the UCLA Policy Evaluation Committee and hereby acknowledge receipt of 50 cents. Responsibility for its contents is mine.*" After the subject had read and signed the receipt, thus reiterating the three experimental manipulations, he was paid the money. The experimenter then handed the subject a ruled page headed "Open Visitation is a Bad Policy" and a page containing a few anti-visitation arguments, and said: "Remember, what we need from you is the strongest, most convincing essay you can write arguing against open visitation. Here are a couple of arguments that you will want to use to get started; be sure to include these, and add some good ones of your own". Each subject was then allowed 10 minutes to write his anti-visitation essay. At the end of that time, the experimenter collected the essay saying: "The last thing I'd like you to do is this. In addition to having you write that essay, we would like to find out how you personally feel about the open visitation issue. So please take a couple of minutes to fill out this questionnaire . . ." (p. 573, italics added).

This should suffice for the Collins and Hoyt procedure for the subjects who are in a low reward counterattitudinal advocacy condition and where each student is supposed to "take personal responsibility for the important consequences of the essay he chose to write". We cannot but feel very sceptical about the validity of this manipulation of the "personal-responsibility-for-important-consequences" variables. Is it not at least equally plausible to define the precipitating situation to which the student was exposed as quite confusing, upsetting and embarrassing? The student who had completed applications and obtained signed parental consent to live in a dormitory where his girl-friend(s) could visit him around-the-clock and who just a week ago had celebrated the institution of this long expected policy change, happens to be taken in by a research fellow who makes him write some arguments, sign an upsetting receipt and cash fifty cents.

Since the "attitude responses" were tapped in immediate temporal contiguity with the essay written, response contagion theory would equally well predict the Collins and Hoyt results, viz., that under such relative perturbation, evaluative assimilation between the subsequent and prior responses would be greater than in less upsetting or arousing circumstances. It might of course be that arousal in this particular instance is caused by the fact that the subject was told that he chose to write an essay with important consequences and that he was personally responsible for the arguments used, but this does not prove that the theoretical interpretation of the effect obtained has anything to do with perceived responsibility for important consequences *as such*.

We hold that the Collins and Hoyt manipulation is conceptually and functionally equivalent to our "blame and hot-pants" treatment and that a mere evaluative response contagion analysis can integrate the (weak) data into the theoretical framework proposed for all hitherto discussed experiments.

As fas as the Collins and Hoyt evidence for "enduring attitude change", and the practical applications which are documented on the basis of this long term effect, we are not inclined to accept the theoretical and practical conclusions. On the basis of the strong evidence produced in our delayed *first* attitude response condition (Table 22), we argue that no long term effects would have been assessed if the subjects had not been invited to evaluate the open visitation issue in close temporal contiguity with the essay. Moreover, the mere evaluative verbal response change should be considered as highly specific and any stability over time of the changed "attitude" response should be thought as conditioned by the very class of responses emitted immediately after the experimental treatment. The Collins and Hoyt "delayed post-test" was indeed, not a "delayed *first* attitude response condition", but a mere *third* (pretest-treatment-post test) assessment of the same attitude responses over a five week period.

Since the Collins and Hoyt treatise presents to our knowledge the most recent and comprehensive effort for reconciling the post-advocacy persuasion literature, we will conclude this reinterpretation section with the statement that the above considerations incite us to reject their final conclusion, viz., "The personal responsibility-for-important-consequences formulation eliminates the confusion in the forced compliance literature, clarifies dissonance and attribution theories, and offers a wide variety of theoretical and practical applications" (p. 587) whereas a response contagion interpretation seems to offer a more parsimonious explanation of a wide variety of relevant data.

Conclusion

At the end of this extensive research report, we will not recapitulate the conclusions which were already formulated at various stages throughout the exposé. Rather we invite the reader once more to recognize the psychological reality of the truly fascinating symptoms of self-persuasion which were assessed both in the laboratory and in the field. There can be no doubt that we succeeded in drastically manipulating the students' "freely" expressed favourability towards the reform of the university exam system, an issue which was important above many others and about which they uniformly had firm and deeply entrenched convictions. Typically, students who were strongly against the traditional exam system, after only half an hour's treatment could be predicted to change this extreme negative attitude into a much milder, almost neutral position. After one particularly perturbing treatment (see Experiment Nine) more than half of the students described themselves as being neutral or even in favour of the traditional exam system whereas no one expressed a strongly negative attitude. At the same time the students invariably claimed a maximum degree of perceived decision freedom with regard to the treatment, thus illustrating a complete lack of awareness of the situational determination of their behaviour. Throughout this research project, analogous effects were assessed for more than one hundred individually treated students. In some other conditions, the opposite effect, i.e., an intensification of the pre-experimental position was predicted and produced.

One might better grasp the relevance of these findings when reminded of the following specifications. In none of the experiments, was the student exposed to explicit influence attempts by another person; social desirability cues were carefully eliminated and controlled; the experimenter did not provide any arguments: the student had to rely completely upon himself and had no access to external sources. Neither reward or punishment was contingent upon the quality of his verbal behaviour or upon the expressed favourableness towards the issue. The students agreed that they were not forced into the treatment and were fully informed about the specific features of the task before deciding to lend their cooperation. In some experiments where similar effects were produced, the students did not even realize that they were subjects nor that an experimenter was doing research with their collaboration, the treatment thus being in all aspects a carefully controlled "real life" experience. Finally, the experimental treatment not only enabled us to predict an important change in the favourableness towards university reform as expressed immediately after the treatment, but presumably much more importantly these very symptoms of manipulated self-persuasion were still reproducible ten weeks later, even when assessed in another "real life" situation totally unrelated to the laboratory treatment by a foreign interviewer interested in the use of drugs during exam periods (see Experiment Thirteen).

The profound psychological validity of these findings leaves no doubt. Repeatedly we have expressed our confusion when witnessing the predictability of the change in the "candid" evaluation of an important issue. Again and again it was depressing to predict the respectable confidence with which the students claimed their personal integrity in important and very consequential matters and the equally predictable almost complete situational determination of their real life behaviour with regard to the same values.

The central focus of our research however, was not the successful production of long term pro- or contra university reform attitude change, but the enhanced understanding of the phenomenon and its underlying processes. It is obvious that the concrete content, i.e. university reform, of the attitude object as such was irrelevant for our purposes—the major concern being to analyse the phenomenon in its most general and fundamental constituents. We started this endeavour with a systematic confrontation between our data and a cognitive dissonance view of the attitude change process. A progressive conceptual analysis of the necessary and sufficient conditions for the remarkable experimental effects obtained led to the rejection of the prevailing theoretical explanations offered in the relevant literature and prepared the stage for a fundamental response contagion reinterpretation of the phenomenon under study. The key operation for achieving this was a radical shift from the classical social attitude paradigm to a mere verbal evaluative response paradigm.

On the basis of the experimental evidence reported in Chapters Three and Four, we strongly suggest abandoning the social attitude concept because it is both misleading and useless for predicting, controlling and understanding social behaviour. Of course, the concept can continue to serve as a parsimonious label for merely descriptive studies of the way individuals or groups say they think, feel or are inclined to behave with regard to some value. Also, psychologists who are interested in the evaluative shifts of verbal behaviour might still profit from some classical attitude change studies. It seems to us, however, that social scientists, fundamental and applied—including those with clinical and educational interests—should seriously question any understanding or practice which is based on classical social attitude assumptions. The pervasiveness of these assumptions throughout all areas of applied psychology might be seriously underestimated. Social scientists should become aware of the fact that the wide use in mass media and social or clinical action of such terms as "attitude change", "sensibilization", "mental (re-)conversion" and "indoctrination" does not prove by itself that these terms have any scientific value for theory or application.

We finally stress the point that our experimental evidence and its interpretation, should not be considered as a trivial artifact which typically contaminated American forced compliance research. It seems to us that an adequate elaboration of the rudiments of response contagion theory, as developed in the last part of this research report could contribute to a better integration of social and general psychology and to a better understanding of such seemingly diverse phenomena as, for example, the (very limited) effect or absence of expected effects of verbal psychotherapy and behaviour therapy (as a function of, for example, novelty and unusual nature of the situation and the specific response changes induced), praying and meditation (for example, under peculiarly emotional conditions), campaigning or advertising (under hectic and arousing circumstances), and the emotional mobilization of masses who can be made to intensily profess a great variety of slogans (evaluative verbal responses) with predictable impact upon specific verbal and non-verbal forms of behaviour.

Are we utterly oversimplifying complex psychological phenomena? After exposing ourselves again and again to the data discussed in this report, we learned that the apparent oversimplifying approach was more adequate in dealing with the observed facts. Couldn't it be, after all, that human behaviour is less complex than most psychologists had hoped for?

References

Abelson, R.P. *et al.* (1968). (Eds), *Theories of Cognitive Consistency: A Sourcebook.* Rand McNally, Chicago.

Aronson, E. (1966). The psychology of insufficient justification. *In* S. Feldman (Ed), *Cognitive Consistency: Motivational Antecedents and Behavioural Consequences.* p. 115–133. Academic Press, New York and London.

Aronson, E. (1968). Dissonance theory: progress and problems. *In* R.P. Abelson *et al.* (Eds), *Theories of Cognitive Consistency: A Sourcebook.* p. 5–27. Rand McNally, Chicago.

Aronson, E. (1969). The theory of cognitive dissonance: A current perspective. *In* L. Berkowitz (Ed), *Advances in Experimental Social Psychology.* Vol IV. p. 1–34. Academic Press, New York and London.

Aronson, E., and Carlsmith, J.M. (1963). Effect of severity of threat on the valuation of forbidden behaviour. *Journal of Abnormal and Social Psychology,* **66**, 584–588.

Baron, R.M. (1968). Attitude change through discrepant action: A functional analysis. *In* A.G. Greenwald, T.C. Brock and T. Ostrom (Eds), *The psychological Foundations of Attitudes.* p. 297–327. Academic Press, New York and London.

Beckers, A. (1969). Onoprecht pleidooi, beloning en attitudgedrag. Sociaal-psychologische experimenten in verband met Festinger's cognitieve dissonantietheorie. (Counterattitudinal advocacy, reward and attitude response. Social-psychological experiments with relation to Festinger's theory of cognitive dissonance.) Unpublished doctoral dissertation, Laboratorium voor Experimentele Sociale Psychologie, Leuven.

Bem, D.J. (1965). An experimental analysis of self-persuasion. *Journal of Experimental Social Psychology,* **1**, 199–218.

Berger, S.M. (1973). Observer arousal and learning. Research Grant GS 2746 from the National Science Foundation, University of Massachusetts, mimeographed.

Berkowitz, L. (1969). Social motivation. *In* G. Lindzey and E. Aronson (Eds), *The Handbook of Social Psychology.* Vol. III. (2nd ed.). p. 50–135. Addison-Wesley, Reading, Mass.

Berlyne, D.E. (1968). The motivational significance of colltaive variables and conflict. *In* R.P. Abelson *et al.* (Eds) *Theories of Cognitive Consistency: A Sourcebook.* p. 257–266. Rand McNally, Chicago.

Bramel, D. (1968). Dissonance, expectation, and the self. *In* R.P. Abelson *et al.* (Eds), *Theories of Cognitive Consistency: A Sourcebook.* p. 355–365. Rand McNally, Chicago.

Brehm, J.W. (1966). *A Theory of Psychological Reactance.* Academic Press, New York and London.

Brehm, J.W., and Cohen, A.R. (1962). *Explorations in cognitive dissonance.* Wiley, New York.

Brock, T.C. (1962). Cognitive restructuring and attitude change. *Journal of Abnormal and Social Psychology,* **64**, 264–271.

Carlsmith, J.M. (1968). Varieties of counterattitudinal behaviour. *In* R.P. Abelson *et al.* (Eds), *Theories of Cognitive Consistency: A Sourcebook.* p. 803–809. Rand McNally, Chicago.

Carlsmith, J.M., Collins, B.E., and Helmreich, R.L. (1966). Studies in forced compliance: I. The effect of pressure for compliance on attitude change produced face-to-face role playing and anonymous essay writing. *Journal of Personality and Social Psychology,* **4,** 1–13.

Chapanis, N.P., and Chapanis, A.C. (1964). Cognitive dissonance: Five years later. *Psychological Bulletin,* **61,** 1–22.

Cohen, A.R. (1962). An experiment on small rewards for discrepant compliance and attitude change. *In* J.W. Brehm and A.R. Cohen, *Explorations in Cognitive Dissonance.* p. 73–78. Wiley, New York.

Collins, B.E. (1969). The effect of monetary inducements on the amount of attitude change produced by forced compliance. *In* A.C. Elms (Ed), *Role Playing, Reward, and Attitude Change.* p. 209–223. Van Nostrand, New York.

Collins, B.E. (1968a). Studies in forced compliance: III and VIII. The effect of true-persuasive instructions, public-private essays, and financial inducement on attitude change produced by forced compliance. Unpublished manuscript, University of California, Los Angeles.

Collins, B.E. (1968b). Studies in forced compliance: IV. An epitaph for the commitment (public-private) interpretation of forced compliance experiments. Unpublished manuscript, University of California, Los Angeles.

Collins, B.E., and Helmreich, R.L. (1966). Studies in forced compliance: II. Contrasting mechanisms of attitude change produced by public-persuasive and private-true essays. Unpublished manuscript, University of California, Los Angeles.

Collins, B.E., and Hoyt, M.F. (1972). Personal responsibility-for-consequences: An integration and extension of the "forced compliance" literature. *Journal of Experimental Social Psychology,* **8,** 558–593.

Cowen, E.L. (1952). The influence of varying degrees of psychological stress on problem-solving rigidity. *Journal of Abnormal and Social Psychology,* **47,** 512–519.

Cré, J. (1970). Dissonantie en frustratie. Kritische replicatie van een experiment over attitudeverandering. (Dissonance and frustration. Critical replication of an attitude change experiment.) Unpublished dissertation, Laboratorium voor Experimentele Social Psychologie, Leuven.

Davis, K.E., and Jones, E.E. (1960). Changes in interpersonal perception as a means of reducing cognitive dissonance. *Journal of Abnormal and Social Psychology,* **61,** 402–410.

Dumez. C. (1970). Kritisch onderzoek van Daryl J. Bem's herinterpretatie van cognitieve dissonantie-experimenten. (Critical study of Daryl J. Bem's reinterpretation of cognitive dissonance experiments.) Unpublished dissertation, Laboratorium voor Experimentele Sociale Psychologie, Leuven.

Edwards, A.L. (1957). *The social desirability variable in personality assessment and research.* Dryden Press, New York.

Eeckhout, D. (1965). Festinger's cognitieve dissonantietheorie. Kritische replicatie van twee experimenten. (Festinger's theory of cognitive dissonance. Critical replication of two experiments.) Unpublished dissertation, Laboratorium voor Experimentele Sociale Psychologie, Leuven.

Elms, A.C. (1967). Role playing, incentive, and dissonance. *Psychological Bulletin,* **68,** 132–148.

Elms, A.C. (1969). *Role Playing, Reward, and Attitude Change.* Van Nostrand, New York.

Feldman, S. (Ed), (1966). *Cognitive consistency: Motivational antecedents and Behavioural Consequents.* Academic Press, New York and London.

Festinger, L. (1957). *A Theory of Cognitive Dissonance.* Stanford University Press, Stanford.

Festinger, L., and Aronson, E. (1960). The arousal of dissonance in social contexts. *In* D. Cartwright and A. Zander (Eds) (1960), *Group Dynamics,* (2nd ed.). p. 214—231 Row Evanston, Ill.: Peterson.

Festinger, L., and Carlsmith, J.M. (1959). Cognitive consequences of forced compliance. *Journal of Abnormal and Social Psychology,* **58**, 203–210.

Festinger, L., Riecken, H., and Schachter, S. (1956). *When Prophecy Fails.* University of Minneapolis Press, Minneapolis.

Freedman, J.L. (1963). Attitudinal effects of inadequate justification. *Journal of Personality,* **31**, 371–385.

Freedman, J.L. (1965). Long-term behavioural effects of cognitive dissonance. *Journal of Experimental Social Psychology,* **1**, 145–155.

Helmreich, R.L., and Collins, B.E. Studies in forced compliance: Commitment and magnitude of inducement to comply as determinants of opinion change. *Journal of Personality and Social Psychology,* **10**, 75—81.

Hess, E.H. (1962). Ethology: An approach toward the complete analysis of behaviour. *In: New Directions in Psychology.* p. 157–266. Holt, Rinehart and Winston, New York.

Hornbeck, F.W. (1967). Studies in forced compliance: IX. The effects of deception, commitment, and incentive on attitude change produced by writing a counterattitudinal essay. Paper presented at meeting of *Western Psychological Association,* San Francisco, May 1967.

Hovland, C.I., Janis, I.L., and Kelley, H.H. (1953). *Communication and Persuasion.* Yale University Press, New York.

Janis, I.L. (1967). Effects of fear arousal on attitude change: Recent developments in theory and experimental research. *In* L. Berkowitz (Ed), *Advances in Experimental Social Psychology.* Vol. III. p. 166–224. Academic Press, New York and London.

Janis, I.L., and Gilmore, J.B. (1965). The influence of incentive conditions on the success of role playing in modifying attitudes. *Journal of Personality and Social Psychology,* **1**, 17–27.

Janis, I.L., and King, B.T. (1954). The influence of role playing on opinion change. *Journal of Abnormal and Social Psychology,* **49**, 211–218.

Kelley, H.H. (1967). Attribution theory in social psychology. *In* D. Levine (Ed), *Nebraska Symposium on Motivation.* Vol. XV. p. 192–238. University of Nebraska Press, Lincoln.

Kelman, H.C., Baron, R.M., Sheposh, J.P., Lubalin, J.S., Dabbs, J.M., and Johnson, E. (1969). Studies in attitude-discrepant-behaviour. United States Public Health Service Grant MH-07280-07, National Institute of Mental Health, mimeographed.

Kiesler, C.A., Pallak, M.S., and Kanouse, D.E. (1968) The interactive effects of commitment and dissonance. *Journal of Personality and Social Psychology,* **8**, 331–338.

Kiesler, C.A. and Sakumura, J. (1966). A test of a model for commitment. *Journal of Personality and Social Psychology,* **3**, 349–353.

Le Bon, G. (1896). *The Crowd.* Unwin. London. (Translated from *Psychologie des foules.* Oleon, Paris, 1895.)

Lependorf, S. (1964). The effects of incentive value and expectancy on dissonance resulting from attitude-discrepant behaviour and disconfirmation of expectancy. Unpublished doctoral dissertation, State University of New York at Buffalo.

Linder, D.E., Cooper, J., and Jones, E.E. (1967). Decision freedom as a determinant of the role of incentive magnitude in attitude change. *Journal of Personality and Social Psychology,* **6**, 245–254.

Lumsdaine, A., and Janis, I.L. (1953). Resistance to "counterpropaganda" produced by a two-sided "propaganda" presentation. *Public Opinion Quarterly,* **17**, 311-318.

McGuire, W.J. (1964). Inducing resistance to persuasion. *In* L. Berkowitz (Ed), *Advances in Experimental Social Psychology*, Vol. I, p. 191–229. Academic Press, New York and London.

Mertens, M. (1967). Attitudeverandering na strafbedreiging. Kritische replicatie van een experiment over cognitieve dissonantie bij kleuters. (Attitude change after threat of punishment. Critical replication of a cognitive dissonance experiment using nursery children.) Unpublished dissertation, Laboratorium voor Experimentele Sociale Psychologie, Leuven.

Miller, N., and Levy, B.H. (1967). Defaming and agreeing with the communicator as a function of emotional arousal, communication extremity and evaluative set. *Sociometry*, **30**, 158–175.

Mintz, P.M., and Mills, J. (1971). Effects of arousal and information about its source upon attitude change. *Journal of Experimental Social Psychology*, **7**, 561–570.

Nel, E., Helmreich, R., and Aronson, E. (1969). Opinion change in the advocate as a function of the persuasibility of his audience: A clarification of the meaning of dissonance. *Journal of Personality and Social Psychology*, **12**, 117–124.

Nuttin, J.M., Jr. (1964). Dissonant evidence about dissonance theory. Paper presented at Second Conference of *European Association of Social Psychology*, Frascati, Italy.

Nuttin, J.M., Jr. (1965). A critical replication of Rosenberg's "When dissonance fails". Communication at the 1965 *APA Convention* in Chicago.

Nuttin, J.M., Jr. (1966). Attitude change after rewarded dissonant and consonant "forced compliance". *International Journal of Psychology*, **1**, 39–57.

Orne, M.T. (1962). On the social psychology of the psychological experiment: With particular reference to demand characteristics and their implications. *American Psychologist*, **17**, 776–783.

Riecken, H.W. (1962). A program for research on experiments in social psychology. *In* N.F. Washburne (Ed), *Decisions, Values and Groups*. Vol. II, p. 25–41. Pergamon Press, New York.

Rosenberg, M.J. (1956). Cognitive structure and attitudinal affect. *Journal of Abnormal and Social Psychology*, **53**, 367–372.

Rosenberg, M.J. (1960). An analysis of affective-cognitive consistency. *In* M.J. Rosenberg *et al.* (Eds), *Attitude Organization and Change*. p. 15–64. Yale University Press, New Haven.

Rosenberg. M.J. (1964). When dissonance fails: On eliminating evaluation apprehension from attitude measurement. Technical Report No. 3, Contract Nonr 495(24), Office of Naval Research, mimeographed.

Rosenberg, M.J. (1965). When dissonance fails: On eliminating evaluation apprehension from attitude measurement. *Journal of Personality and Social Psychology*, **1**, 28–42.

Rosenberg, M.J. (1966a). Some limits of dissonance: Toward a differentiated view of counterattitudinal performance. *In* S. Feldman (Ed), *Cognitive Consistency: Motivational Antecedents and Behavioural Consequents*. p. 135–170. Academic Press, New York and London.

Rosenberg, M.J. (1966b). A research programme on consistency and change in social attitudes. Technical Report No. 4, Contract Nonr, 495 (24), Office of Naval Research, mimeographed.

Rosenberg, M.J. (1968). Hedonism, inauthenticity, and other goads toward expansion of a consistency theory. *In* R.P. Abelson *et al.* (Eds), *Theories of Cognitive Consistency: A Sourcebook*. p. 73–111. Rand McNally, Chicago.

Rosenberg, M.J. (1970). The experimental parable of inauthenticity: Consequences of counterattitudinal performance. *In* J.S. Antrobus (Ed), *Cognition and Affect*. Little, Brown and Co, Boston, Mass.

Rosenthal, R. (1963). On the social psychology of the psychological experiment: The experimenter's hypothesis as unintended determinant of experimental results. *American Scientist*, **51**, 268–283.

Rosnow, R.L., and Robinson, E.J. (Eds), *Experiments in Persuasion*. Academic Press, New York and London.

Schachter, S. (1959). *The psychology of Affiliation*. Stanford University Press, Stanford.

Schachter, S. (1964). The interaction of cognitive and physiological determinants of emotional state. *In* L. Berkowitz (Ed.), *Advances in Experimental Social Psychology*. Vol. I, p. 49–80, Academic Press. New York and London.

Schachter, S. (1971). *Emotion, Obesity, and Crime*. Academic Press, New York and London.

Schachter, S., and Singer, J.E. Cognitive, social ,and physiological determinants of emotional state. *Psychological Review*, **69**, 379–399.

Schachter, S., and Wheeler, L. (1962). Epinephrine, chlorpromazine and amusement. *Journal of Abnormal and Social Psychology*, **65**, 121–128.

Scott, W.A. (1957). Attitude change through reward of bveral behaviour. *Journal of Abnormal and Social Psychology*, **55**, 72–75.

Scott, W.A. (1959). Attitude change by response reinforcement: Replication and extension. *Sociometry*, **22**, 328–335.

Turner, E.A., and Wright, J. (1965). Effect of severity of threat and perceived availability on the attractiveness of objects. *Journal of Personality and Social Psychology*, **2**, 128–132.

Verhaeghe, H. (1970). Beloning en onoprecht gedrag. Kritische herformulering van de kognitieve dissonantie verklaring vanuit de attributietheorie. (Reward and counter-attitudinal behaviour. Critical reformulation of the cognitive dissonance explanation from the attribution theory.) Unpublished dissertation, Laboratorium voor Experimentele Sociale Psychologie, Leuven.

Webster's Third New International Dictionary of the English Language. (1961). (Unabridged). Merriam, Springfield, Mass.

Wheeler, L. (1966). Toward a theory of behavioural contagion. *Psychological Review*, **73**, 179–192.

Zajonc, R.B. (1968). Cognitive theories in social psychology. *In* G. Lindzey and E. Aronson (Eds), *The Handbook of Social Psychology*. (2nd ed.). Vol. I. p. 320–411. Addison-Wesley, Reading, Mass.

Zimbardo, P.G. (1960). Involvement and communication discrepancy as determinants of opinion conformity. *Journal of Abnormal and Social Psychology*, **60**, 86–94.

Zimbardo, P.G. (1965). The effect of effort and improvisation on self-persuasion produced by role playing. *Journal of Experimental Social Psychology*, **1**, 103–120.

Zimbardo, P.G., and Ebbesen, E.B. (1970). Experimental modification of the relationship between effort, attitude and behaviour. *Journal of Personality and Social Psychology*, **16**, 207–213.

K

Appendix to Chapter One: fact and fiction in a scientific review

The two most comprehensive and authoritative source books on attitude change and cognitive consistency theory (Feldman, 1966 and Abelson *et al.*, 1968) include a contribution by Rosenberg in which our replication (Chapter One, Section 3) is treated in such a way that the reader can use the qualifier of his own choice, but which we prefer to define as "unusual", thus expressing the hope that little of the criticism we and all readers are bound to find in second hand sources, would be of a similar nature.

Since Rosenberg's reply is most extensive in his article in the Feldman book on "Cognitive Consistency", and no new arguments are introduced in Rosenberg 1968, we will comment upon each of the points raised by Rosenberg in his lengthy 1966 discussion of our replication.

(1) The first objection made by Rosenberg is formulated as follows: *In a most important and relevant aspect, the Nuttin experiment is inadequate as a replicative design; the two-experiment disguise does not seem to have been carried out properly* (Rosenberg, 1966, p. 158, italics added). The arguments used in support of the above statement reads:

'In my own study [Rosenberg, 1964–65] . . . there was no direct contact and little meaningful relationship between the essay-eliciting and attitude-measuring experiments. In Nuttin's study, however, the experimenters were rather closely linked. The attitude-measuring experimenter actually escorted the subject to the essay-eliciting experimenter (who thereupon, as Nuttin discloses, 'thanked me for not having forgotten his need' (Nuttin, 1964, p. 13)). After the completion of the essay, the latter experimenter delivered the subject back to the office of the former and, as I have already noted, expressed his thanks and his hope that he might have access to additional subjects later on. *The arousal of an evaluation apprehension pattern of suspicion would certainly have been greater in these circumstances than in the earlier experiment* (Rosenberg's own) *that was supposedly being put to replicative test (ibid.*, p. 158, italics added).

It is obvious that we cannot "prove" that the direct contact between the two experimenters did not arouse an evaluation apprehension pattern of supicion, neither can Rosenberg prove that it did or that his perceptual separation was perfect. But we have good reasons to assert that our perceptual separation was

223

at least as carefully and successfully materialized as the one of the Rosenberg experiment.

For the reader who is already familiar with our procedure for the perceptual separation phase (cf. supra, p. 29–30) it will be obvious that Rosenberg's quotations on the direct contact between the two experimenters are manifestly severed out of their context, and even give a distorted view of what actually happened. Rosenberg's comments do indeed suggest that the first experimenter "escorted" the subject to the office of the essay-eliciting experimenter, but even the summary description of the instructions in the mimeographed (Nuttin, 1964) outline on which Rosenberg's comments are based, were very clear in this respect: "The subject was delivered to experimenter 2 . . . who took the subject to his own office in the opposite part of the building. Experimenter 2 continued to play the role, asking for example what kind of studies the subject was doing, for which experiment he was scheduled, etc. As soon as they arrived in the study of experimenter 2 . . ." (ibid., p. 13).

More important is that the context of the quotations makes it very clear that the denounced physical (and minimal) contact between the two experimenters was precisely a consequence of the fact that the physical distance between the two offices was brought to an (acceptable) maximum level, whereas the "psychological" or "perceptual" separation, which really is the main point, was supposed to be enhanced by experimenter 2's "thanking for not having forgotten his need" and expressing his hope for "additional subjects later on", as well as by the many other elements of the two-experiment disguise not mentioned by Rosenberg.

We could even argue that a reader of Rosenberg's 1964 report and of our 1964 outline (or the more complete description of our experimental procedure in Eeckhout, 1965) would agree that there are objective indications which point in the opposite direction. As a matter of fact, Rosenberg does report that "two subjects were discarded from the analysis because they evidenced virtually complete and *spontaneous* insight into the deception (two-experiment disguise) that had been employed (Rosenberg, 1964, p. 35). Furthermore, after the experimenter told the subjects in the debriefing phase about the deception used, "a few subjects, two or three per group, claimed to have had suspicion suggestive of what had now been revealed". Although we completely agree with Rosenberg that it is very difficult to interpret the latter non spontaneous findings, we merely want to point to the fact that despite our efforts in a permissive and relaxed interview situation, not a single subject did claim, neither spontaneously nor after probing, any insight into the two-experiment disguise.

Another objective indication of our explicit care to realize an effective perceptual separation, is that we purposely and for obvious reasons, omitted part of Rosenberg's instructions (which otherwise were followed as close as possible), viz., when experimenter 1 says to the subject before sending him to experimenter 2 "I don't know what it's about exactly except that it has to do with attitudes and that's why he called me, *because my research is in a similar area as you'll see later*" (Rosenberg 1965, p. 33–34, italics added). The subsequent information about possible monetary rewards has been retained, because of the possible effect of differences in reward expectations which might be created.

Our most important but probably least convincing argument against this aspect of Rosenberg's misrepresentation of our research endeavour is similar to the one we used (cf. supra, p. 21–22) in support of Festinger and Carlsmith when Rosenberg deals in an equally subjective manner with their manifest effort for perceptual separation, by saying that "the degree of separation may well have been insufficient because the experiment did not involve disguising the two phases as two different studies conducted in two different departments (1965, p. 32). It is evident that we, even more than Festinger and Carlsmith, were committed to realize a "perceptual separation" since we explicitly wanted to *manipulate experimentally* the very factor under consideration. After several pilot-studies, the described procedure proved to be adequate for our explicit purpose. Not a single subject did evidence any insight. We had the opportunity to comment amply on the face validity of our manipulation in public discussion and private communication with Rosenberg at the occasion of a debate scheduled at the 1965 APA convention. One just cannot prove that any manipulation of this sort was perfect. But shouldn't there be a minimum of confidence in one's colleagues explicitly stated research policy?

What then can be the value of Rosenberg's statement that our replication "was inadequate in a most important and relevant aspect"? It clearly was a very easy way to dispose of embarrassing data, especially when the chances for a rejoinder were almost non-existing for a non-publishing psychologist who, at the time, had lost his interest in dissonance research.

(2) The second objection formulated by Rosenberg probably sets a record of misinforming the reader who is motivated to learn about "scientific facts". Since this objection was based on two distinct errors of fact, we will deal first with the following quotation: "*An equally important methodological failing in Nuttin's study concerns the absence of the conventional sort of control group.* In most other studies involving some form of counterattitudinal advocacy (i.e., the studies by Festinger and Carlsmith; Cohen; Rosenberg; Carlsmith, Collins and Helmreich) baseline data are obtained from a group of subjects who do not perform any counterattitudinal advocacy and who receive no reward; instead they merely respond to the attitude measure that serves for the experimental group as the source of dependent variable data. *Nuttin did not run such a group*" (*ibid.*, p. 158, italics added).

The reader who is familiar with the report of our first experiment, will know that this is simply not true. Our "conventional control group", which is exactly comparable to the ones used by Rosenberg and all the studies which he refers to, is probably one of the most reliable "conventional baseline" sources of the relevant literature, since the data were collected individually on one hundred and twenty subjects, taken at random from the same pool as the subjects for the experimental condition (cf. supra, p. 34).

Rosenberg presumably must have overlooked what was clearly written on page 22 of the mimeographed 1964 outline which he used as basis for his discussion: "The very last rating for all subjects (of our Festinger and Carl-smith replication) was the critical item of our Rosenberg replication".

The weight Rosenberg attaches to the first part of his argument will become clear in its second part:

> Instead, each member of his "control group" wrote a "consonant essay" (i.e., an essay supporting his own attitude) without any promise or receipt of a reward. *The writing of this sort of essay would be likely to move these subjects toward intensification of their original attitudes and thus toward a scalar extremity greater than that found in the control group of comparable studies. In turn, then, this would tend to increase the differences between the mean attitude position obtained from this group and from the experimental group in which counter-attitudinal essays were written.* Thus, statistically significant magnitudes of attitude change that might be shown by any of the experimental group (if one relies upon the "control group" data as a baseline) *would not actually be significant in any relevant sense* (*ibid.*, p. 159).

It should be first made clear that this argument is not directly relevant for the critical issue of our replication of Rosenberg's experiment, which, as far as Rosenberg is concerned, focuses on the validity of *his* thesis, that Cohen's data are due to the uncontrolled effect of two denounced biasing research contami-nants. In as much as our replication of the Cohen data, however, can be seen as strengthening our refutation of the Rosenberg "biasing factor" thesis, it is understandable that Rosenberg wants to show that we did not replicate the Cohen findings. In this context he accuses us of using an unconventional control group which would facilitate the production of significant differences "which would not actually be significant in any relevant sense".

To begin with, it can be argued that even if Rosenberg was right (which he is not, as will become clear in a moment) his argument bears only on the comparison between the baseline-control and the experimental conditions and does not deal with the significant differences between high and low reward conditions which lie exactly in the direction opposite to his results. Whatever the baseline data might be, the crucial facts of the controversy with Cohen remain the inverse or direct relation between size of reward and magnitude of attitude change.

The important point however, is that *our data* prove that Rosenberg's assertions about the significance enhancing effect of our "pseudo-control" condition are simply in error. As a matter of fact, the mean attitude response of our 120 baseline subjects is 2.6 (see a detailed report on these data in Eeckhout, 1965, p. 203) whereas the mean attitude response of the denounced control group is 2.7. The difference, if any, is exactly in the opposite direction of the one on which Rosenberg's second argument is based.

We admit of course the fact that our experimental design did include a control group "consonant or pro-attitudinal essay, no reward" and that its methodological usefulness was defended and still has been in this monograph. But to conclude from this that we have omitted to collect the conventional baseline data and that therefore our data would not be significant in any relevant sense, is an utterly unwarranted conclusion. It would indeed have been a serious error from our side if we had claimed to run a close replication of the Cohen and Rosenberg experiment without having arranged for the type of baseline data which were used in these studies. It would have been utterly unfair indeed, if we had neglected to report any difference between these two types of control conditions, in order to enhance the significance of our replicated Cohen findings.

That we did not neglect the conventional baseline type of control group, especially for comparison with the replicated studies, can further be shown in Nuttin, 1966, which is a publication of part of the 1964 outline, and where a basically similar design was used with regard to our Festinger and Carlsmith replication. There too we have a consonant role playing zero reward condition in the design, but for purposes of comparison with the original study, only the "no role playing—no reward" condition, which is exactly similar to the original Festinger and Carlsmith baseline, was used.

This should suffice to make it clear that Rosenberg's second accusation of an "equally important methodological failing" has no basis whatsoever in the objectively established facts to which Rosenberg had easy access, more than anyone else and certainly more than his readers, since he was among the first to receive a copy of the 1964 outline with the personal assurance that any further information would be provided with pleasure.

(3) Rosenberg's third attack is introduced by the following clearly misleading and distorted judgement of our 1964 research endeavour: "*However, there is a far more serious problem in these data* (more serious than the problems raised by the previous arguments), *though Nuttin does not comment upon it in his report*" (*ibid.*, p. 160). Then Rosenberg presents our data for the zero reward counter-attitudinal plea condition, conveying the impression that he has seen a problem for dissonance theory which "Nuttin did not comment upon". It will be remembered that the 1964 mimeographed outline to which Rosenberg is constantly referring, is a hastily written memo which was distributed to members of a small working conference. The mimeograph had only a pro-cedure and main results section and no discussion of the results was presented for obvious reasons: the data were barely collected before the conference. But for anyone who has an objective look at the design of the studies and to the title of the paper (dissonant evidence about dissonance theory) it will become clear that the major emphasis of the paper is not the Rosenberg-Cohen issue, but an experimental analysis of the basic postulates of dissonance theory concerning the consonance of the reward and the role attributed to the "central dissonance" in the Cohen and Festinger and Carlsmith type of experiments. We have never claimed that dissonance theory was corroborated by the totality of our data. A quite different statement is that the Cohen results were replicated when restricting ourselves to the original conditions used. It was evident that we added a zero dissonant essay condition and several rewarded consonant con-ditions for the sole reason of assessing the validity of the dissonance view (see for example, the discussion in Nuttin, 1966), and that the overall results of our experiments were never presented as corroborating dissonance theory. It is thus highly suprising to find Rosenberg saying that "Nuttin did not comment" upon

the fact that there were serious problems with the dissonance interpretation of his data.

So far we have discussed the arguments presented by Rosenberg in an effort "to develop the groundwork of conclusions by a close and, at times, perhaps almost exegetical examination of the research findings and interpretive controversies . . . and that, as I see it, recommend those conclusions as *necessary* ones" (Rosenberg, 1966, p. 136, italics not added).

After having commented upon all arguments presented by Rosenberg, we should quote Rosenberg's "necessary" conclusion: "On the basis of the foregoing close analysis of the Nuttin study, then, the most parsimonious conclusion would seem to be that, *because of its various inadequacies of method and design*, it has yielded data that are quite inconclusive. Whether these data reflect great random error only, or whether they also bespeak the influence of some suspicion arousal in the high reward condition, remains an open question. *At any rate, Nuttin's data do not seriously challenge the conclusion that I have drawn from my own study*—that is when true counterattitudinal advocacy is undertaken for incentives of varying strength, consequent attitude change based on self-persuasion is a positive function of the magnitude of the incentive" (*ibid.*, p. 160).

Before closing the Rosenberg dossier we would however like to point to a last, most discouraging and surprising aspect of Rosenberg's defence strategy.

At no point of his lengthy and "almost exegetical" discussion of our replication of his study, does Rosenberg even hint at the fact that we did experimentally manipulate his "perceptual separation" and "actual delivery of reward", the two denounced procedural sources of evaluation apprehension and negative effect arousal. Not only does he withhold this information from his readers, but, and this is really a puzzling move in strategy, just before starting the discussion of our paper, he suddenly, in a most candid way, informs the reader that *he himself did manipulate experimentally the* "*perceptual separation*" by running "*as part of his study,* 'one-experiment' versus 'two-experiment' disguise groups' " (Rosenberg, 1966, p. 154, italics added). Although this part of his chapter does not directly attack our own research, its content is so intimately related to the above discussion and is so characteristic of the flavour of Rosenberg's defence strategy, that we cannot refrain from commenting upon it.

First, it should be made clear that Rosenberg never referred to these quite important data, "run as part of his study", neither in his 1965 article, nor in the 1964 ONR technical Report, nor in his extensive 1966 final report on his 1961–64 "research programme on consistency and change in social attitudes" (Rosenberg 1966b.). As a matter of fact, he explicitly discussed in the introduction of his study (Rosenberg, 1965, p. 30) the possibilities for checking upon the presence of the denounced sources of contamination" (evaluation apprehension and negative affect arousal). The only two ways he considers are: (1) "by asking the subject how he interpreted the purpose and meaning of the experiment". The difficulties with this approach are however so serious that this alternative is rejected; (2) "by conducting an altered replication of the original experiment, one in which we redesign those of its aspects that are presumed to have fostered the contaminating processes". So, no hint at the desirability of a balanced design in which the presumed procedural aspects would be manipulated, and *a fortiori* no reference to the fact that it has been done "as part of the study".

Moreover, in the discussion section of his article (Rosenberg, 1965, p. 38) he elaborates at length on the various ways in which further investigation of these contaminating processes (which he considers as the primary purpose of his study) should be pursued. Talking about more direct investigations of the contamination effects, he summarizes the design of two recent studies which he undertook and in which "*by intention* rather than by inadvertence possible cues for contamination were supplied". Again no mention whatsoever is made of the intentional manipulation of the Cohen-contaminating variables which are disclosed in his 1966 chapter. Let us see how these new data are brought into the discussion.

The occasion offered is the argument presented by Aronson (1966, p. 123) in another chapter of the same book, stating that Rosenberg should have manipulated experimentally the presumed source of evaluation apprehension. This was the first and main argument for our Rosenberg replication (Nuttin, 1964, p. 4, Aronson acknowledges the use made of our 1964 mimeographed outline). Amazingly enough, Rosenberg considers the argument of Aronson to be "a perhaps more important point", although he never mentions this aspect of our own research, which was the only study providing experimental data on the problem.

After having acknowledged the importance of the problem, he candidly goes on by saying that "in fact, because this (the importance of the argument) was recognized, one-experiment groups (without perceptual separation) were run as part of my study. However, the postexperimental questionnaire revealed that a large number of the subjects, unlike those run under the two-experiment disguise, did not perceive themselves as having been free to refuse to write the counterattitudinal essay" (*ibid.*, p. 154). In footnote, he gives then the results: the combined $.50–$1.00 reward group show a significative change in the advocated direction. "The $5.00 group, *however*, is not significantly different from the control group" (*ibid.*, p. 154, italics added). We wonder why Rosenberg writes "however" instead of . . . "whereas" the $5.00 did not differ from the control group? These data are indeed just beautiful dissonance data.

Why did Rosenberg refrain from reporting these most interesting results as part of his original study? The reason advanced is, he says, that, "these data did not seem appropriate for testing the hypothesis that the relationship supporting the dissonance prediction would be obtained in a situation in which no attempt was made to limit the operation of the evaluation apprehension artifact" since . . . "perceived freedom is a necessary condition if dissonance reduction is to be sought through attitude change" (*ibid.*, p. 154). So, Rosenberg did not want to abuse experimental data *in support of* Cohen's study, because his postexperimental questionnaire revealed that these subjects felt less free in their decision to write the essay.

The important facts however are, (1) that Cohen did *not* include any post-experimental check concerning perceived decision freedom in his study; (2) that Rosenberg did use instructions which were "modelled word-for-word" after the ones of the Cohen experiment (Rosenberg, 1965, p. 34); (3) that Rosenberg himself did not report at all on the perceived freedom of choice of the subjects run in his own experiment.

So, the case seems very clear: since Cohen did not check the perceived freedom, and since Rosenberg *did* replicate Cohen's results under experimental conditions identical to the original ones, he should have reported these most interesting results obtained for the no perceptual separation conditions as "part of his study" (Rosenberg, 1966, p. 154).

We really wonder why Rosenberg refrained even from hinting at the data of these conditions from his nicely balanced design, which would have allowed him to show that the Cohen data are replicated if "evaluation apprehension" was aroused by the absence of the "perceptual separation" and that the Rosenberg theory (both his affective-cognitive consistency theory and his evaluation apprehension hypothesis) was confirmed if "evaluation apprehension" was eliminated as a result of the two-experiment disguise and the actual delivery of the reward.

Rosenberg had indeed no reason to bother with postexperimental questions on perceived freedom, not only because Cohen did not check for it, whereas he had realized a word for word replication of the Cohen experiment, but, most important, *because he could easily have interpreted the differences in perceived freedom by pointing to the crucial difference brought about by the two-experiment disguise.* As a matter of fact, it is not surprising at all that the subjects of the one-experiment (no perceptual separation) conditions did feel less free in their decision to write the essay, since this was *the* experiment for which they had signed up. So the subjects did not have much choice not to comply with the experimenter's request. In contrast however, the subjects of the two-experiment disguise, had committed themselves to participate in an unforeseen experiment "while they had to wait anyway". They had indeed not signed up for this unforeseen experiment, but had accepted to participate in it upon the suggestion of the experimenter (Rosenberg), and it is quite normal that they did express (to Rosenberg) a relatively higher perceived decision freedom than the subjects of the "no perceptual separation" condition.

So the best guess Rosenberg was perfectly enabled to make, was that the felt decision freedom in his "no-perceptual separation" conditions would be more comparable to the decision freedom of the original Cohen subjects.

It is interesting to note that Rosenberg concludes his paragraph concerning this late disclosure by stipulating "I should not wish to make any major claims for these data" (Rosenberg, 1966, p. 154). We cannot but feel highly puzzled by the fact that a scientist does not want to make major claims for data which confirm his central hypothesis.

Author Index

Subject Index

A

A-cognitive process, 108, 137, 155, 198

Advocacy,
  active v. passive, 59, 205
  anonymous v. identified, 52, 65–83, 142, 184, 185
  counterattitudinal v. pro-attitudinal, 43–51, 85, 92–100, 105, 145, 146, 203
  elaborate v. assertion, 1, 5, 59, 87, 205
  free, 160, 173–175, 183
  private v. public, 58, 100–106, 114, 115, 127, 142
  radio v. TV, 65–83, 95, 101, 103, 105, 108, 114, 122, 155, 160, 162, 184, 185

Affect,
  negative affect arousal, 11–13, 15, 16, 37, 39, 50, 106, 221, 222

Affective-caognitive consistency, 10, 15–18, 20, 23, 24, 37, 54, 59, 87

Arousal,
  (cognitive) dissonance, 13, 18, 24,, 50 51, 53, 55, 63, 64, 68, 82, 93
  effect on attitude change, 197, 201
  emotional, 129, 131, 138, 141–143, 149, 171, 181, 182, 195
  evaluation apprehension, 11–13, 37, 39
  fear, 131
  physiological, 201–203
  sexual, 149
  suspicion, 12, 13, 63, 117

Assimilation. see Evaluative assimilation

Attitude, definition,
  evaluative verbal response paradigm, 157, 175–181, 187–191, 216

Attitude related rating, 143, 165–167, 176–178

Attitude response,
  attitude related response v. attitude response proper, 143

baseline, 3, 34–36, 67, 78–81, 94, 96, 98, 103, 123, 134, 171, 175, 198
  delayed, 163, 165, 168, 175
  delayed first, 147, 163, 170, 171, 175, 212
  second, 169, 170, 173, 174
  long term persistency, see Long term persistency
  third, 173, 174, 212

Attractiveness of experimenter, 61, 62, 106

Attribution theory, 213

Audience,
  consequences to, see Consequences

B

Blame, 132, 138, 173, 195, 203, 205, 207
  "dissonant", see "Dissonant"

Behaviour,
  attitude discrepant, 95, 105, 108, 123, 139, 145
  attitude related, 159, 164, 181
  overt v. attitude response, 164, 181, 186, 188, 190
  "real" v. "intentions", 118
  therapy, 216
  unpredicted, see also Unpredicted responses, 182, 183, 187, 195

Bribe, 111   124

C

Coercion, 128, 129, 187, 188

Cognitive dissonance
  see also Dissonance, "Dissonant"
  arousal, see Arousal
  and effort, 297–209
  interpretation, 2, 4–10, 18, 23, 48, 50, 55, 68, 81, 88, 92, 95, 107, 108, 155, 208
  operational definition, 93
  prediction, 4, 9, 15, 18, 35 39 41 42 48–51 54 68 93 98 109 110 127 203

233